KV-108-797

Governing Scotland

The Invention of Administrative Devolution

James Mitchell
Department of Government
University of Strathclyde, Glasgow
UK

EDINBURGH UNIVERSITY LIBRARY

WITHDRAWN

© James Mitchell 2003

All rights reserved. No reproduction, copy or transmission of this publication may be made without written permission.

No paragraph of this publication may be reproduced, copied or transmitted save with written permission or in accordance with the provisions of the Copyright, Designs and Patents Act 1988, or under the terms of any licence permitting limited copying issued by the Copyright Licensing Agency, 90 Tottenham Court Road, London W1T 4LP.

Any person who does any unauthorized act in relation to this publication may be liable to criminal prosecution and civil claims for damages.

The author has asserted his right to be identified as the author of this work in accordance with the Copyright, Designs and Patents Act 1988.

First published 2003 by
PALGRAVE MACMILLAN
Houndmills, Basingstoke, Hampshire RG21 6XS and
175 Fifth Avenue, New York, N.Y. 10010
Companies and representatives throughout the world

PALGRAVE MACMILLAN is the global academic imprint of the Palgrave Macmillan division of St. Martin's Press, LLC and of Palgrave Macmillan Ltd. Macmillan® is a registered trademark in the United States, United Kingdom and other countries. Palgrave is a registered trademark in the European Union and other countries.

ISBN 0–333–74323–7

This book is printed on paper suitable for recycling and made from fully managed and sustained forest sources.

A catalogue record for this book is available from the British Library.

Library of Congress Cataloging-in-Publication Data
Mitchell, James, 1960–
    Governing Scotland: the invention of administrative devolution/
James Mitchell.
        p. cm.
    Includes bibliographical references and index.
    ISBN 0–333–74323–7 (cloth)
        1. Great Britain. Scottish Office – History. 2. Decentralization in
government – Scotland – History. 3. Scotland – politics and government –
19th century. 4. Scotland – Politics and government–20th century. I. Title

JN1231.M58 2003
320.9411—dc21   2003045686

10 9 8 7 6 5 4 3 2 1
12 11 10 09 08 07 06 05 04 03

Printed and bound in Great Britain by
Antony Rowe Ltd, Chippenham and Eastbourne

EDINBURGH UNIVERSITY LIBRARY
WITHDRAWN

Governing Scotland

Also by James Mitchell

CONSERVATIVES AND THE UNION

STRATEGIES FOR SELF-GOVERNMENT

SCOTLAND DECIDES (*co-author*)

POLITICS AND PUBLIC POLICY IN SCOTLAND (*co-author*)

This book is dedicated to my Aunt Margaret Boath, Margaret and Sarah Paterson and to my late Uncle Alex

Contents

List of Tables   viii

Preface   ix

1. Introduction   1
2. The Origins of the Scottish Central Administration   11
3. Settling Down to Business   29
4. Educational Administration   50
5. Administering Agriculture, Health and the Highlands
   and Islands   74
6. MacDonnell, the Boards and the 1928 Act   92
7. The Reorganisation Debate and Gilmour   117
8. The Origins and Development of the Goschen formula   149
9. Scottish Office Ministers   182
10. Conclusion   207

Notes   216
Bibliography   246
Index   254

List of Tables

4.1 Meetings of the Committee of the Privy Council on
     Education in Scotland   51
4.2 Numbers and ranks of SED Staff based in Edinburgh,
     1908 and 1912   69
5.1 Comparison of Scottish and English/Welsh rates   77
7.1 Edinburgh offices, addresses and staff, 1923   125
8.1 Population of United Kingdom by constituent nation   152
8.2 Goschen losses, 1892–94   156
8.3 Goschen loss/gain, 1894–96   156
8.4 Local taxation (Scotland) Account, Financial Year
     ending 31 March 1901   160
8.5 Comparison of grants for Scottish and English and
     Welsh Education, 1901–02   165
8.6 Comparison of figures used by Mr D.M. Wilson at Oban
     EIS Congress on 18, April 1911 with those of
     Accountant's Report for 1908–09. Selective Examples
     from table   167
8.7 Percentage which receipts from Exchequer bear to
     total in various years, prepared by SED including
     Local Taxation monies, 11 April 1923   171
8.8 Percentage which receipts from Exchequer bear to
     total in various years, prepared by SED excluding
     Local Taxation monies, 11 April 1923   171
8.9 Expenditure per head of population from public funds
     using 1921 census   172
8.10 Note Marked 'confidential' initialled R.T.H. (Hawkins),
     23/3/26   173
8.11 Statement of services in Scotland to which the
     Goschen formula applies with expenditure on those
     services in the financial years, 1930–34   179
9.1 Background, incumbencies and future offices of
     Scottish Secretaries, 1885–1939   184

Preface

In 1980, in a bibliographical essay, it was noted that though the Scottish Office was the 'most influential institution in Scotland' it was 'among the least analysed'.[1] This is remarkable not least because it was the focus of much political activity in Scotland. There have been two books on the history of the Scottish Office. The first was published in 1957 as part of a series on Whitehall Departments and written by Sir David Milne, then Scottish Office Permanent Secretary.[2] The other was written by John Gibson, a retired Scottish Office civil servant who had been commissioned to write it in celebration of the Office's centenary.[3] Despite perennial debates on Scotland's constitutional status there was little academic consideration of this key institution despite the fact that its importance was recognised in a number of works.

For those interested in the subject, there are a number of interesting works. William Smith's *The Secretary for Scotland*, published in 1885, was guide to the legislation with a useful introductory essay providing background to the Office's establishment. John Percival Day's Public Administration in the Highlands and Islands of Scotland, published in 1918, is probably the best work on not only the public administration of the Highlands and Islands but on Scotland published up to that point in time and, indeed, for many years after. It details the structure of government, its functions and finances. Works cited in the bibliography by Grierson, Jeffrey, Laird, Peck and Rose are uncritical for the most part and written from the inside but helpful. The work of Ian Levitt, notably his collections of National Archives of Scotland papers is underutilised by historians. He appears to have looked at many of the public papers that I have used in this book.

Twenty years ago, I was fortunate to receive a Fullerton, Moir and Gray scholarship from the University of Aberdeen to allow me complete a D.Phil. at Nuffield College, Oxford. I chose to study the early history of the Scottish Office. Having completed the thesis I moved on to other matters only returning to this study many years later. I was grateful to receive the support of the Leverhulme Trust under its Nations and Regions programme which allowed me to do work on territorial public finance. Chapter 8 is the outcome of that work.

Many individuals helped in the production of this book, some directly, others indirectly. Few of those who were key to the events that are discussed in this book were alive when I started this work. John Aglen, secretary to the Gilmour Committee, which reported in 1937, was the sole survivor but he sadly passed away before I could reach him. I was fortunate to have had a lengthy interview with Sir William Murrie in January 1983. He had begun his career as a public servant in the Scottish Office in the inter-war period and was to go on to become Permanent Secretary later. Grant Jordan at Aberdeen University has been a great support throughout my academic career and commented many years ago on chapters of the thesis. So too did Nevil Johnson of Nuffield College acting as my University supervisor. David Butler's role as College supervisor ensured that my interests were never too narrowly focussed. Iain MacLean and James Kellas were my examiners and I have maintained contact sporadically with them. From their different perspectives they have been important contributors to our understanding of the territorial nature of the United Kingdom.

Back then I approached the study as an historical institutionalist though I did not know so at the time. My awareness of this literature came later as indeed did much of the literature. Another set of literature I owe a debt to and, again, one that I grew to know better after I had completed the original thesis, was the territorial politics literature. The work of Michael Keating, Jim Bulpitt, Richard Rose, James Kellas, Charlie Raab and others associated with the old UK Politics group and the revived Territorial Politics group, under Jonathan Bradbury's guidance, proved very useful. David Heald read versions of the chapter on finance.

Particular mention must be made of the work of Stein Rokkan and Derek Urwin, most notably the distinction they drew between the union and unitary state. I first applied this distinction in papers I was writing in the early mid-1980s on the subject of devolution. I reached the conclusion some years ago that the notion of the union state needed to be fleshed out. I have applied it in this study to the Scottish case in a manner not done before. This idea still has much mileage and, I believe, is of great value in making sense of the United Kingdom. Rokkan and Urwin deserve greater credit than they are generally given for introducing the notion and defining what they mean by a union state. Credit would best take the form of further elaboration of the idea, its implications and application.

In time the notion of the union state has moved from having been an idea that a small handful of territorial politics specialists knew about or cared about to the situation in which it is now widely used even approaching having become an orthodox view. That change was reflected in the reception to the idea that the United Kingdom is a union state. Initial reactions verged on outright rejection. Today, opposition is muted. In large measure this reflects the better appreciation of the territorial dimension of politics. Much remains unclear and more work needs to be done to elaborate on our understanding of the United Kingdom. I intend to produce a further volume, currently nearing completion, that will explore the idea in a wider, UK context.

Finally, I would like to refer to debts of a quite different kind. While in Oxford I made frequent visits to north Oxfordshire to visit my Uncle Alex, Aunt Margaret, cousin Margaret and her daughter Sarah. My late uncle always ensured that my visits were fun, as important to any doctoral student as any intellectual guidance. Sarah is now an academic herself. I dedicate this book to them for the most enjoyable moments of my period as a graduate student. Finally I should thank my immediate family – Laura, Euan and Kirsty: Laura for encouraging me to return to this work and complete it as well as for long discussions on aspects of it, notably historical institutionalism; Euan and Kirsty for being the best tonics available after hours on the computer or in the office.

JAMES MITCHELL
Strathclyde University

1
Introduction

Throughout its existence, the Scottish Office embodied the UK's willingness to acknowledge Scottish distinctiveness but, as part of Whitehall and accountable to Parliament at Westminster, it also represented the unity of the state. Founded in 1885, the Scottish Office's jurisdiction grew throughout its existence. At its inception, its work was held to be 'not very heavy'[1] and the Duke of Richmond and Gordon, the first Scottish Secretary, doubted whether there was a need for it.[2] By the early 1980s, one estimate suggested that the Scottish Office had responsibilities equivalent to approximately eleven other Whitehall Departments.[3] James Kellas went so far as to suggest that the Scottish Secretary had become Prime Minister for Scotland.[4] As a domestic territorial department, the Scottish Office was unique until the Welsh Office was set up in 1964. The Northern Ireland Office (NIO), established after the collapse of Stormont in 1972, is another example of a domestic territorial department. The NIO was created to bring about 'direct rule' from London while Scottish and Welsh Offices were described as 'administrative devolution'. There were certainly major differences between the Scottish Office, Welsh Office and NIO but the simplest explanation for the direct rule/administrative devolution distinction is historical. The NIO came into existence following a period of legislative devolution and its political heads have never come from Northern Ireland.

The Welsh Office resembled the development of the Scottish Office condensed in form and telescoped in time.[5] The Scottish Office served as a precedent for the establishment of both the Welsh Office and the NIO. The model adopted in 1964 when the Welsh Office was established was, in its essentials, that of the 1939 Scottish Office. This model was advocated as one for a reformed NIO by James Molyneaux, then leader of the Ulster Unionists, in 1983.[6]

1

The Scottish Office was important in a number of ways. It represented an unusual means of organising central government responsibilities. It is not unusual that a Department has a client group with which it interacts forming a series of policy communities, but the Scottish Office was unusual in that this client group was a nation. The Scottish Office was in many respects a pressure group representing Scottish interests within British central government. It was a department which could mobilise a resource, national sentiment, unavailable to other departments. It was more than simply an example of what has been termed 'field administration'.[7] National sentiment played an important part in its emergence and development. The existence of the Scottish Office encouraged a conception of Scotland as a political and not merely a cultural entity. Ironically, those who sought to mitigate Scottish nationalism with a measure of administrative devolution gave credence to the case for Scottish self-government by officially recognising a distinct Scottish dimension to politics. However, as John Mackintosh noted, the existence of the Scottish Office had no effect in reducing or preventing the rise of nationalist feeling.[8] Jack Brand pointed out that by the time that the Scottish National Party (SNP) had begun to grow in the 1960s, it was accepted that 'public affairs in Scotland should be conducted in a special way'.[9] Though this in itself is insufficient in explaining the rise of the SNP, as Brand noted, it was an important factor. The Scottish Office is, therefore, of importance not merely to students of public administration but also those of nationalism.

Territorial organisation of central government

The organisation of modern states requires, in all but the very smallest, a significant territorial dimension. This applies to dictatorships and socialist republics as much as liberal democracies. Administrative efficacy requires that certain functions are performed beyond the centre. The nature of territorial divisions of functions and powers varies considerably though terms such as 'decentralisation' are commonly used.[10] A highly centralised state may prove to be an administrative nightmare to govern and provoke secessionist movements or, at least, demands for radical decentralisation. On the other hand, stress on a state's indivisibility may help to bind it together.

Unitary states, according to King, supposedly display 'one supreme, ultimate and unified centre of authority'.[11] King's 'supposedly' is understandable. The notion of sovereignty is out of place in the modern world, if it was ever relevant. The great difference in the approach to territorial politics which exists across those states which might be characterised as unitary range from those which have permitted a fair degree of sub-state autonomy, at least as great as under many federal systems as witnessed in the case of Stormont in the fifty years up to 1972, to the mythical French education system in which the Minister could look at his watch at any time and tell what was being taught in schools throughout France. Unitary states are more clearly recognised for what they are not than what they are. The categorisation into unitary, confederal and federal relationships is inadequate.[12] In trying to make sense of the United Kingdom with its territorial dimension requires a greater degree of sophistication than is permitted by such notions.

The UK is a union state, achieved by a treaty where integration is 'less than perfect' with the preservation of pre-union rights and institutional infrastructures which 'preserve some degree of regional autonomy and serve as agencies of indigenous elite recruitment'.[13] Crucial to this understanding is an appreciation of the importance of history. The unitary-union state distinction was initially put forward by Stein Rokkan and Derek Urwin.[14] Since then it has been applied to debates on constitutional reform. In order to understand the United Kingdom, the concept of the union state now needs to be developed in different directions. First, its historical dimension needs to be fleshed out. The UK has been a dynamic union. Its features and dimensions have changed over time. Second, it needs to be developed comparatively and the concept tested against the experience of different parts of the United Kingdom. This book attempts to fill a gap in the literature with regard to the first aspect as applied to Scotland.

The central argument is that the establishment of the Scottish Office and its development to 1939 are central to understanding the union state. The picture that emerges challenges simplistic notions that have underpinned discussions of a unitary United Kingdom.

Themes

The Scottish Office did not emerge in a vacuum. It grew out of a distinctly Scottish apparatus of administration. To a large extent, this was based on the nascent structure of Scottish local government. Central administrative boards existed but the bulk of work was done at local level. This local apparatus had its roots in the organisation of the Church of Scotland. Its *mores* were based on Presbyterianism. In many respects, it differed from that which existed in England. It is not the purpose of the book to search ever further into the past to discover the historic roots of the separate Scottish central administration.

The primary purpose is to make sense of the manner in which Scotland was governed in the twentieth century, particularly its basis in the last quarter of the nineteenth century and first half of the twentieth. No attempt to make sense of the development of the Scottish Office after its establishment is possible without some appreciation of the background to its creation just as any understanding of Scotland today requires an understanding of the recent past. What emerges from the outset is the importance of symbols in the Scottish Office. Stressing the Scottishness of the structure of government, before and after the establishment of the Scottish Office, has been a constant theme. Institutions that might in another context be deemed dry administrative apparatus became important conveyors of national identity.

Public opinion was important as a dynamic force in central administrative development from before the Scottish Office was established. The public in question changed over time, most notably it became a wider, more democratic public, but public demands for changes to accommodate Scottish interests were consistently voiced and fed into debates on reform. This public pressure was generally incoherent and its demands imprecisely defined but, in the nature of national sentiment, its importance lay in its persistent, even pervasive nature rather than its ability to produce clear blueprints for reform. It could not be combated by simple logic. Arguments that a Scottish Office was unnecessary might have had a logic behind them but could not overcome the power of national sentiment. The cost of resisting the establishment of the Scottish Office was higher than simply conceding its establishment. Whether Lord Salisbury and the Conservatives would have been so willing to set up the new office had they been able to communicate with future generations of Conservatives can be speculated upon but at the time there was little expectation that it might feed, rather than appease national sentiment. Little wonder that Salisbury did not fear Scottish nationalism given that the Scottish home rule movement barely existed as a serious political force until after the First World War.[15] Moreover, scholars of nationalism have long noted that there is no clear relationship between the development of national sentiment and conceding ground to it.[16]

However, evidence from Scotland would suggest that concessions have fed demands but that may be too simple. It is difficult to prove that any relationship between developing national political sentiment and concessions is anything more than coincidental. But the circumstantial evidence is powerful and a theoretical link can be provided. The Scottish Office was a political institution and became a focus of political pressure. Pressure groups, political parties, those seeking policy change as well as those opposing initiatives focus their attention on government institutions in which decisions are made. Over time, the range of policies that were covered by the Scottish Office grew and with it the Scottish Office as the focus of attention. It matters less whether the Scottish Office could influence matters, whether its powers were less than its responsibilities. It does not even matter whether or not it was an innovative department. So long as the perception existed that it made a difference or represented an opening in the decision-making process, it would attract pressure from groups and individuals and, in turn, assume a significant place in the life and politics of Scotland.

As later chapters show, the establishment of the Scottish Office had implications for other political institutions. Political parties and pressure groups would require to operate on a Scottish level. Parliament too would have to accommodate this territorial department. Questions to government ministers, committees dealing with Scottish legislation and debates on Scottish matters would be required, enhancing the sense of a Scottish political community. It is little wonder that James Kellas, doyen of students of Scottish politics with his keen historical understanding, should give the Scottish Office central place in the development of what he termed the Scottish political system.[17] We may argue about whether what emerged constitutes a political system[18] but, however conceived, a distinctive Scottish politics exists rooted in recent history and the Scottish Office was central to this.

The emergence of the Scottish Office grew out of pressure to take greater account of Scottish distinctiveness, address grievances that Scotland was neglected and was based on pre-existing structures of distinct, if rudimentary machinery of government. The new office assumed a role as guardian of Scottish interests as well as having administrative duties and responsibilities. Within a very short period of time any sense that the office would have little to do was disproved. It settled into a pattern that was to remain with it throughout its existence. Its primary purposes would be threefold:

(i) it was an institutional expression of the union state demonstrating that Scotland would be treated distinctly but within a centralised state;
(ii) it articulated Scottish interests especially in the cabinet and Whitehall, at the heart of government;
(iii) it had administrative duties, initially mainly concerned with education, but in a short time others were added which provided precedents for future developments.

The Scottish Office was set on a clear path, at least one that appears clear in retrospect. Even before its establishment, but certainly from its early days, the Scottish Office's functions, in the widest sense as listed above, were evident. Education had been the Office's first main administrative responsibility. In the chapter that focusses on education, Bagehot's distinction between the 'dignified' and 'effective' branches of government is useful.[19] The Committee of the Privy Council for Scottish Education existed in little more than name, in common with other aspects of central government. It did so alongside the newly established Scottish Office. But education in the early years of the Scottish Office is important in other respects. First, many later debates were rehearsed around educational administration and articulated more fully in these early debates than they were later. Whether the office should be based in London or Edinburgh, for example, was discussed at length with respect to education before the First World War. A more general debate took place after the war. Second, the issue of who should control education policy – the bureaucrats, politicians or the public – became politically sensitive, again presaging later debates. These early debates reverberated throughout the twentieth century and ultimately contributed to the establishment of the Scottish Parliament.

Third, as again became common across Scottish central administration, the development of educational apparatus owed more to compromises than principles. This is not to criticise the thousands of public servants who worked tirelessly or the tens of Ministers, nor even to suggest that the structure was incapable of meeting the needs of the country. Merely, its *ad hoc*, incremental development was not envisioned by 'founding fathers' but emerged piecemeal. Fourth, a tension that became common throughout the development of Scottish central administration between what might be called the Whitehall view and the Scottish view was evident during the early post-1885 development of Scottish educational administration. The Whitehall view can be summarised as the need for administrative efficacy while the second was the need to accommodate Scottish distinctiveness. The tension between the two runs throughout the development of the Scottish Office. It proved a creative tension with neither view dominating.

The development of administration for agriculture, health and the highlands and islands shows the manner in which earlier precedents allowed the machinery of government to deal with these matters in a Scottish context. An alternative scenario is conceivable in which Ministries of Agriculture and Health for Britain as a whole would be established rather than, as happened, separate Scottish administration for these purposes. Repercussions for other parts of the UK is hinted at in the early development of the Scottish Office. Treating Scotland differently created precedents of three sorts.

First, it created a precedent for how new or expanding areas of public policy should be organised. If education, local government and other matters were to come under the Scottish Office then why not agriculture and health? With the Scottish Office's establishment it would be difficult at least to avoid consideration of separate Scottish machinery for new or expanding areas of policy. Second, the Scottish Office created precedents for other parts of the UK. If Scotland should have its own Minister why not Wales? That question emerged in debates when health matters were under discussion and would be heard again and again. But it should not be assumed that the establishment of the Scottish Office set Scottish administration on some ineluctable course. Separate Commissions were established for Insurance but in time these disappeared and national insurance became consolidated and centralised across the UK after the Second World War. Concessions to the Scottish view could and were reversed. In addition, limits were placed on the extent to which the Scottish view could prevail over the Whitehall view. Allowing Scots to administer animal health raised fears in Whitehall that this would lead to lax controls and the danger of diseased animals straying over the Anglo-Scottish border. Notably, no one seems to have suggested that separate administrative arrangements might lead to lax controls in England. Consequently, while agriculture was to be organised by nation for many purposes, animal health was to be organised on a British basis. This only changed following the recommendation of the Royal Commission on Scottish Affair in the mid-1950s.[20]

The Highlands and Islands represents an example of distinctiveness within distinctiveness. The peculiar and often desperate problems of the Highlands and Islands demanded special treatment and this included the provision of separate administrative machinery. The existence of the Scottish Office also created a third kind of precedent in ensuring that the Highlands and Islands was, where necessary, to be dealt with by special machinery. If Scotland is treated differently, why not regions within Scotland? The administration of the Highlands and Islands was set to be for Scotland what Scotland was for the UK. Once more, this was a theme that ran throughout the twentieth century.

The tensions between the Scottish and Whitehall views were at their height in debates on reform of the central administration after the First World War. The professionalisation of the civil service which had begun with Northcote–Trevelyan in the nineteenth century passed much of

Scottish central administration by until relatively late. This made Scotland different and resulted in politicians who would otherwise be expected to oppose a system of government based on patronage defending this on the grounds that it was Scottish. It was the Conservatives who were the reformers at this stage and they reformed in a typically conservative manner in keeping with British traditions. The process of removing the patronage boards and replacing them with departments was approached gradually and in a piecemeal manner. Compromises with the Scottish view were found in the establishment of advisory boards.

Having faced strong criticisms in the early stages of this process, advocates of reform learned lessons. The second stage of reforms was prepared more carefully in advance. First, consensus was sought through the establishment of a cross-party committee. Second, it was advocated in terms of the Scottish view though, in truth, what was being attempted was a move towards the Whitehall method of government. The invention of the notion of 'administrative devolution' was part of this process. However intractable the many social and economic problems appeared to be in the 1930s, territorial management was remarkably successful. The backdrop was propitious for the development of political protest. The reforms could easily have been presented as anti-Scottish, as had happened a decade before, but instead a reform that 'modernised', to adopt an over-used word, Scottish government was instituted with remarkable ease. In some senses, this was the apogee of the union state from a Scottish perspective.

Treating Scotland differently had implications for public finance. Again, this was not something that emerged from the existence of the Scottish Office but preceded it and was part of the pre-existing structure already noted of treating Scotland as a political unit. Public finance reflected the union state. London dominated decision-making but a Scottish dimension had to be developed and, again, this was not static. Myths grew up around the system of grants. Of all aspects of Scottish government, this was the one that has been least understood, largely because it was most neglected by scholars, politicians and the public. Those who knew the system best were inside government. Again, in common with debates on how Scotland should be governed, public finance debates often operated on two levels. First, within Whitehall there were debates between the Treasury and the Scottish Office (or parts of it), the latter as a spending department, on how much and what mechanism should be used to determine Scottish expenditure. Second, there were debates amongst Parliamentarians and (an admittedly very small) public. There were moments when these two levels of debate resembled each other but often the connection appears tangential. The Goschen formula is fascinating both from a public policy perspective but also in terms of symbolic politics and public perceptions. Additionally, here was institutional incrementalism at its most obvious.

Reinforcing the limited nature of administrative devolution were the politicians who filled the office of Scottish Secretary in these formative years up to 1939. These were not impressive figures. Most gained a place in the cabinet that would never have been within their reach but for the existence of the Scottish Office. Only one – A.J. Balfour – went on to become Prime Minister and he was at the Scottish Office for only seven months. A few other (usually minor) stars shone brightly and briefly at the Scottish Office. Walter Elliot is generally seen as a great success on the basis of little including credit for the 1939 reforms that should, in fact, be credited to his predecessor Godfrey Collins. In total, the twenty men who held the office of Scottish Secretary from 1885 to 1939 were not a very impressive lot. A quarter were promoted to a more senior office of state. A few were highly competent administrators – notably Sir John Gilmour and Collins – but few would leave a legacy and association with major policy change in any of the fields over which the Scottish Office had jurisdiction. Tom Johnston, in the unusual circumstances of war, did that and Willie Ross, later in the 1960s and 1970s could claim to have enacted truly distinctive policies addressing Scottish needs that amounted to more than (financial) extensions of policy for England.

Conclusion

Administrative devolution was established during the period up to 1939. It was the most manifest institutional form of the union state. Scotland's distinct status within the United Kingdom was acknowledged in its existence but so too was the centralised nature of the UK's system of government. 'The union state' as Rokkan and Urwin defined it, was 'not the result of straightforward dynastic conquest. Incorporation of at least parts of its territory has been achieved through personal dynastic union, for example by treaty, marriage or inheritance. Integration is less than perfect'. [21] No understanding of Scotland's position within the twentieth-century United Kingdom can fail to take account of that background. The Scottish Office grew out of this. Again, as Rokkan and Urwin noted, of the union state, 'While administrative standardization prevails over most of the territory, the consequences of personal union entail the survival in some areas of pre-union rights and institutional infrastructures which preserve some degree of regional autonomy and serve as agencies of indigenous elite recruitment.'[22] That did not amount to a federal constitution or anything close to it though there may have been elements to Scotland's position that resembled federal arrangements. Crucially, Scotland remained part of a state with a centralised system of government and in which Parliament at Westminster enshrined that centralisation and greatly limited the degree of autonomy. Scotland did not have autonomy other than the autonomy to ask for and often receive more favourable treatment. That would in time prove a frustrating limitation.

2
The Origins of the Scottish Central Administration

Introduction

The origins of Scotland's distinctive structure of government are elusive. The office of Scottish Secretary, created in 1885, might seem a logical starting point but a structure of administrative boards based in Edinburgh existed before this. It might, therefore, seem sensible to start by considering why and when these came into existence. What is discovered is that there were different starting points for the various boards and that they emerged from a pre-existing set of institutions. It proves extremely difficult to find any single or clear origin. The temptation is to go as far back as the Treaty of Union, 1707 and the provisions within it for maintaining Scottish institutions. However, perhaps more useful than trying to find an elusive starting point is a quest to make sense of the continuation of Scottish institutions. It is not so much that some formative event or decision or set of events and decisions set a path which led ineluctably to a highly differentiated system of government in Britain. A mixture of chance, opportunities and cumulative decisions resulted in a system in which Scotland was treated as a distinct unit for a wide range of administrative functions.

Government growth is crucial to any understanding of the development of the system of British government and Scotland's place within it. However, this did not always mean that as government intervention increased so too did the Scottish dimension. But any attempt to understand the evolution of territorial politics within the British system of government over the course of the late nineteenth and early twentieth centuries must take account of the changing nature of government intervention. Debates on what government should do were more important than how it should be done. Nonetheless, having determined to

11

intervene, government had to determine the most appropriate, not always the best, methods of delivery. This explains how the union state developed from its foundations in the nineteenth century.

Historians have remarked on the lack of Scottish central administration during the middle part of the nineteenth century following the demise of the Scottish Manager and the passage of the Great Reform Act. Hanham remarked that for half a century after the 1832 Reform Act, the Scots 'were amongst the least governed people in Europe'.[1] Pryde had commented:

> Virtually leaderless, and without an official spokesman in Parliament, Scottish affairs were entrusted to a series of statutory boards and commissions, comprising ex-officio and appointed members, paid and unpaid, including such experts as lawyers, doctors and scientists, and meeting generally in Edinburgh. Almost inevitably, they got the name of being arbitrary, remote and bureaucratic.[2]

The Boards and local administration

The Scottish boards that emerged in the nineteenth century[3] owed their existence as separate institutions to the distinctiveness of Scots law and local administration. The idea of local government in Scotland as a creature of statute based mainly upon a system of local rates was described in 1935 as a 'comparatively modern idea'.[4] Founded mainly by royal charter and without much direct contact with Whitehall before the nineteenth century, central control emerged as the functions of Scottish local government increased. That the form of central administration which emerged differed from that in England was to be expected given the distance from Whitehall, the distinctiveness of local government with which it would be intricately involved, and the different practices and ideals in Scotland manifested particularly in education and the poor law. Notably, the system of central government administration that developed in the nineteenth century was very limited.

A Board of Supervision for the relief of the poor in Scotland was created in 1845 for the central administration of the poor law. Argument preceding the establishment of this board had been about whether a voluntary or compulsory system should operate to finance poor relief. The latter was adopted after the Disruption in the Church of Scotland in 1843 which had resulted in the secession of a large number of churchmen making the voluntary system unworkable.[5]

The three distinctive features of nineteenth-century welfare provision in Scotland have been listed by Levitt: the lack of overt control; the individualistic ethos of the welfare administrators; and the preference for voluntary assistance by the administrators.[6] The Scottish poor law administration never reached the level of notoriety of the English system which has been explained, at least to some extent, as a result of the lack of overt control exerted by the Scottish Board of Supervision.[7] Writing at the beginning of the twentieth century on local government in Scotland, Mabel Atkinson maintained that 'central administrative control practically begins with the institutions of the Board of Supervision'.[8]

Initially it had been assumed that the main form in which central control would be exerted would be judicial control. Recognising that it would be highly unlikely that a private individual would sue a defaulting local authority, the central board was charged with the power to prosecute. However the extent of central control by this means was thought by one commentator to have been negligible by the fact that the Board of Supervision only prosecuted two authorities between 1845 and 1870.[9] With the Board's powers statutorily limited to ensuring proper poorhouse management, making determinations in cases of inadequate relief, dismissing incompetent inspectors of poor and distributing the medical relief grant, Levitt drew the conclusion that the central administration was 'largely conducted through advice, recommendations and rules based on established practice'.[10]

The Camperdown Commission on Civil Service Departments in Scotland which reported in 1870 noted that much of the work of the Board of Supervision involved acting as arbitrator in legal disputes between parochial boards.[11] It was an unobtrusive regulatory body. As with other Scottish boards there was continuing pressure to change the composition and remit of the Board of Supervision. This came from Scotland, not Whitehall. The composition of the Board of Supervision and certain poor law practices as well as the more limited powers of the Scottish central administration also set the Scottish system apart from that of England and Wales. In his observations on the Secretary for Scotland Act of 1885, William Smith noted that the English Local Government Board was represented in Parliament by its President and its *ex officio* members, all of whom were Cabinet members:

The Board of Supervision, on the other hand, is not a departmental staff, but a deliberative committee of nine members, six of whom sitting by virtue of public office in Scotland – viz., the Lord Provosts of Edinburgh and Glasgow, the Solicitor-General for Scotland, and the Sheriffs of Perth, Renfrew, and Ross and Cromarty – and three of them nominated by the Crown, one of whom is chairman with a salary. The chairman is not eligible for Parliament.[12]

Under the Lunacy (Scotland) Act, 1857 a General Board of Commissioners in Lunacy for Scotland was established. Again, as with poor law, the central board's influence over the local administration, which in the case of lunacy meant twenty-two districts in Scotland each with a local lunacy board, was to take the form of judicial control through the Court of Session. By 1885, the General Board had never actually used this judicial device.[13] It consisted of five Commissioners nominated by the Crown: three paid, two unpaid and with the assistance of two deputy Commissioners, both medical officers, and a paid secretary with a staff of clerks and was responsible to Parliament through the Home Secretary until 1885.

The administration of prisons in Scotland had also evolved in a distinct manner. The Prisons (Scotland) Act, 1877 established the Prison Commissioners for Scotland who included three Crown appointees plus the Sheriff of Perthshire and the Crown Agent for Scotland. As with the other boards, an annual report was produced and presented to Parliament. A Fishery Board came into existence with a new constitution in 1882. The Board preceding it had covered England and the Isle of Man until 1849 and 1868 respectively, after which time it dealt exclusively with Scotland. The Board consisted of three Sheriffs and seven Crown appointees including a secretary.[14] Until 1885 Crown appointees were made on the recommendation of the Lord Advocate, though officially through the Home Secretary.

Educational administration

In 1884, the year before his appointment as Secretary of the Scotch Education Department, Henry Craik wrote about the two centuries of Scottish 'national education' and contrasted this with only fourteen years in England.[15] Craik described the Scottish system 'national in the sense that it was established by law: was in theory co-extensive with the country; and drew its resources from a statutory assessment'.[16] A Committee of the Privy Council had been created in April 1839 'to superintend the application of any sums voted by Parliament for the purpose of promoting Public Education'[17] which covered both England and Scotland.

Attempts in Parliament to establish a Board of Education for Scotland in 1854 and 1855 had narrowly failed but the Royal Commission under the Duke of Argyll, appointed in 1864, to investigate Scottish education led to the recommendation that a Board of Education should be created as an administrative adjunct to the Committee of Council. The Argyll Commission had noted the 'extreme variation'[18] that characterised Scottish education:

At present there is no competent authority to initate, to administer, or to superintend. Schools spring up where they are not required and there are no schools where they are required. The buildings may be good or they may be unsuitable. The school apparatus may be adequate, or there may not be a bench to write at or a blackboard or map throughout the length and breadth of a whole district. The teachers may be good or they may be utterly incompetent: they may be wealthy men, or they may be starving: they may be under official supervision, or the entire management of the schools may devolve upon themselves, and they may be responsible to no one. The children may attend school or they may not attend, but grow up in absolute ignorance. All these evils are due to want of organisation, and suggest the necessity of some central authority to regulate the education of the country.[19]

It may have been a 'national' system but it was far from uniform.

The Commission, therefore, proposed that a Board of Education should be established with investigative, supervisory and advisory powers.[20] Additionally, they called for a census of accommodation and supervision of the building of schools. Notably, the Commission saw the Board as complementing, rather than superseding, the Committee of Council.[21] In 1869, a year after the Commission reported, the Duke of Argyll introduced a bill on Scottish education. Despite having the support of the Lord Advocate, the bill fell with other unfinished business after it had been returned to the Lords in a much amended form from the House of Commons.

In 1870, an Education Act was passed for England and Wales[22] which was followed by the introduction of a Scottish bill by George Young, the Lord Advocate. As the Education (Scotland) Act, 1872, it was to be 'far and away the most ambitious and statesmanlike measure affecting Scottish education before the twentieth century'.[23] Criticism of the bill had concentrated on the proposed new department. Young had envisaged the main central governing body for Scottish education to be a Committee of the Privy Council which, along with its civil servants, was to be known as the Scotch Education Department.[24] One notable critic of this proposal was the Duke of Richmond and Gordon, later to become the first Secretary for Scotland and Vice President of the Scotch Education Department in 1885. The provision of a Committee of the Privy Council for Education in Scotland, which came into existence on August 9, 1872, was not regarded as likely to be of any value by the Duke, 'It means simply a room in Whitehall, with the word 'Scotland' painted on the door. It is a sham, and can be nothing but a sham.'[25]

In addition to the Committee of Council, which Young explained was required to administer the imperial funds voted by Parliament, a Board of Education in Scotland, opposed by Young, was to be included in the Act after an amendment was successfully moved in the Lords. By Orders in Council its life was extended by two years and then a further year by another Act in 1877. The Board was dissolved in 1879 but only after attempts to give it a permanent status had failed. The Act of 1872 instituted the 'framework of the new system'[26] and while the central bodies were important, the major institutional achievement of the Act was the provision of 984 districts, each to be managed by a school board elected triennially. Centrally, the Act established a 'Scotch Education Department' in London, as well as a temporary Board of Education in Edinburgh. The Committee of Privy Council charged with distributing grants, framing a code for grants, and regulating examinations for the teachers' certificates of competence attracted criticism and Scottish MPs insisted upon the acceptance of the Lords' amendment to include a Board of Education, as had been proposed by the Argyll Commission.

The Scotch Education Department (SED) existed only in name, creating dissatisfaction with the system of government which found expression in Parliament. The critics of the SED saw the retention of the temporary Board of Education as the best prospect for Scottish education.[27] In reply to a question in March 1877, Viscount Sandon, Vice President of the Council, told the Commons that the Scottish Committee had not met the previous year at all:

> It has not been considered necessary, nor would it have been in accordance with usage, to summon, under ordinary circumstances, to Whitehall the other members of the Scotch Department; but other members of that Department have been consulted on details with which they were specially conversant, or when matters of general policy respecting Scotch Education have arisen.[28]

In effect, the Scotch Education Department, like its English counterpart, had a largely nominal existence.

During the debate on Scottish education grants, the lack of a 'really Scotch element in the administration of the Scottish system of Education' was criticised.[29] In reply, Sir Stafford Northcote, Chancellor of the Exchequer, maintained that a Scotch Education Department did exist and named the members at that time to be the Lord President, the Prime Minister (First Lord of the Treasury), the Lord Advocate, Lord Gordon of Drumearn and himself.[30] The Chancellor also told the Commons that with the demise of the Education Board in Edinburgh there would be more for the Committee to do. In addition, he announced that from the following year there would be a separate vote for one of the Assistant Secretaries, who would be specially engaged on Scottish business, instead of the then existing practice of taking the estimates altogether: 'So that there would be a Scotch administration, he would not say all composed of Scotchmen, but of men conversant with Scotch business.'[31] Notably, the Lord Advocate did not automatically become a Privy Councillor, but with the creation of the Privy Council Committee on Scottish Education and the decision to include the Lord Advocate as a member, Scotland's principal law officer and, until 1885, the individual acting as 'Scotland's Minister', became a Privy Councillor *ex officio*. In reply to a Parliamentary Question, Gladstone had explained the position of the Lord Advocate:

> The practice, I believe, has been this – that the Lord Advocate has never been appointed on accession to Office to the Committee of Council on Education. He has been appointed of late years after holding Office for a certain time.[32]

In 1937 when the proposals of the Gilmour Committee were being discussed, the Lord Advocate noted the risk of future Lord Advocates losing the *ex officio* Privy Councillorship.[33] In fact, Lord Advocates appointed following the Reorganisation of Offices (Scotland) Act, 1939, continued to be made Privy Councillors.

Dissatisfaction with the Scottish central administration

It can, therefore, be seen that even before 1885, Scottish administration was different from that south of the border. Demands for special treatment were strengthened by the very existence of an already separate set of central administrative bodies. For the most part, these were administrative boards operating from Edinburgh answerable to Parliament through the Home Secretary, which effectively meant the Lord

Advocate. Education was exceptional in that its central organisation and co-ordination was centred in London. Scottish administration followed the English pattern after 1832 with Boards becoming Ministries. Education, however, stood out and seems to have acted as a catalyst reinforcing the case for a special Scottish Minister despite some Scottish educationalists' insistence that a British-wide Education Ministry should be set up.

In the nineteenth century, dissatisfaction with the method by which Scotland was governed was expressed periodically. The Lord Advocate had come to dominate Scottish political life by the beginning of the century after the abolition of the Scottish Privy Council in 1708 and the Secretaryship of State in 1746.[34] The office of Scottish Manager which followed reached its apogee under Henry Dundas, first Viscount Melville.[35] In 1804 in a discussion in the House of Commons Charles Hope of Granton, the Lord Advocate described his duties as 'extensive beyond conception' and stated that he performed duties in 1804 which before the Union were performed by the Lord High Chancellor, Lord Justice Clerk, Lord Privy Seal as well as the Lord Advocate.[36]

Criticism of the Lord Advocate during the early part of the nineteenth century did not lead to demands for the abolition of the office, but for a definition and limitation of his functions. The Whig journal, the *Edinburgh Review* was one of the strongest critics of the functions of the Lord Advocate's office.[37] But there appeared to be little desire to see the return of the office of Secretary of State for Scotland:

> In the first place there is no necessity for such a Secretary. There is no more need of a separate Secretary for Scotland, than for Yorkshire, Northumberland, or Wales. Everything that Scotland requires to be done can easily be accomplished by the general Secretary for the whole kingdom, and by the other establishments with which the country is now quite familiar ... In the second place, if we must have a separate Secretary, we are very clear that, let it be given to whom it may, this office ought never to be united with that of Public Prosecutor.[38]

Criticism ebbed with the passage of the Jury Act in 1825 which stemmed the extent of the Lord Advocate's judicial influence. The struggles surrounding the Reform Act also served to demote the issue of Scottish administration. The discredited system of Scottish government dominated by a single Manager had almost come to an end after the death of Henry Dundas, although his son Robert acted as Manager until 1827 but without the near omnipotence of his father. It was in the period after the

Great Reform Act of 1832 and with the demise of the Scottish Manager that Scotland appeared to be an 'ungoverned' nation. Nevertheless, the incorporation of Scottish affairs within the responsibilities of the Home Office, acting through the Lord Advocate, deprived Scotland of much of the Scottish central administration and direction of earlier years:

> Even in the first days after 1832 it is well known how sick and tired Jeffrey became of his position of Lord Advocate, in which he was blamed if anything went wrong, but in which he had little power to make anything go right. Both he and Cockburn came to the conclusion that it was indispensable to have, besides the Lord Advocate, some other parliamentary representative of the general interests of Scotland.[39]

The vacuum created by the abolition of the Scottish Manager was not felt to have been adequately filled when Canning had transferred Scottish affairs to the Home Office and appointed Lord Althorp as Scotch Lord of the Treasury. One MP described the new post as 'somewhat shadowy and mysterious', a 'sort of assistant to the Lord Advocate'.[40] During the 1850s, concern was increasingly expressed that Scotland was ignored and forgotten in London. In 1851, the Convention of Royal Burghs asked for the political and legal functions of the Lord Advocate to be separated and for the appointment of a Secretary of State for Scotland. The Home Secretary had replied that he was the Secretary of State for Scotland.

In November 1853 a public meeting, organised by the non-party National Association for the Vindication of Scottish Rights, was held in Edinburgh, attended by over 2000 people.[41] The Association was short-lived but presented a petition in the Lords that included a call for the appointment of a Secretary of State to preside over the administration of Scottish affairs.[42] This general dissatisfaction was expressed in 1857 in the first issue of the *Journal of Jurisprudence* in which the author did not complain of a lack of Scottish legislation passed by Parliament, but found fault with the legislative and judicial processes:

> What we want at present is not so much new laws as the consolidation of those we have; and, more particularly, the rendering of the machinery by which they are worked, a little less cumbrous and uncertain.[43]

Coupland described the Scottish Rights Society as the 'First Nationalist Movement' and the campaign for a Secretaryship of State for Scotland as the 'Second Nationalist Movement'.[44] This may have exaggerated the links between these developments in Scottish politics but many of the personalities engaged in the Scottish Rights Society were to be found campaigning for a Secretary of State in the 'Second Movement' and there was overlap in their demands. Motions calling for the re-establishment of the office of Secretary of State for Scotland and for an Under Secretary of State were proposed in Parliament in 1855 and 1858 respectively.[45] The Scottish Rights Society and the romantic nationalism associated with it were all but forgotten in the upsurge of British nationalism following the outbreak of the Crimean War in 1854 and the Indian Mutiny in 1857.

In 1858, William Baxter MP argued that the matter was not one of Whig versus Tory 'but a question of administration'. He described the Lord Advocate as the 'political monarch and dictator of Scotland [who] had the entire charge of all the legislative business affecting Scotland, and was the sole organ of his Administration in either House of Parliament',[46] and drew a picture of Scottish administration reminiscent of the days of the Scottish Manager. The Lord Advocate combined the roles of public prosecutor and chief law officer with that of a 'Minister for Scotland', receiving deputations from Scotland, attending to business in the House and ensuring that Scottish business was not neglected in London. The motion, however, was defeated by 174 votes to 47.[47] The view prevailed that there would be insufficient work for an Under Secretary of State for Scotland to do and that the Home Office, Lord Advocate and Edinburgh Boards were adequate.[48]

In June 1864, Sir James Fergusson moved a resolution in the House of Commons calling for a Select Committee: 'to inquire how far the number of the Members of the Administration charged with the conduct of the affairs of Scotland, and having seats in Parliament, is commensurate with the requirements of that part of the United Kingdom'.[49] In reply, the Lord Advocate, James Moncrieff had described his 'usual course':

> I have come up to London in the second or third week in February, and remained until the 20th March. Sometimes I may have borrowed a day or two after that date when the Court of Session rises for the jury trials, which then immediately commence; but never, so far as I am aware, to the detriment of public business or the inconvenience of the House. I have always been in my place after Easter, and have remained till at least the 20th July; and then, when the Scotch Members are generally more intent on preparation for the 12th of August than on legislative action, I have sometimes gone to Scotland immediately after that date.[50]

In 1867 Baxter asked questions in Parliament aimed at securing support for the appointment of a Scottish Minister, particularly as the Lord Advocate was not then represented in the Commons.[51] The Home Secretary, Spencer Walpole, accepted that Scottish Members in both parties favoured an inquiry into Scottish administration and reflected a general discontent in Scotland.[52]

In a joint letter to Gladstone in March 1869, Sir Robert Anstruther and Mr Edward H.J. Craufurd,[53] representing around two-thirds of the Scottish Members, asked for the appointment of a Chief Secretary for Scotland with functions similar to that of the Irish Secretary plus matters including education, factories and mines. Anstruther and Craufurd were critical of the system of management which operated without any direct responsibility to Parliament and of the Lord Advocate's inability to undertake all duties associated with the office. The MPs listed the 'multiform' duties of the Lord Advocate including acting as Attorney-General for Scotland, Public Prosecutor, uniting functions of a grand jury and coroner, dealing with appeal cases in the Lords, being the Scottish legal adviser to the Crown, as well as having a large private practice. Having conferred with the Chief Secretary for Ireland, Anstruther and Craufurd maintained that there would be little difficulty in defining the work of the civil and legal officers so that they should discharge their respective duties to greater advantage.

In 1869, Prime Minister Gladstone conceded that an inquiry into the Scottish Boards should be conducted during the recess. He told the House that the inquiry 'did not arise from any observations made by the Government themselves, but arose out of a variety of communications made to us by Scotch Members'.[54] The inquiry was conducted by Lord Camperdown and Sir William Clerke who concluded, largely, in favour of the status quo. They reported in March 1870 after interviewing Edward Craufurd MP, Duncan McLaren MP, Sir Robert Anstruther MP and William Baxter MP in London and officials of the Scottish Boards in Edinburgh.[55] The Commissioners were required to consider the possibilities of effecting economy by means of concentrating the duties of the boards under a Parliamentary head and generally to inquire into the constitution, establishments and duties of the boards.[56]

The main supporters of change from whom the inquiry took evidence differed in their objections and proposals. The main objection of Craufurd and Anstruther was that the boards were inefficient. Despite presenting a detailed scheme of reform, McLaren failed to convince the Commissioners that he really understood the workings of the boards. Neither was Baxter able to convince the Commissioners that he understood the weaknesses of the existing system. This lack of expertise made their estimated calculation of savings lack credibility. As the Commissioners remarked: 'it is difficult to see how any calculation as to prospective saving can be trustworthy which is not founded on an intimate knowledge of the duties of the various departments.'[57] Opponents of any radical change, though willing to consider minor alterations in the composition of the boards and particularly the amalgamation of the Lunacy Board with the Board of Supervision, included MPs and former MPs such as Sir William Gibson-Craig, Peter McLagan MP and Nisbet Hamilton, the Lord Justice General and, notably, Edward Strathearn Gordon MP, who had been and would again become the Lord Advocate. Expertise lay on the side of the status quo. The Camperdown Report concluded that the Lord Advocate was, in practice, the 'Scotch Minister' but found that:

> the Home Secretary should be in fact, as he already is in theory, Minister for Scotland, having two advisers – the Lord Advocate and a Civil Parliamentary Officer attached to the Home Department – who would consult together on all questions of Scotch business and legislation, and between whom, in cases of difference, the Home Secretary would ultimately decide, and either or both of whom he might consult, according to his discretion, with reference to the distribution of patronage. . . It does not appear to us necessary or advisable to appoint for Scotland an independent and highly paid officer answering to the Chief Secretary for Ireland.[58]

The Commissioners maintained that criticism of the Scottish administration did not come from the Scottish people but chiefly from Scottish MPs and others who had contact with the authorities in Edinburgh and London. They found that a major source of complaint was the preponderance of the legal profession in the administration of Scotland in the shape of the Lord Advocate and membership of the boards. Camperdown felt that there was no argument against the amalgamation of the Lunacy Board with the Board of Supervision and in general the work of the boards was found to be done well and economically.[59]

The Government accepted the central findings of the inquiry, though on the detailed proposals they differed with Camperdown: the Lunacy Board survived intact despite the Commission having given, as the Duke of Argyll described it, 'a kind of half opinion that one Lunacy Commissioner would be sufficient'.[60] Baxter and McLaren appear to have been conscious of the divergent principles involved in consolidating the Scottish administration under a single Parliamentary head while attempting to maintain something more than a semblance of Scottish administration in Scotland. Opposition to the abolition of the boards had been expressed in terms of defending devolution. In 1858, the MP for St Andrews stated that he 'viewed with great jealousy any attempt to transfer the administration of Scotland from Edinburgh to London.'[61] F.M.G. Willson has stated that it is misleading 'to speak of British administrative development; a review of the use of ministries and boards must take account of national differences.'[62] While the Government endorsed Camperdown's approval of the Scottish boards in 1870, there had been a tendency away from such a system of administration in England and the growing acceptance of the doctrine of individual ministerial responsibility especially from the 1853 Northcote–Trevelyan Report which had criticised the patronage associated with boards.[63] In June 1870, Northcote–Trevelyan progressed further: competitive tests for admission to certain departments and situations were made obligatory. Although Camperdown expressed the view that the Home Secretary ought to act as Scottish Minister responsible for the Scottish boards, thus concurring with the doctrine of individual ministerial responsibility, the practicalities of such a proposition, given the multifarious duties involved, meant that it was doubtful whether anything could really be expected to change as a result of the Commissioners' proposals. The popularity of Lord Advocate Moncrieff, who had retired in 1869, and the abilities of his successor, George Young may well have concealed, as William Smith suggested, the need for change in the same direction as England.[64]

Fifteen years after the Camperdown Report, the Secretaryship for Scotland was created due to the pressures from Scotland rather than pressure to introduce individual ministerial responsibility and to dispose of the Edinburgh boards. Indeed, London remained hostile to the establishment of a Scottish Office detached from the Home Office. Resolutions continued to be presented in Parliament and questions asked urging the creation of an office with special responsibility for Scotland.[65] On the whole, the same grievances as before were heard: partly a feeling of neglect, partly injured pride but largely dissatisfaction with the system of administration. In Parliament criticism of the dominance of the legal profession was voiced. In 1881, Rosebery argued that the dominance of the legal profession was 'almost unequalled in history' and the only other example of a government restricting its offices was the Government of the Holy See. Scotland had been 'handed over to the legal rather than to the spiritual arm'.[66] The view that Scottish affairs were not being dealt with adequately was heard and demands were made for providing Scotland with some measure of influence in London.[67] In 1872, Sir David Wedderburn listed Scottish grievances – the lack of any official representative in the Cabinet; the lack of efficient machinery for giving Scotland the benefit of UK legislation; the probability that Scottish MPs would be outvoted by English and Irish Members even when the Scots were unanimous; and insufficient time and attention given to Scotland by Parliament.[68] The demand for a Scottish Secretary became the solution to many problems on which the hopes and expectations of many Scottish MPs increasingly concentrated.

Specific matters causing discontent fed the general feeling of dissatisfaction. Education was, as previously noted, a major source of discontent throughout the 1870s and early part of the next decade. The office of Lord Advocate continued to cause disquiet amongst Scottish MPs, partly because of the perennial question of the functions attached to the office and also because of the inadequate facilities provided for the Lord Advocate in London. Camperdown remarked in 1881 that meetings between the Lord Advocate and Scottish Members would take place 'in a tea-room, or some other hole-and-corner place, where they could collect together'.[69] At the second reading of the Local Government Board (Scotland) Bill, Dalrymple noted that the 'separate residence of the Lord Advocate was abolished, and he was made the occupant of a very small and, he believed, unwholesome room in the Home Office. That went far to impair the dignity and the power of the Lord Advocate.'[70] William Smith, in his book on the Scottish Secretary, published just after its creation, quoted Dalrymple's speech but adds an adjective: 'small, damp, and unwholesome room'.[71] An important piece of criticism of the Scottish administration was to be found at the end of Omond's history of the Lord Advocates of Scotland written in 1883:

> Since then [1834] the machinery of Government has become more and more complicated, and almost the whole management of Scottish affairs has been thrown upon the Lord Advocate. The result has been that, not by the fault of the Lord Advocates, but by the force of circumstances, these affairs have been to a great extent neglected. There has been no system. Useful legislation has been frequently delayed. Scottish bills in Parliament have been considered of little importance. The one official member for Scotland has been overworked and burdened with an undue proportion of duties and responsibilities.[72]

The campaigns for a Secretaryship of State in the 1880s

In 1878, Sir Richard Cross, the Home Secretary, introduced a bill for the creation of an additional Under Secretary for Home Affairs with responsibility for Scotland but it was not proceeded with. No more was heard on the matter during the Conservative Administration which ended in March 1880.[73] Gladstone's antipathy and Whitehall inertia were powerful counters during Liberal Governments to the considerable body of support for change.[74] Rosebery's intervention was to provide the cause with an important ally who, during his appointment as Under Secretary at the Home Office from August 1881 to June 1883, argued for change within the Government.

The Earl Fife brought the attention of the Lords to the question of the Scottish administration in June 1881.[75] This debate was to be an important juncture in the campaign. The Scottish press, led by Charles Cooper of the Scotsman, 'took the cue'.[76] It was around this time also that the 'slippery slope' argument was turned on its head. As Rosebery had warned during the debate, 'the words "Home Rule" have begun to be distinctly and loudly mentioned in Scotland' and a Secretary of State was needed to stem this growing demand'.[77] That year a resolution had been brought before the Convention of Royal Burghs urging a separate and subordinate legislature. Land agitation in Ireland was at its height and the Irish Question dominated politics. It was also recognised, even by opponents of a Scottish Secretary, that discontent was 'very deeply rooted in Scotland, and it was daily finding more forcible expression'.[78] This ensured that the Government would not treat the claims lightly. Nevertheless the Earl Granville, for the Government, could only promise the 'fairest and fullest consideration' and reminded their Lordships that the Government had been asked to create Ministers of Justice, Education, Agriculture, Commerce and Mercantile Marine.[79]

Rosebery's appointment to the Home Office had been made on the understanding, at least by Rosebery, that arrangements for Scottish business were temporary and that reforms would be instituted at an early date. However, with little evidence of progress, resignation became inevitable. Gladstone viewed Rosebery's support for a Scottish Office as Rosebery's strategy to enter the Cabinet.[80] Robert Rhodes James described the differences:

all proposals foundered on Gladstone's refusal to accept a separate Scottish Ministry and Rosebery's determination not to accept anything else. In these circumstances the numerous letters and memoranda which sped to and fro, the meetings of senior Ministers and the draft proposals which everyone was drawing up were somewhat unreal.[81]

A number of Scottish pieces of legislation were passed in 1882: the Educational Endowments Act, Fisheries Board Act, Entail Act, Citation Amendment Act, Teachers' Tenure Act and other less important pieces of legislation were all passed. In its New Year edition 1883, the *Times* looked back over the first complete year in which an Under Secretary at the Home Office had responsibility for Scottish affairs and noted the quantitative improvement in the legislative programme for Scotland:

> By very general consent these successes are ascribed to the end of last year in the arrangements for conducting Scottish business. The management of Scottish affairs was then divided between the Lord Advocate and an additional Under-Secretary in the Home Department. . . . The benefits, both legislative and administrative, which Scotland has derived from the change have given force to the demands for a more permanent and more worthy recognition of Scotland's claim on the Government.[82]

In early May 1883, the Cabinet discussed a scheme to create a Local Government Board for Scotland with a Parliamentary President. Some members of the Cabinet – Dilke, Chamberlain, and Harcourt – supported the measure as a means of retaining Rosebery.[83] However, Rosebery had already decided to make the 'meaningless gesture'[84] of resignation, though within a month Harcourt introduced the Local Government Board (Scotland) Bill. The bill was to create a Local Government Board for Scotland consisting of a president with a seat in Parliament, the Lord Advocate and some *ex officio* Cabinet members. Gladstone's offer of the position of Scottish Minister in the unlikely event of the bill's passage was refused by Rosebery.[85] The bill was neither regarded as adequate by those who wanted a Secretary of State nor really desirable by the Government. As William Smith commented 'The Bill was introduced by the Home Secretary in a singular speech, from which it might be inferred that he did not regard the change as one of serious importance,[86]

On January 16, 1884 a meeting was held in Edinburgh, bringing together the various supporters of a Secretaryship of State. Chaired by the Conservative Marquess of Lothian and addressed by Conservatives and Liberals, the meeting adopted resolutions demanding the unconditional appointment of a Secretary of State for Scotland.[87] The meeting in the Free Assembly Hall had been organised by the Convention of Royal Burghs who had sent invitations to numerous individuals and bodies in Scotland. Even the *Times* accepted that 'these were responded to so fully as to justify the assumption by the meeting of the title "national" '.[88] An impressive gathering, including 132 Scottish burghs and with eighteen MPs,[89] was told by Lothian that the meeting 'was the largest and most universal gathering that had ever taken place in Scotland'. The only dissentient note appears to have been that of a letter from the ever intractable Earl of Wemyss which declared that the existing machinery was 'amply sufficient if judiciously and efficiently worked'.

In a more perceptive editorial than was probably appreciated at the time, the *Times* noted the diversity of claims and demands being made of the proposed Secretaryship for Scotland:

> when we examine the demands of those who ask for a Scottish Minister, we find them incoherent and undefined. Some want a man to push measures through the House of Commons, some want a man to energize local government, and some want to lay the foundation for creating a separate Scottish bureaucracy, which they would speedily seek to locate in Edinburgh, thus wantonly splitting every branch of administration in two for no better end than the multiplication of offices. Of the three classes the last one really defined its own aims, though it judiciously veils them under vague and confused clamour for a Minister who, it is popularly supposed, would in some way add to the importance and foster the nationality of the Scotch. A Scottish Minister could not stem the flood of talk in the House of Commons or induce Mr Parnell to cease from obstruction; therefore he is useless for hastening the passage of Scotch Bills. He could not improve local government, because his interference would be usurpation, and the task, moreover, would be beyond his power. But what he could do, and is meant to do by those who have set this agitation on foot and worked it up to something like popularity, is to become the nucleus of a separate central administration, to culminate in due time to costly and superfluous apparatus resembling that now at work in Ireland.[90]

The meeting demanded the introduction of a bill early in the next session, recommended that Parliament and the Prime Minister be petitioned by the bodies represented in the hall. After such success in uniting such a diverse body and having agreed to constitute a committee to further the aims of the meeting, the Government had little choice but to meet the representatives. In February, a deputation communicated the resolutions to the Prime Minister. A.J. Balfour and Lord Balfour of Burleigh, both of whom had spoken at the Edinburgh meeting, urged Salisbury to support the creation of a Secretaryship for Scotland. The new bill was brought forward in 1884 and had both Conservative and Liberal support. The Earl of Dalhousie made clear, in presenting the bill, that the Government sought cross-party support for the measure.[91] Presented initially in the Lords on 8 May, the Secretary for Scotland Bill differed from the previous year's Local Government Board (Scotland) Bill in that individual ministerial responsibility, missing from the earlier bill, was basic to the new proposals. The bill was amended in committee to add law and justice to the office's responsibilities. Rosebery had moved the amendment supported by Lords Huntly, Lothian, Aberdeen and Salisbury. The Government yielded and agreed to the additional functions being transferred. Balfour of Burleigh's amendment to include the transfer of the General Register of Sasines was carried despite Government opposition. However, Huntly's amendment transferring elementary education to the new department was rejected by thirty-two votes to eighteen.[92] At report stage, Camperdown successfully moved an amendment omitting the part of the schedule of the bill which would have transferred the management of endowed school education in Scotland from the Committee of Council to the new Secretary.

In July, Gladstone announced the withdrawal of the Government's legislative programme after the defeat of its Franchise Bill. After this 'massacre of the innocents', the Government agreed to re-introduce the Secretary for Scotland Bill at a later date.[93] It was to be the only one of the late Government's proposed legislation to survive. Even after the fall of the Gladstone Administration and the return of Salisbury, Rosebery continued to pilot it through the Lords. On August 14, the Royal Assent was given and the Secretary for Scotland Act, 1885 established an office which was at first to be occupied by the Duke of Richmond and Gordon, who had opposed its establishment. The Act's main responsibility was education – the Secretary for Scotland being the Vice President of the Scottish Education Department. Law and justice, which Rosebery's amendment had included in the bill of 1884, had been withdrawn 'rather than run the risk of losing the Bill on account of one particular provision.'[94] However within two years an amendment Act was passed to include law and justice under the auspices of the Secretary for Scotland. The creation of the office no more defined a lasting and precise delimitation of the powers and responsibilities of the Secretary for Scotland any more than it was to appease Scottish national sentiment or satisfy Scottish grievances.

3
Settling Down to Business

In 1925, an article in a popular Scottish periodical described the Scottish Office as 'a mysterious Department in London which came into existence in a casual kind of way forty years ago'. The Scottish Secretary 'is a mysterious potentate who is known to exercise great power in certain spheres, but the nature of whose functions, powers and responsibilities is little understood by the people he is supposed to govern as a minister responsible to the Imperial Parliament. It is amazing how little the machinery for the government of Scotland is understood either in England or in Scotland, how antiquated it is, how patched up and improvised, how much of a makeshift'.[1] Looking back from 1925, such a description of the developing Scottish administration had much validity: there had been no guiding principles in the thinking behind the development of the office of Secretary for Scotland. The origins of the office had been a response to Scottish grievances rather than a desire to devise a scheme for administrative efficacy. Its uncertain responsibilities and the different proposals that initially emerged suggest that issues of good government were secondary. Campaigners for a Scottish Minister had not detailed the powers and responsibilities of the proposed office.

There were different interests amongst supporters of the office which partly explains the impression conveyed by those who advocated the creation of a Scottish Office that they were confused as to its purpose, functions and future. In addition, Hanham has maintained that it took four years, from 1883 to 1887, to reach agreement on three fundamental matters: the status of the Scottish Minister; the office's role in educational matters; and the amount of Home Office work to be done by the Secretary for Scotland.[2] While a fair degree of agreement was reached and this lasted for some time, none of these matters was finally resolved. The resolution of the differences concerning the status of the office did not occur until from 1892 the Scottish Secretary established himself continually in the Cabinet, War Cabinets apart. The office was elevated to that of a Secretary of State in 1926 and the Scottish Secretary of State only received the same remuneration as other Cabinet Ministers in 1937. Additional educational responsibilities were handed over to the SED including responsibility for the Science and Art grants in 1897 and university education only transferred in the 1980s. Powers and responsibilities continued to be added to the Scottish Office for the rest of its history.

In other respects too, the Scottish Office moved away from its original conception by the outbreak of the Second World War. The relations with the boards had not been clearly set out in the Act of 1885 and the initial appearance of an office superimposed on the boards developed into a much more integrated structure by 1939. The site of the Scottish administration appeared to be settled in 1939, but St Andrews House which opened that year never did become the home for all of the staff of the Scottish Office in Edinburgh.

A number of unforeseen consequences of the creation of a territorially defined office emerged over the first fifty years of its existence. The establishment of the Scottish Office further legitimised the argument that Scotland should be treated as a separate entity. When consideration was given to the creation of new administrative bodies which normally would have been organised on a British or United Kingdom basis there was normally some plea for a Scottish body. Further to this, there developed demands for Scottish statistics and information which could only enhance the notion of an emerging Scottish politics and in Parliament there were calls for Scottish special treatment. The Scottish Office also provided a focus for attention and for grievances concerning matters that were both within and outwith the statutory limits of its responsibilities. Matters were not resolved soon after the office was established. The establishment of the Scottish Office had far-reaching implications and its development challenge any idea that its creation placated the Scots.

The Acts of 1885–89

A bill introduced in 1884 intended to give the Secretary for Scotland responsibility for law and justice but not education. The following year a new bill, which became the Secretary for Scotland Act, excluded law and justice but included education. These measures were a response to general Scottish grievances, not even related to the responsibilities proposed for the office. If anything, pressure existed to exclude functions from the Secretary's responsibilities. According to Sir Lyon Playfair, education was only included because lawyers had successfully argued that law and justice should be removed, 'so that education has been thrown to him [Secretary for Scotland] as a *corpus vile*. Schoolmasters and Professors are not as powerful as lawyers in this House'.[3] He prefaced his remarks by mentioning the 'good many Parliamentary vicissitudes' which had finally resulted in the situation.

Playfair, regarded as a keen defender of Scottish education, complained about education's subsidiary status, as he saw it, implied in the Act. He noted the increasing tendency to create Education Ministries in other countries:

> But Scotland alone, which above all other countries is essentially educational, is in future to have a Minister made up of a large variety of heterogeneous materials mixed up like a Scotch haggis, and then salted with education to give it a flavour.[4]

Playfair would have preferred that the Scottish Office had not been established but argued in a letter to Gladstone in December 1884 that if education had to be included it would be necessary to have the Minister in the House of Commons.[5] Opposition to the bill, and particularly the separating of Scottish and English education led Playfair to announce that he would not be seeking re-election as the Member for the Scottish Universities.[6]

In 1884, a Select Committee under the Chancellor of the Exchequer, Hugh Childers had concluded that 'primary education in England and Scotland should be under the control of the same Minister' though it conceded that 'it would be well to have a distinct Permanent Secretary for Scotland, responsible to the Minister of Education'.[7] Sir Francis Sandford, Chief Secretary of the Education Department, believed that the administrative distinction between Scottish and English education was 'nominal'.[8] Although accepting that the education systems and ideals of Scotland and England were so different that 'we could not get on without some Scotchmen exclusively devoted to Scotch work',[9] Sandford opposed the idea of separate departments for England and Scotland.[10] Notably, Mundella, the Vice President of the Committee of Council on Education, was disposed to establishing a board for educational administration in Edinburgh similar to that which had existed temporarily after the 1872 Education Act.[11] Sandford's successor at the Education Department, Patrick Cumin also agreed with the re-introduction of a board in Edinburgh which he hoped would act, as had the previous one, as a 'considerable safeguard to the department, because it was a kind of buffer between the local authorities and the central department'.[12]

However, Scottish administration was not well understood. When William Forster MP, who had served as Vice President for Education from 1868–74, gave evidence to the 1884 Select Committee, the committee and he appeared to know little about the temporary Education Board that had existed in Edinburgh during the previous decade.[13] At the committee stage of the Secretary for Scotland Bill in the Commons, it was alleged that 'Scotch evidence had been tendered to the Committee and refused' though this was denied by Playfair.[14] The unanimous proposal of the Select Committee for a British Minister for Education, which Playfair cited in argument against the Secretary for Scotland Bill, and Gladstone's stated intention to adopt the proposal in November 1884,[15] were, however, set aside in the creation of the office of Secretary for Scotland.

In Scotland, dissatisfaction with educational administration did not mean that there was support for the transfer of education from the Privy Council to the Scottish Office. The Educational Institute of Scotland (EIS), the professional body of Scottish teachers, was strongly opposed to the move and school boards were, on the whole, opposed. Even strong advocates of a Scottish Office recognised this opposition. Lord Balfour suggested strengthening the Scottish Committee of the Privy Council.[16] Unlike the transfer of the poor law and prisons to the protection of wild birds and the fishery board, education was included under the remit of the new office in the Act itself rather than in a schedule.[17] Rosebery explained this as a simpler manner of transferring education 'bodily' to the control of the new Secretary despite his preference for a more 'distinct way by scheduling the Education Act'.[18]

Argument surrounding educational responsibilities demonstrated the importance of appearance over substance. There had been some confusion in the Lords when the Earl of Minto had noted at report stage that an amendment passed in committee assigned the Secretary for Scotland the position of 'President' of the SED but had appeared in the amended bill as 'Vice President'. Rosebery explained that the change had been made at the insistence of the Lord President of the Council, Viscount Cranbrook, so that the Scottish Committee of Council was formally headed, as the English Committee, by him.[19] Nevertheless, Rosebery supported the amendment later moved by Minto which sought to remove the word 'Vice' from the Act thus creating a post of 'Secretary for Scotland and President of the Scottish Education Department'.

Rosebery argued that the examples of the Local Government Board and Board of Trade demonstrated that a Committee of Council could have a president other than the Lord President of the Council and that implicit in the term 'Vice President' was 'some idea of keeping up fancied connection with English Education'.[20]

Viscount Cranbrook's opposition was notable:

> What it amounted to was this – that no one but a Scotsman was to be considered fit to administer Scottish Education. He [Cranbrook] wished to know whether the noble Earl would like to exclude Scotsmen from interfering with, or exercising any influence on, English Education; or would take it out of the power of Scotsmen to administer Education in England – from his noble Friend (the Duke of Argyll), who had been head of the Council, or from his noble Friend (the Earl of Rosebery) who had attained a distinguished position as a Scotsman – a position which they did not at all grudge him?[21]

This issue would return a century later.

Having received the Royal Assent on 14 August, 1885, the Act came into operation with the appointment of the Duke of Richmond and Gordon. As he made clear in his letter of acceptance, he thought the office was unnecessary,

> You know my opinion of the office, and that it is quite unnecessary, but the Country and Parliament think otherwise – and the office has been created, and someone must fill it. Under these circumstances I am quite ready to take it, and will do my best to make it a success (if this is possible!).[22]

The office had been created out of general grievances, it had imprecisely defined responsibilities and the expectations of it were considerable. Within two years an Amendment Act had to be passed to clarify conflicting responsibilities of the Scottish and Home Offices concerning law and justice. The original bill, as Lord Lothian wrote in a memorandum to the Cabinet in July 1887, had been 'ill-drafted, and passed at the fag end of the Session of 1885'.[23] Revision of the Act was also because of the interpretation initially applied by the Home Secretary:

> The office only exists within certain Statutory powers. The Secretary has no jurisdiction whatever beyond what is specially imposed upon him by the Act. In every other respect, until experience has shown

the necessity for alteration in the Law, and the Law has been altered accordingly, the Secretary of State must still remain responsible.[24]

A.J. Balfour became Scottish Secretary in late July 1886 and during his seven months at the office he gave the 'first intimation of his real ability'.[25] In November 1886, Salisbury invited Balfour to join the Cabinet:

> In view of the fact that much of our impending legislation had a Scotch side – & Scotland being in no way represented in the Cabinet – I thought it expedient that you should become a member of it.[26]

The elevation to the Cabinet of the Scottish Secretary would go some way to placate the Lord Advocate whose sensibilities had been hurt at the prospect of having to deal with a Minister outside the Cabinet. Discontent in the Crofting Community during the early 1880s and the eruption of violence in 1882 with the Battle of the Braes on Skye,[27] was the background to the candidatures of four Independent Crofters and two Highland Land Leaguers in 1885. The frustratingly anomalous division of responsibilities, with the Home Office retaining responsibility for law and order and the Scottish Office responsible for local government and the local police,[28] was compounded by the stubborn objections of the Home Office and Lord Advocate to any further transfer of powers. The consequent inaction resulting from inter-departmental stalemate demanded resolution.

The problem had been apparent when the office was established. J.H. MacDonald, as Lord Advocate, had been required to send an explanation of the respective legal positions of the Home Secretary and the Scottish Secretary to Sir Richard Cross, the Home Secretary. MacDonald summarised the situation:

> The Commissioners under the Duke are responsible for the provision and proper working of the police force. The Sheriffs, Judges, and Secretary of State are responsible for the maintenance of the law, and as such have the police force at their disposal.[29]

Within a fortnight of taking office, Balfour wrote a memorandum for Cabinet explaining the problems and outlining his solution.[30] Accepting that legislation would be required to place the matter on a 'proper footing', Balfour argued that the 'extreme inconvenience, and even danger, of leaving things precisely as they are in the present disturbed condition of certain parts of Scotland' required some immediate 'mutual agreement' between the two offices.

Balfour recommended that the Secretary for Scotland ought to be the 'chief executive central authority'.[31] For him, the motive for change was clearly that of efficiency and not sentiment: 'To have two Chief Secretaries for Scotland, one sitting at the Home Office, the other at Dover House, is as insane as it would be to have two Chief Secretaries for Ireland, with different offices and different staffs'.[32] The Scottish Secretary's view suggested that the problem of finding a role for the office and determining its remit, apparent in debates before the establishment of the office, remained unresolved. As Balfour indicated in a memorandum for Cabinet, there was a gap between the expectations of the office and its legal remit: 'though nominally in charge of Scottish affairs, he has nothing to do with the most important portion of Scotch Government'.[33]

In order to clarify the situation along the lines proposed by Balfour, a much wider conception of the office's remit was needed. Balfour's two recommendations – that the Scottish Secretary should determine when and how the 'forces of the Crown are to be sent in aid of the local authority' and that the Lord Advocate should 'inform or consult' the Scottish Secretary rather than the Home Secretary – would mean that the Scottish Office was no longer merely a Scottish Education Ministry with some other responsibilities. The question of extending the sphere of the Scottish Office in the two years immediately after its inception involved the Scottish Secretary using his most potent, but rather risky, means of influence. In a letter to Salisbury, Prime Minister and his uncle, Balfour's veiled threat of resignation was an early, and most probably the first, example of the use of this power by a Scottish Secretary: 'I think you will find more difficulty than you anticipate in overcoming the red tapism of your cabinet; – and if you fail it becomes rather an interesting question what I ought to do'.[34] Cabinet acceptance of Balfour's demands allowed the Scottish Secretary to use his newly acquired powers to impress the Prime Minister. Though the lull in the land agitation was temporary, Balfour's success in asserting law and order and his initiation of plans to ease population pressure through his discussions with the Canadian and New Zealand High Commissioners in London for state-aided emigration, served to raise his standing and the status of the office.[35] Balfour's success at the Scottish Office did not mean that he was to remain there for long. In March 1887, far more challenging issues of land agitation and national sentiment were presented to Balfour in his next post as Chief Secretary for Ireland.

The Act of 1887

In his memorandum of August 1886, Balfour argued that the transfer of law and justice to the Scottish Office required legislation to 'place it on a proper footing'[36] though he viewed a Cabinet decision as sufficient for temporarily altering the situation. The Cabinet decided in September 1886 that 'it was essential that, in practice, there should be no division of authority'[37] and agreed the *de facto* transfer to the Scottish Office. Despite this Cabinet decision, the Lord Advocate in a memorandum in March 1887[38] argued against the *de jure* transfer of those functions:

> If the Secretary for Scotland were to exercise powers which are not conferred on him by Statute under which his office came into existence his action would be irregular, and I should think invalid. Delegation by an officer of state of duties imposed on him by Statute or ancient custom is plainly illegal.[39]

This had been written even though what Lord Advocate MacDonald had described as illegal had been in operation for six months. MacDonald's reply to Balfour's Cabinet memorandum of eight months before was legalistic and much concerned with the position of the Lord Advocate. The Act of 1885 had explicitly protected the Lord Advocate's situation:

> Nothing in this Act contained shall prejudice or interfere with any rights, powers, privileges, or duties vested in or imposed on the Lord Advocate by virtue of any Act of Parliament or custom.[40]

The Lord Advocate pointed out that the transfer of law and justice to the Scottish Office would affect his position, 'holding an ancient and important office, [the Lord Advocate would] be responsible to an official who is not a Secretary of State'.[41]

During the passage of the bill in 1887, Donald Crawford, who had been legal secretary to the Lord Advocate from 1880–85, moved an amendment to remove the exemption from transfer of the exercise of the prerogative of mercy to the Scottish Office.[42] Crawford's successful amendment avoided the anomaly whereby the Home Secretary would have had responsibility for a matter for which he would have had no direct means of acquiring any information. Reports by judges and law officers were made to the Scottish Secretary from whom the Home Office would have had to acquire the information. The reason for the proposed retention of this power in the Home Office had been that only a Secretary of State had a right at all times to approach the sovereign. This would provide some problems for the Scottish Secretary, though the occasions when the prerogative of mercy would need to be invoked would be few.

By the time legislation was being considered, Lord Lothian had succeeded Balfour as Scottish Secretary. Lothian was in the fortunate position of arguing for a change which had, in effect, already been brought about. His submission to the Cabinet was critical of the narrow conception of the office and argued that 'by the mere fact of his appointment' the Scottish Secretary was concerned with the 'whole business arising out of his connection with Scotland as its proper and direct Administrator'.[43] This view, according to Lothian, was generally accepted:

> The Treasury, other State Departments, public authorities, and private individuals have not, however, taken this restricted view of the Secretary for Scotland Act, and have accordingly been in the habit of addressing this Department direct on matters in any way connected with the business of Scotland.[44]

Lothian cited three examples of general business which 'in spite of every obstacle, flowed, by a gradual process' into the Scottish Office. The Crofters' Commission, postal mail services for the Western Hebrides and Peterhead Harbour were all outwith the Scottish Secretary's competence yet these matters had been 'settled and disposed of by the Secretary for Scotland'. He listed those matters that should be exempt from the transfer, which were to appear subsequently in section 3 of the Amendment Act. An alternative proposal suggested by Lothian, which he preferred[45] that he did not expect would be acceptable judging by the scant attention paid to it in his memorandum, was to make the Scottish Secretary 'one of Her Majesty's Principal Secretaries of State, that is, Secretary of State for Scotland'.[46]

At the second reading of the Amendment Bill in the Commons, the Home Secretary gave two reasons for opposing the upgrading office and thus avoid the need to detail powers to be transferred or retained. Matthews' first reason was that of expense: 'He did not believe in the possibility of keeping the Secretary of State of so important a country as Scotland permanently at a lower or different level than other Secretaries of State.'[47] His other explanation was that 'Cabinets were already large enough'.[48] In effect, the Scottish Secretary should have a lower status and a lower salary.

James Caldwell, MP for Glasgow St Rollox, moved an amendment in the Committee attempting to make the Scottish Secretary a Secretary of State basing his case on the need to 'confer upon him the status of Cabinet rank'.[49] The amendment was withdrawn after W.H. Smith stated that the Secretary for Scotland would 'almost uniformly'[50] be a member of the Cabinet but that it would be both unusual and undesirable to lay this down by Act of Parliament. The *Journal of Jurisprudence* saw things differently. The objection, they maintained, was to paying 'a man £5000 a year when they can obtain his services for a smaller sum. The other reason is that the Government dislike to increase the necessary number of the Cabinet'.[51]

Rosebery maintained that the Scottish Secretary would 'by the very force of circumstances, attract to himself all those other attributes which we wished to have been given to him by the Bill of that time, and which it is now found necessary to give him'.[52] The flow of functions would not be ended by the Amendment Act which explains why the Home Secretary emphasised that the new Act was not to be regarded as a final measure.[53] Another probable reason for stressing that further legislation would follow was to satisfy those who wanted the office to become a Secretary of State. Lothian had ended his Cabinet memorandum of July 1887 with a plea for a more comprehensive measure that would have avoided constant problems arising over definition of powers:

> I feel bound to point out that I foresee difficulties and intricacies which it will not entirely remove, and that consequently future legislation may even then still be necessary. It is, therefore, a matter for grave consideration whether it would not be better to make the Amending Act a complete and effective measure, and one which would be thoroughly acceptable to the people of Scotland, by the creation of a Secretary of State.[54]

In introducing the bill, Lothian had recommended two 'considerations' to the Lords in support of the bill: the sentimental consideration, recognising the Scottish and English administration were 'entirely distinctive and different' and the practical consideration which had arisen from the problems in the Western Highlands.[55] However, the sentiment that lay behind the bill would not disappear and practical considerations would remain so long as central government expanded its role. Many of the inadequacies which critics of the original and later Acts identified remained after the passage of the Amendment Act and continued to provoke discontent. Opponents of the office remained sceptical, seeing the office as an expensive encumbrance usurping the role of the Lord Advocate. The Earl of Wemyss had argued in 1887 that since the office's creation Scottish business had not been conducted any better but he estimated its cost 'something like £10,000 a year for the Scottish Office'.[56] Although Lothian disagreed and suggested that the 'additional expense did not really exceed £7,000',[57] an answer given to a Parliamentary Question only five days later had estimated that:

> the total additional charge on the Estimates may (therefore) be put at £11,800. It must, however, be observed that the relief afforded to the Education Office, the Home Office, the Local Government Board, and the Board of Trade by the transfer of the Scotch work from them only provided for extra work in the Departments for which extra staff would certainly have been required had the transfer not taken place.[58]

Many MPs expressed regret that the office had failed to live up to their expectations, though this probably reflected unrealistic expectations rather than the failings of the Scottish Secretary. This disappointment was evident during the debate on the Scottish Estimates in December 1888, only sixteen months after the Amendment Act had received its Royal Assent. The MP for Elgin and Nairn complained that they had 'shut up the Secretary for Scotland in a private room at Whitehall, where nobody could approach him, and consequently, he was not open to that criticism which was brought to bear upon other officials'.[59] Peter Esslemont, Liberal MP for Aberdeen, seemed to view the creation and extension of the Scottish Office as diversionary:

> the result had been simply to promote a few more things to lay in the Scotch Office, and to close the mouths of the Scotch Representatives, instead of encouraging legislation by placing more power in their hands.[60]

Such criticism arose out of policy disagreements as much as dissatisfaction with administrative machinery. Advanced Liberals could hardly have been expected to support the Government of Lord Salisbury and the lack of Scottish measures, as perceived by these MPs, made for a feeling that Scotland was neglected.

The boards were almost unaffected by the Scottish Office and criticisms continued to be heard. Being responsible to the Scottish Secretary did not alter their internal organisation or their work practices. The Fishery Board was particularly criticised. It was felt by a number of Scottish MPs that the fishing industry was neglected and dissatisfaction with the operation of the board was periodically heard in Parliament.[61] Dr Charles Cameron, Gladstonian MP for the College Division of Glasgow, argued in the Scottish Estimates debate in 1888 that the Edinburgh Boards should be 'annexed' to the Scottish Office with the Scottish Secretary always a member of the Commons and responsible for all Scottish business.[62] James Barclay, Forfarshire's MP, went further and argued that the Edinburgh Boards should be abolished and created into Departments under a strengthened Scottish Secretary in Edinburgh.[63] Cameron was clear in 1888:

> ... to make the Department a reality they must annex to it a number of these Edinburgh Boards, the business of which might be much better administered from the Scottish Office. In that way a saving would be effected which would go far to make up for the cost of the Office ... If they wished to make the Scotch Office valuable they should concentrate in the hands of the Secretary for Scotland, who should be a Member of the House of Commons, the whole of the Scotch Business. It had been done already to some extent, but he desired to see the concentration carried further.[64]

In 1885, Playfair had pointed out that the creation of a Scottish Office in London could not be, as Salisbury had suggested, portrayed as a case of decentralisation. Transferring matters 'from one side of Whitehall to the other side of Whitehall'[65] was not decentralisation but represented a case of administrative concentration of quite multifarious functions previously under the aegis of various Whitehall departments with their common feature being their application to Scotland. As this was the only characteristic shared by those matters transferred to the Scottish Office, it was not surprising that demands would be made to go further and 'repatriate' the Scottish administration. Demands to have the Scottish Office and the Board of Education sited in Edinburgh were overruled in the early days. The Marquess of Lothian was adamant that the office should be based in London.[66] Disagreements over the siting of the office were not resolved and there were many calls for the Scottish administration to be moved north over the years. Calls for the Scottish Secretary to be appointed from the Commons continued to be made especially when members of the Lords held office: Marquess of Lothian 1887–92; Lord Balfour of Burleigh 1895–1903; Marquess of

Linlithgow 1905; Lord Pentland (formerly John Sinclair MP) 1909–12; Viscount Novar 1922–24.

Educational administration, which had attracted particular criticism in the period leading up to 1885 continued to be a cause of discontent. Questions in Parliament concerning the functions, responsibilities, membership and number of meetings of the Committee of Council on Education in Scotland were asked fairly regularly. In 1888, James Caldwell, one of the most vehement critics of Scottish educational administration, was told that the Government would not alter the membership of the Committee by replacing the Chancellor of the Exchequer and Home Secretary by Privy Councillors more acquainted with Scottish affairs as the 'presence of these Ministers on the Committee is essential, in view of the questions relating to finance, and to the administration of the Factory and similar Acts which come before the Committee'.[67] However, Smith's failure to provide information on the attendance of these Ministers at Committee meetings weakened this argument.[68] Dissatisfaction with the Committee of Council also kept questions of reform open. Additionally, the strains evident between the Scottish MPs and the Scottish Office, regardless of which party was in office, concerning the financial relations within Britain and the perceived unfair representation of Scotland in Parliament continued to act as a pressure on Scottish administration. Any notion that the Amendment Act had settled matters was soon dispelled.

The Act of 1889

The Home Secretary had been right to emphasise that the 1887 Act was not the conclusion of legislative deliberation on the office of Secretary for Scotland. Only two years later it was necessary to pass an Act explaining the Secretary for Scotland Act of 1887. This Act of 1889 was short and simply stated that,

> Nothing in the Secretary for Scotland Act, 1887, shall affect or be deemed to have affected any powers, duties, or functions of any of Her Majesty's Principal Secretaries of State as Secretary of State for the War Department.[69]

The need for the 1887 Amendment Act had been the limited powers of the 1885 Act while the need for the 1889 Act was the implicit limitlessness of the 1887 Act. In April 1889, a memorandum to the Cabinet noted that the 1887 Act had specifically excluded certain Home Office functions from the transfer to the Scottish Office but,

> The words of the Act, however, are so sweeping, that they appear to include powers and functions hitherto exercised by the Secretary of State for War in Scotland, and to transfer them to the Secretary for Scotland.[70]

The earlier Act had comprehensively transferred 'all powers and duties vested in and imposed on one of Her Majesty's Principal Secretaries of State by any Act of Parliament, law or custom, so far as such powers and duties relate to Scotland'.[71] It had failed to distinguish between the various offices of state and had thereby implicitly included, matters such as the control of forts, barracks, and other military buildings, and responsibilities for dealing with deserters, lunatics and prisoners under the Army Discipline Acts in Scotland. Such wide-ranging powers had never been intended and it was clearly another case of poor draftsmanship. The definition of the Scottish Office's jurisdiction had in only four years developed from its initial functional basis to a territorial basis before returning once more to a more functional basis, though much more extensive than before.

In 1889 there were five Secretaries of State but three of them – those with responsibilities for the Colonial, Foreign and India Offices – had no functions relating to Scotland or departmental work in Scotland. Only the Home Office, which was dealt with in the original Amendment Acts, and the War Office, which appeared to have been overlooked, had responsibilities in Scotland. The 1889 Act had gone far enough. Any additional new Secretary of State would be deemed to have a British or UK remit unless otherwise stated. When one was created, under the Air Force (Constitution) Act, 1917, there was no need for a specific mention in the legislation of its application in Scotland.

The Scottish Grand Committee

One grievance of the campaign in the 1850s had been the under-representation of Scotland in Parliament. In 1863 this had been largely rectified by an increase in the number of Scottish MPs from fifty-three to sixty in a House of 658 and then again to seventy-two in a House of 670 in 1885, but this 'in itself, of course, could not safeguard Scottish affairs from the insufficient attention paid to them by Parliament'.[72] Dissatisfaction and persistent demands for change continued to be heard even after the establishment of the Scottish Office. Salisbury's cynical remark that the expectations of the Scottish people were 'approaching the Arch-angelic'[73] had some truth in it. Evidence of this was expressed in an editorial in the *Journal of Jurisprudence* in 1887 discussing the Amendment Act:

> There is, it is true, a person now charged with the duty of looking after Scotch business, but as he has no power to force the Government to introduce Bills to remove grievances, – or, having introduced them, to press them on, – matters are in no better position than they formerly were.[74]

In 1882 Gladstone had moved a resolution in the Commons to appoint standing committees 'for the consideration of all Bills relating to Law and Courts of Justice, and to Trade, Shipping, and Manufactures, which may be committed to them respectively',[75] conforming with Sir Erskine May's suggestions for the alleviation of Parliamentary congestion. Sir George Campbell, Liberal MP for Kirkcaldy, moved an amendment removing the limit on the number of committees in the hope that the 'principle of territorial division of work, as distinguished from division by subjects'[76] would follow from the extension of the proposed scheme of standing committees. However, he later withdrew his amendment realising it would fail. He had hoped that a committee on Scottish business would be established. Campbell was a Scottish home ruler which made his proposal suspect in the eyes of his fellow Parliamentarians and although he contended that his proposals would not 'necessarily lead to Home Rule'[77] he did not win the support of many MPs. An interesting detail, in light of later developments, was his suggestion that, 'if the Grand Committees which he proposed succeeded, they might sit at Edinburgh and report the result of their deliberations to the House'.[78]

Six years later, in March 1888, Campbell once more attempted to increase the number of Standing Committees, and moved an amendment calling for a committee to consider 'all Bills relating to Scotland only'.[79] On this occasion, there was a division and the proposal was defeated by 214 votes to 137. Unlike the campaign for a Scottish Secretary, the debate on the establishment of a Scottish Grand Committee divided on party lines. Though Liberals, including Gladstone, had opposed Campbell's proposal in 1882, they came to accept the proposition of a Scottish Standing Committee when the issue was debated in 1888. Notably, this was during Salisbury's Conservative Administration when the Liberals and Crofters had 44 Scottish MPs and the Unionists, including Liberal Unionists, had 28 Scottish MPs in Scotland.

Some informal procedures for Scottish matters appear to have existed. References were made to the 'tea room meetings' when Scottish MPs would meet and settle Scottish matters and according to some accounts, even resulted in new Scottish legislation. In 1888, the Postmaster General, Henry Raikes had described the arrangement regarding Scottish Bills:

> Members representing Scotch constituencies found opportunities for discussing certain Bills among themselves, they then brought these Bills before the Secretary for Scotland, and in the end they passed through the House after some merely formal debate. He was not aware that the fact that there was no prolonged discussion in the House in any way diminished the value of a measure when passed.[80]

This description of what happened, suggesting the existence of an informal Scottish Grand Committee, was challenged by Campbell who described them as an 'illusion'.

Sir George Trevelyan, who had briefly been Scottish Secretary, linked the Scottish Secretaryship with the demand for a Scottish Grand Committee. Trevelyan noted the disappointment caused when the Scottish Secretary was present in the Lords and was not in the Cabinet. He remarked that the 'Scottish Executive was not dependent upon the majority, but the minority of the Scottish Representatives'.[81] Trevelyan's observation that had the Secretary for Scotland Bill gone to a Scottish Grand Committee then 'it would have come out a very different one'[82] ignored the report and third reading stages which would still have been taken on the floor of the Commons. The return of the Liberals in the 1890s under Gladstone, and later by Rosebery, provided a Parliamentary majority for supporters of a Scottish Grand Committee. A petition presented to Gladstone in December 1892 signed by Scottish MPs expressed dissatisfaction with the conduct of Scottish business and the 'Cabinet could not but admit the gravity of the case'.[83] The Cabinet aimed to improve the arrangements for Scottish business hoping to 'have a wholesome effect in checking the growth of crude desires on proposals with reference to what is called Home Rule for Scotland'.[84]

Gladstone changed his mind on a Scottish Committee. Five days before his retirement as Prime Minister, he stated that the Government intended to introduce a Scottish Grand Committee.[85] Rosebery's accession to the premiership in March 1894 could only improve the opportunities for specifically Scottish matters. In April 1894, Sir George Trevelyan, moved a motion to create a standing committee consisting of 'all the

Members representing Scottish constituencies, together with fifteen other Members, to be nominated by the Committee of Selection'.[86] The following year a similar resolution was passed but instead of fifteen added Members it was agreed that there should be twenty. [87]

Two of the most persistent home rulers, Gavin Clark and James Weir, argued that as six Government Ministers had Scottish seats and were unlikely to attend meetings this would, effectively, give the Conservatives a majority.[88] George Goschen observed that Grand Committees normally consisted of a reflection of the House plus fifteen specialists while the Scottish committee would consist of seventy specialists with 'fifteen ignoramuses from England'[89] and William Hunter claimed that the insistence on a committee composition corresponding with that of the Commons did not really conform to precedent.[90]

An unfavourable comparison was drawn by W.A. Hunter, MP for Aberdeen North, with John Bright's proposal of 1886 for Irish and Scottish Committees.[91] Bright's proposal was more radical in proposing to make the committees permanent, that they should be composed only of MPs from the respective nations, that they should take the second readings of bills, and that all bills concerning Scotland and Ireland exclusively should be referred to the committees. Trevelyan's scheme only set up the committee by sessional order and included added Members, second reading stages to be taken by the whole House and 'most important of all', as Hunter stated, bills would be referred to the committee by Order of the House of Commons.[92]

Many comments reflected the absence of rigidly applied rules and conventions. It is often unclear whether speakers in the debates were referring to the Grand Committees abolished in 1832, the standing committees established in 1833, select or *ad hoc* committees when they were drawing comparisons and citing precedents. In July 1895, Salisbury and the Conservatives were returned bringing an end to the experiment. The Scottish Grand Committee had been credited with success in its work on the Local Government (Scotland) Act, 1894 but the Liberals had not attempted to make the Committee a permanent feature of Parliament.

In 1907, under Liberal Prime Minister Campbell-Bannerman, the Scottish Grand Committee became an established part of the Commons committee system. Whereas when it had existed in the 1890s it had been created by sessional orders it was established by standing order in 1907. Pressure had also come from outwith Parliament. In April 1906 the Convention of Royal Burghs passed a resolution calling for a Scottish Grand Committee consisting entirely of Scottish MPs.

Debating the Scottish estimates

The establishment of the Scottish Office did not affect the funding of Scottish administration and policy. Each of the Boards was financed separately by an annual Parliamentary vote and the creation of the office of Scottish Secretary only added a further vote to those that already existed. There was no consolidation of these votes and in the published estimates, as well as in the ordering of the Parliamentary timetable for their consideration, the various votes were classified under the usual headings such as the salaries and expenses of the civil departments; law and justice; education; science and art. There was, however, some movement of votes between the different classes of expenditure.[93]

In 1897, Campbell-Bannerman urged the Government to give more time to Scottish supply debates, in light of the limited time available the previous year.[94] But the most vigorous criticisms of the lack of time given to debate Scottish votes came during Campbell-Bannerman's own premiership from 1905 to 1908. In March 1907, Campbell-Bannerman declined to provide a day for the discussion of Scottish estimates.[95] Three months later he again rejected a proposal that more time should be provided for the discussion of Scottish votes. That year only three of the twelve votes had been debated.[96] One MP was ruled out of order when he attempted to raise a Scottish Local Government Board matter during the supply debate on the Fishery Board for Scotland both under the responsibility of the Scottish Secretary.[97]

In 1908, frustration with the rigidity of Parliamentary procedures, which served only to compound the feeling that Scottish affairs were being neglected, was once more evident. A ruling from the chair that fisheries could not be brought up was described by Duncan Pirie as 'another example showing the difficulty Scottish Members had in calling attention to matters relating to the administration of Scottish affairs'.[98] His protest was in vain and his claim that there had been no limit on the range of responsibilities debated on the Chief Secretary for Ireland's vote was denied by the chairman. Prime Minister Asquith conceded another half day for the discussion of Scottish estimates but this failed to satisfy Scottish MPs.[99] When Pirie called for a return showing the dates on which discussion had taken place on Scottish votes and the amount of time allotted to these over the previous decade, the Scottish Secretary John Sinclair answered that such a return would be unnecessary as the information could be obtained from Hansard.[100] Pirie's promise to raise the question again, which he did five days later, until he received the information was evidence of the growing resentment with the allocation of Parliamentary time.

The following year in the supply debate on the Scottish Secretary's office there was further reason for complaint from Scottish MPs. John Sinclair had been given a seat in the Upper House, as Lord Pentland, while retaining the office of Scottish Secretary. Comparisons were once more made with Ireland.[101] A.C. Morton warned that the Government was losing support in Scotland and noted that over the four years of that Parliament 'we never had the Law Officers vote before us at all' as these were 'guillotined out of existence'.[102] The annoyance felt was evident again in 1910 but the critics concentrated their attention on the call made in a petition signed by forty-two Scottish MPs proposing that the headquarters of the Scottish Office should be moved from London to Edinburgh. During the debate the chairman had to interrupt speakers on twelve occasions in a relatively short debate to bring them to order and prevent them straying beyond the strictly defined boundaries of the Scottish Secretary's vote.[103] Duncan Pirie continued his campaign to change the procedure and increase the time given to Scottish estimates. He remarked on the perennial difficulties which Scottish MPs had in raising matters including some which had not been discussed under a vote in the Commons for over a decade.[104]

Around this time, home rule for Scotland became an issue in Scottish politics. A Scottish Nationalist Committee, consisting of nineteen Liberal and two Labour MPs, was formed in June 1910 partly for fear that the 'Home Rule cause should not receive adequate backing in Scotland once Irish Home Rule was out of the way'.[105] Asquith considered a federal structure with Parliaments for Scotland and Wales. Problems associated with such a proposal, which impaired the progress of similar proposals later, were recognised by Winston Churchill in Cabinet memoranda in February and March 1911.[106] Many of the same MPs who had campaigned for a Scottish Grand Committee, who sought to extend its functions who had tried to ensure that its membership would consist only of those MPs with Scottish seats and who had been unceasing critics of the lack of time allocated to Scottish estimates were also Scottish home rulers, including Duncan, William Gulland and Sir Henry Dalziel.[107] But the prospect of a measure of Scottish home rule was entirely contingent on developments in Ireland before the First World War. Scottish nationalism was a 'cold, imitative, artificial thing'.[108] In 1914, the Asquith Government's commitment to Scottish home rule was weak. In reply to a Parliamentary Question the Prime Minister explained that no pledge had been given 'as regards time'.[109]

Parliamentary procedure remained a grievance up to the First World War. In July 1912, Sir George Younger, a prominent Unionist MP, joined

Pirie to press the Speaker for greater latitude in debates on the Scottish votes. The Speaker recognised that this was the prerogative of the Chairman of Ways and Means and urged them to consult him but nevertheless stated that:

> if both sides of the House comes to an agreement, with his [Chairman of Ways and Means] assent, to use one Vote for the purpose of a general discussion ranging over all the Scotch Votes, then there could be no objection.[110]

However, the following day the Chairman of Ways and Means, rejected the proposal for a general discussion as there was 'not a general agreement' in favour.[111]

Later that month in an adjournment debate, Scottish MPs complained that half of the only day allotted to Scottish estimates had been lost because of a debate on a strike in the Port of London. The absence of both the Prime Minister and Scottish Secretary from the adjournment debate, though both were 'supposed to be Scotch Members',[112] added to the complaints. Munro-Ferguson, who later became Scottish Secretary, argued that the problem had been aggravated since the creation of the Scottish Office and recalled the days 'when the Scottish Members were able to consult with the Lord Advocate in this House, and arrange their business in some way'.[113] The Unionist MP for Glasgow Bridgeton, Charles Scott Dickson reminded Scottish Liberals that their party had an overwhelming majority in Scotland and suggested that they ought to copy the Irish – 'a good Scottish Nationalist party to give effect to their views in the House of Commons', as Dickson stated, which would make sure that 'it would not be tolerated for a moment that the Scottish Estimates should be treated as they are'.[114] Parliamentary Questions asking for the number of hours devoted to Scottish votes since 1900 and calls for a separate sessional volume containing the proceedings relating to Scotland continued to be demanded by James Hogge MP during late 1912.[115]

Conclusion

By the outbreak of war in August 1914, it was obvious that the Scottish Office had not removed Scottish grievances but had provided a focus for them. Successive Governments had to admit that there had been a neglect of Scottish business but were adamant that Scotland was not deliberately ignored. Asquith's candid observations in presenting the

Government of Ireland Bill in April 1912 recognised the failings in Westminster's over-strained proceedings. It was hardly an exaggeration, the Prime Minister told the Commons, that:

> when the season annually comes round for compiling the King's Speech, the practical question for those concerned with its composition is what is the least instalment of that which is admittedly overdue by which England, Scotland, and Wales can respectively for the Session be bought off.[116]

He referred to the dismay at having to vote sums of public money undebated each session. The Parliamentary procedure for debating estimates had not been organised on a territorial basis but reflected the organisation of government by function. With the Scottish Secretary charged with responsibility for votes in various classes of expenditure there was neither the appearance nor the reality of a consolidated administrative structure. By 1914, however, a tendency towards a more territorial basis was evident. Home rule, the Scottish Grand Committee, demands for wide-ranging discussions of the Scottish estimates, and the perceived neglect generally of Scottish affairs all tended towards the emphasis of the territorial at the expense of the functional basis within Parliament. Once established the Scottish Office was a focus for grievances and an alternative to the functional organisation of government.

4
Educational Administration

Background to state involvement in Scottish education

State intervention in education emerged out of the activities of the Churches across Europe. Scotland was no exception. The parish was the basis for educational organisation and indeed finance. Co-ordination had initially been provided by the Kirk but over time the state at the centre adopted an increasing role in education. The organisation of the state's involvement, therefore, had its basis in the organisation of the Kirk. In the words of George Elder Davie, the Anglo-Scottish union was a 'unity of politics combined with a diversity in what may be called social ethics'.[1] That was especially true in education with its 'presbyterian inheritance'. It was this basis that also provided the base of distinctiveness in Scottish educational provision. Early central grants had come about largely as a result of pressure for England with a consequent need to provide something comparable for Scotland. Inevitably, only the rudiments of a national system existed. Anything approaching a national system only emerged after the 1872 Education (Scotland) Act. The central administration of education in Scotland followed the existence of local provision and it was no surprise, therefore, that its role was often ill-defined and even merely symbolic.

The Committee of Council on Education in Scotland

Theoretically, Scottish education, as English education, was administered by a Committee of the Privy Council. There were two reasons why this form of administration was attractive to central government. It avoided the establishment of a formal Ministry which would mean that Governments were accepting direct responsibility for the development of education. Second, education was bound up in religious rivalries and a Committee of Council, with an imprecise membership, was attractive to Government. In reality, the Committees of Council dealing with English and Scottish education represented, in Bagehot's term, 'dignified' rather than an 'effective' branch of Government.[2] Behind the facade a pattern of bureaucratic government developed.

From 1895 to 1914 the Committee met on nineteen occasions: on four occasions it discussed Fettes and Dollar Endowments; in March 1887 the Coal Mines Regulations Bill was considered;[3] but most of the meetings dealt with financial matters (Table 4.1). A fortnight lapsed between two meetings held in November 1888 and again in May 1889

Table 4.1 Meetings of the Committee of the Privy Council on Education in Scotland

7 December 1885
Considered and approved the scheme for the Fettes Endowment and proposals for inspection of Higher Class Schools

9 March 1886
Fettes Scheme again considered. Dollar Institution scheme considered

1 April 1886
Dollar Institution Scheme considered and approved

16 March 1887
Coal Mines Regulation Bill considered

7 May 1887
Limit of fee in Scotch Schools considered

15 July 1887
Approval of Educational Endowment Schemes considered

23 April 1888
Limit of fee in State-aided Schools considered

14 July 1888
Difficulties of School Boards in insular parishes considered

13 November 1888
Difficulties of School Boards in insular parishes considered

27 November 1888
Difficulties of School Boards in insular parishes considered

12 April 1889
Application of part of Probate Duty Grant towards relief of school fees considered

6 May 1889
Application of part of Probate Duty Grant towards relief of school fees considered

20 May 1889
Application of part of Probate Duty Grant towards relief of school fees considered

EDINBURGH UNIVERSITY LIBRARY
WITHDRAWN

Table 4.1   (Continued)

5 March 1891
Relief of fees considered

11 December 1891
Question of assistance to secondary education considered

19 March 1892
Court of Session Judgement regarding election of School Board for Port Glasgow
considered

14 July 1893
Terms of reply to Address of the House of Lords in regard to Minute of 1 May on
Secondary Education considered

3 March 1899
Minute for distribution of grants for Secondary or Technical Education under
2(4) of Local Taxation Account (Scotland) Act, 1898 discussed and approved

12 February 1913
The Defences to be lodged in regard to Dalziel School Board versus Scotch
Education Department were considered.

Note: Nineteen meetings in total in 32 years, of which 12 were concerned with purely
financial matters, 4 with Fettes and other Endowments where the matters arising would be
mainly financial.

Source: National Archives of Scotland, SOE 2/12.

but such frequency only occurred when there was unfinished business.
It was more usual for the Committee to meet two or three times each
year until about 1891. Thereafter meetings became less regular and less
frequent. After a meeting on 3 March, 1899 there was only one other
meeting when, on 12 February, 1913, the Committee considered the
defences to be lodged in the legal case of the Dalziel School Board versus
the Scotch Education Department.[4] This final meeting of the
Committee had been called to discuss a case that concerned the infre-
quency of its meetings. In 1912, the School Board of Dalziel had dismissed a schoolteacher from Knowetop Public School in Motherwell
because she had joined the Roman Catholic Church. The teacher had
appealed to the Scotch Education Department under the provisions set
out in the Education (Scotland) Act, 1908. This had resulted in the
Department insisting that the School Board should pay the teacher a
sum equivalent to three months salary. In challenging the authority
of the Secretary and Assistant Secretary of the Scotch Education
Department to make such a decision, or indeed the Vice President (i.e.
the Secretary for Scotland), the pursuers maintained that the references
in the legislation were to the Committee of the Privy Council
for Scottish Education and that the 'pretended decisions of the

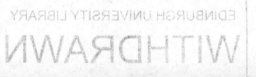
EDINBURGH UNIVERSITY LIBRARY
WITHDRAWN

defenders . . . were not, in fact, decisions of the defenders, but were decisions of the secretary or other official of the defenders'.[5] In defence, the
SED maintained that although the letters to the School Board were
signed by the Secretary and Assistant Secretary of the SED, the decision
had been taken by the Secretary for Scotland as Vice President of the
Committee. Both in the original case and the appeal, the Court found
for the SED. The Committee of Council on Education never met again.

There was never any doubt that the Secretary of the Department was
responsible to the Scottish Secretary and, at least in theory, was accountable to the Committee of the Privy Council on Education in Scotland.
Neither was there ever an occasion when the SED Secretary claimed to
be responsible to the whole (non-functioning) Committee in an attempt
to avoid being accountable to the Scottish Secretary as happened in
1926 when Sir Warren Fisher argued that as permanent head of the
Treasury, he was responsible to the Treasury Board, another 'dignified'
rather than 'efficient' part of the Constitution, rather than directly to
the Chancellor of the Exchequer.[6] At the time of the Dalziel School
Board case there was a feeling in Scotland that the Secretary of the SED,
John Struthers was acting autocratically. This feeling was prevalent in
Scottish local authorities and may have encouraged Dalziel Parish to
challenge the authority of the officials of the SED.

Had it met more frequently there would almost certainly have been
more interest in its composition. The Act of 1872 had defined the Scotch
Education Department as the 'Lords of any Committee of the Privy
Council appointed by Her Majesty on Education' which was amended in
the Interpretation Act of 1889 to mean the 'Lords of the Committee for
the time being of the Privy Council appointed for Education in
Scotland.'[7] The amendment was taken to mean that the Committee
remained in being until a new Committee was appointed, thereby
removing the need for the appointment of a new Committee whenever
a new Government assumed office. Throughout the first fifty years of its
existence there was little consistency in the Committee's membership;
the size varied and the listings of the membership would sometimes be
by office and sometimes by individual names. In the Dalziel School
Board versus SED case in 1914 the Committee of the Privy Council listed
in the case included Lord Shaw, then a Lord of Appeal who had served
as Lord Advocate from 1905–09. The case was heard before the Court of
Session, thus Shaw was not affected in his judicial role as a Lord of
Appeal. Fortuitously, or perhaps with the real prospect of the case being
heard before the Extra Division of the Court of Session, Alexander Ure,
who had been Lord Advocate from 1909–13, was not re-appointed to the

Committee of Council in February 1914. The faintly absurd situation arose after the final meeting of the Committee, when it did not matter who was on it, when an attempt was made to prevent this happening in future. An Order in Council of August 13, 1920 set out the new method of appointment by reference to office, dropping the Lord Advocate and the 'great and good'. A consequence of including former Lord Advocates on the Committee of Council, or more precisely the failure to remove them was that the Committee would normally include a Scottish judge, as it was normal practice for a retiring Lord Advocate to become a Court of Session judge. Every Lord Advocate from the 1880s to the First World War succeeded to the bench in some capacity or other. This practice was formally discontinued when James Clyde, Lord Advocate from December 1916 to March 1920, became Lord President of the Court of Session. The removal of a sitting judge removed the possibility of a member of the judiciary being in the awkward position of being called upon to deal with a case in which the Scottish Education Department was a party.

Membership of the Committee was debated again within the SED in 1929 and 1931 though it had not met for sixteen years and it was agreed then that there was no need for a new Order in Council or reconstitution of the Committee on each occasion that a member changed. Though this protracted and repetitive debate appears pointless there was probably a more serious and practical consideration involved. A genuine fear seems to have existed that the authority of the SED might be challenged in the courts and there was a desire not to stir up unnecessary trouble. Nobody could pretend that the Committee of Council was a functioning part of Scotland's administration. The minutes of the meetings of the Committee of Council recorded in the SED's Minute Book only stated the date and subject discussed.[8] There were no minutes detailing the discussions that took place. A.C. Morton MP questioned McKinnon Wood in July 1912 as to its composition, when it met and what it did and was correct in stating that the,

> 'My Lords' business is a sham and a fraud upon Scotland. Practically they never meet, are never called together, and it would have been much better if the Secretary for Scotland, in answering the question, had told us he was 'My Lords', and that nobody else was concerned in the matter.[9]

However, Morton's description of the Committee of Council had been pre-empted over twenty-five years before by a far more authoritative account of the work of 'My Lords' of both the Scottish and English Committees. This was important not only because it compared the Committees and described their position even then as being largely formal, but also because it was written by Henry Craik who had been the first Secretary of the SED:

> ... at no time has either Committee exercised an authority, or indeed has been summoned except on casual and not very frequent occasions. No quorum is prescribed; no records of proceedings are kept; and even when the advice of certain members has been sought, in view of legislative proposals, they have met rather, perhaps, as a committee of the cabinet than as a Committee of the Privy Council. The practice as regards the composition of the Committees has never been defined, and has varied considerably in regard to the English and Scottish Committees. That for England is composed entirely of certain leading State officers, whose functions are far too great to allow of their assisting at any deliberations thereon, and whose presence on the Committee is little more than nominal. The Committee for Scotland, on the other hand, has always, since 1878, contained members who were unconnected with the Government; and very recently no less than four such members sat on a Committee of nine.[10]

In October 1912, Craik asked McKinnon Wood whether he was 'aware that in years past this committee frequently met, and that minutes of the meetings are preserved among the archives of his Department'.[11] This contradicted his article in *Fortnightly Review* of 1885 quoted earlier. It was generally known that no detailed minutes were kept of the Committee's meetings and those that existed were basic. Craik's intervention in 1912 was probably that of the defensive former SED Secretary.

The transfer of Science and Art Administration

The idea of transferring the Scottish element of the Science and Art Administration from South Kensington to the SED at Dover House had been under consideration for a number of years. Principal Grant Ogilvie of Heriot-Watt College in Edinburgh had supported transferring the Scottish share of the grant to the SED. Craik's supervision of the development of secondary education in Scotland is generally regarded as one of his major contributions to education during his long term as Secretary of the SED. Intricately connected with this were questions regarding the distribution of the Science and Art Department's grant which lay outwith the SED's control. Having enlisted the support and advice of Grant Ogilvie in 1895,[12] Craik became involved in a struggle with South Kensington for the control of the Scottish element in the Science and Art Department's vote.

Grant Ogilvie felt that the distinctive features of Scottish secondary education, as much in the fields of technical subjects as any others, required separate central administrative treatment. Particularly notable was the distinctive local administration of Scottish secondary education and its relationship to organs of central administration which meant both the Science and Art Department and the SED. Scientific education initially had been organised by local voluntary committees aided by Science and Art Department Grants. These local committees were quite distinct from any of the elected bodies empowered to levy rates and their existence was without statutory authority. In Scotland, where the school boards were not confined to elementary education, secondary schools increasingly encouraged the teaching of technical subjects. School boards were almost universal throughout Scotland and tended to take over the work of local Science Committees so that, as an undated and unsigned memorandum for the Scottish Secretary in 1894, written in what looks like Craik's handwriting, stated:

> They have thus come to embrace the whole domain of Education – secondary and elementary: technical and general: and they naturally fail in many cases to draw a distinction between their various functions.[13]

Craik's memorandum explained the complexities of local educational authorities involved in spending funds and put forward a solution:

> The County Council, the School Board, and the County Committees on Secondary Education, have all some part in the administration of such funds, and they are apt to double one another's work. On the other hand, all those local authorities are in direct contact with yourself, either as Secretary for Scotland, or as Vice President of the Scotch Education Department. It would be comparatively easy to bring them into line, and to direct their work, were it not that they have also to deal to some extent with an entirely different central authority.[14]

Craik proposed that 'all Educational subsidies should go to Scotland through this Department'[15] and suggested that a small committee should consider and report on the idea. However, as Craik himself recognised in a note to Trevelyan in February 1895, the 'public representatives do not fully show the urgency of the matter'[16] but this may have been partly compensated for by the cross-party nature of the support that did exist. Arthur Acland, Vice President of the English Committee of the Council on Education during the late Liberal Government, had agreed that the SED should make proposals for taking over all of the work of the Science and Art Department in Scotland but the Secretary of the Science and Art Department, Sir John Donnelly had criticised Acland's decision in a long minute in July 1895 and proposed that a departmental committee should take evidence on the subject. The support of Scottish Conservative MPs proved useful when six months later the Conservatives were returned to power.

In December 1895, Balfour of Burleigh's office received a letter from the Duke of Devonshire, Vice President of the Committee of Council on English Education, proposing the establishment of a committee of three members. A committee was nominated by the Lord President of the Privy Council, nominal head of both Scottish and English Committees, consisting of Craik, Donnelly and Sir Herbert Maxwell, Conservative MP for Wigtownshire. The committee was instructed to consider 'what functions, if any, of the Science and Art Department should be transferred to the Scotch Education Department'. The committee took no evidence and with the entrenched and opposed views of Donnelly and Craik the opinion of Maxwell was pivotal. Maxwell thought that if there was to be a separation in the administration then it should be made with regard to imperial as well as to the local functions of the Science and Art Department. The committee had met from October 1896 to February 1897 and by July 1897 a decision had been reached by the Lord President to transfer the Scottish work of the Science and Art Department from South Kensington to the SED. Excluded from the transfer were functions pertaining to certification, scholarships and training of Scottish teachers and students attending the Royal College of Science in London and courses at the Royal College of Art.

Notably, the views of John Struthers, amongst other inspectors, had been sought by Craik in early 1895. Struthers was clear in his support for the transfer and his reply quoted from the Blue Book of 1887–88 in which he had written that 'it is essential to the thorough inspection of a school that the work be judged of as a whole and not piecemeal'.[17] Struthers' arguments were clearly those of a school inspector who, at the local level, had recognised the duplication and problems of achieving a balanced education through the divided jurisdiction of the SED and the Science and Art Department. Struthers moved south to Dover House to take charge of this new SED responsibility in 1898 after Craik won

Balfour of Burleigh' support.[18] Geographically, the transfer had been one within London and not from London to Scotland. His later opposition to proposals to transfer the work of the SED to Edinburgh would suggest that Struthers would not have given his support to the transfer otherwise.

Bureaucratic despotism and the case for an advisory council

Remoteness and a bureaucratic despotism were often charges laid against the SED and particularly against its secretary. The transfer of Science and Art responsibilities may have had the support of Scottish MPs and the Scottish people, or at least the press in Scotland, but it could only accentuate what critics saw as the SED's main failings. Even more functions were now under the auspices of the SED: though this seems to have been more acceptable than having Scottish matters administered by an 'English' Department, many Scots, including Scottish Liberal MPs felt that the accumulating authority of the SED was quite unacceptable. The Principal of St Andrews University, James Donaldson, for one, regarded the Secretary of the SED as wielding too much more power over Scottish education:

> It is the opinions of this permanent official that are expressed when 'My Lords' are said to determine anything. He wields the entire power which, by any Act of Parliament or provisional order or code, is designed to the Scotch Education Department . . . He has thus absolute control over the entire system of public education, except that he does not appoint the teachers.[19]

The focus of educational policy studies around late Victorian and Edwardian times tends to be on the permanent head of the SED rather than on the Scottish Secretary. Alexander Morgan's *Makers of Scottish Education*, published in 1929, contains chapters on Sir Henry Craik and Sir John Struthers as well as other educationalists in Scottish Universities, schools and the church but in a book on the contributions to education of selective individuals there is not one devoted to the work of any of the Scottish Secretary. Histories of Scottish education similarly devote much more space to the Secretaries than to the Government Minister in charge of education.[20]

In June 1903, Professor S.S. Laurie, a leading critic of the SED, addressed an EIS conference in Edinburgh and attacked the SED's policies of centralisation, Government-by-circular, post-primary division, and 'bureaucratisation'.[21] In one of his last lectures as Professor of Education in Edinburgh, Laurie once more expressed his support for the greatest possible freedom for local authorities:

> The more 'efficient' the Department, the worse for the country. Of course, if the State gives money for schools, it must exercise control of some sort, but there is such a thing as the limits of State activity.[22]

June 1903 had also been a month in which the SED Secretary had been more directly under attack. At an unusual public meeting in Ayr, Craik confronted the criticism in a constitutionally questionable manner. His 'platform defence' of SED policy was, however, badly received. Craik's unusual course of publicly defending the SED in Ayr had probably been felt necessary on the grounds that hostility towards the Department, focussing particularly on himself, had intensified over the preceding months and, as the *Glasgow Herald* commented, had 'appeared to be more bitter than most people could have believed.'[23] However, the *Scotsman* suggested that,

> it is really not methods they are at variance about, but control. Professor Laurie would most conscientiously and cuttingly find fault with any schemes of education that came down cut and dry from Dover House, because the excellent ex-Professor wants to have all schemes of the kind drawn up by a National Board of Education sitting in Edinburgh.[24]

Craik's retirement did not reduce the intensity of opposition to the SED's 'autocracy'. Craik's legacy may have been a greatly expanded secondary education structure in Scotland but also included the SED's reputation for remoteness and 'bureaucratic despotism'. After Struthers' appointment to the Secretaryship in 1904, a nominal change was made so that edicts from the SED were no longer in the name of 'My Lords', but this merely confirmed what was already known, that 'My Lords' had no substantive existence. This change did not appease the critics at all. The Education Bill of 1905 was talked out by its opponents mainly defending the local school boards but, as Findlay noted,

> SED independence and the need for its reduction was a theme also linked with 'enlargement' in one case as a possible means of creating a better local–central balance of power.[25]

Later that year, the *Educational News* argued that Parliamentary procedure was a sham and that SED autocracy was confirmed.[26]

Struthers' influence seems to have been as great as Craik's had been. One study of the local administration of education suggests that it was on Struthers' recommendation, against the judgement of Haldane and Balfour of Burleigh, that the decision was taken by the Scottish Secretary, John Sinclair, not to enlarge the administrative areas in the Act of 1908.[27] The new Secretary had been fairly influential in his role as Assistant Secretary in the five years preceding his promotion. A study of the development of physical education in Scottish state schools credits Struthers with the innovative and important work in that field rather than the Secretary of the SED or the putative head, the Scottish Secretary.[28] The report written by Struthers in 1894, 'The Sloyd and Kindergarten Occupations in the Elementary Schools', based on his knowledge gained from a trip to Sweden in 1890, had been his first major contribution in this field. A Royal Commission on Physical Training was established following the Boer War of 1899–1902. Recruitment had demonstrated the extent of ill-health and unfitness in the population. This was followed in 1903 by the establishment of the Inter-departmental Committee in Physical Deterioration that had included Struthers as a member.

An Act passed in 1908 Act was the culmination of efforts to encourage physical fitness and health through the education system. Providing a broader interpretation of the scope of education, the Act recognised that improving the physical condition of the people was a crucial problem for educationalists. However, Struthers' influence had not been confined to these matters. Bone's work on Scottish school inspection suggests that Struthers had been the 'driving force' behind much of the policy on post-elementary education from his period as senior examiner in 1898,[29] and that there was 'no doubt that it was Struthers' ideas which lay behind the changes which came to teacher training in 1905–06'.[30] The 'despotism' of the SED Secretary and his officials was often of a benevolent kind, as the Dalziel School Board case demonstrated. With regard to local authorities, the SED's autocracy was regarded by one important section of the Scottish educational lobby as definitely benevolent. Scottish teachers could feel more secure in the knowledge that the SED's relatively enlightened and unprejudiced position would mitigate sectarianism common in many school boards and also ensured that teachers were paid a nationally determined amount.

Various proposals had been made over the years to lessen the SED's authority. The Scottish Secretary's responsibilities were regarded to be

too varied and burdensome for any single Minister. This was the fundamental criticism on which proposals for a separate Education Minister
for Scotland or, failing that, an Under Secretary for Scotland devoting
his time solely to education had been made by Principal Donaldson in
October 1892.[31] At the time, Donaldson had argued for a 'constructive
council containing representatives of every kind of educational knowledge and experience of the country'.[32] The idea of establishing a consultative body on education to meet in Edinburgh was quite unattractive to
the SED but the idea percolated down through the years finding expression on occasions in Parliament, the press, in books and at educational
conferences, though was blocked by the SED until in 1918 the proposal
took statutory form in the Education (Scotland) Act.[33] To some extent
the Advisory Council established in 1918 replaced the Committee of
Council – the former met more frequently, produced reports and consisted of educationalists, though its influence in initiating policy during
the inter-war period would not appear to have been very much greater
than had been the Privy Council Committee. The idea of an Advisory
Council was often allied with proposals to situate the department in
Edinburgh rather than in Dover House, Whitehall. Both ideas were
attempts to gain some kind of Scottish control of Scottish educational
affairs.

In a Cabinet memorandum in December 1899, Balfour of Burleigh
argued for a bill to consolidate Scottish educational legislation which
would organise a system for the administration of the various funds for
Higher and Technical Education and would provide representative bodies
to act as local education authorities.[34] Included in the proposals, though
not central to them, and appearing to be almost an afterthought at the
end of the five page memorandum, was the proposal for a consultative
committee which would be similar to a body established under the Board
of Education Act for England. Balfour explained the reasons for including
such a provision:

> I propose this not from a conviction that it is demanded in the inter-
> ests of good administration, but because it commends itself in certain
> quarters, and may be useful in facilitating the progress of the Bill.[35]

The Bill was mentioned in the Queen's Speech but lack of Parliamentary
time rendered its passage impossible. Agitation continued for a consolidating piece of educational legislation and specifically for a clause establishing a consultative body. Concern was consistently expressed not
only regarding the lack of Scottish control but with regard to the lack of

initiative in Scottish education. However, not everyone outside the SED agreed that a national council would 'give to the Department the support that comes with contact with national sentiment and the living interest of the people'.[36] An editorial in the *Scotsman* critical of Professor Laurie's proposals for a consultative body in Edinburgh argued that such a body could prove 'just as meddlesome, as arbitrary, and as bureaucratic as the Department in London, and perhaps, a little less disinterested and biased'.[37]

The precedent set in England in 1899 bolstered the case of advocates of a consultative committee. Support for a council came from R.B. Haldane, prominent Liberal MP, in the preface to a book arguing for Scottish educational reform which included a chapter on the case for a Scottish Council of Education.[38] Similar proposals were made in 1913 by Rev. John Smith, an Honorary Fellow of the Educational Institute of Scotland, who suggested that a 'Scottish Education Committee' should meet 'once a quarter in Edinburgh'.[39] Donaldson, in an address to the Education section of the British Association at Dundee in September 1912 was still arguing for a Minister for Education and a Committee 'principally or solely of a consultative character'.[40] Donaldson had looked further afield than most others. He suggested that two types of committee might be possible: one based on the Supreme Council of Public Education in France consisting of representatives of every class of teachers or one based on the German model consisting of men with wide educational experience, two or three persons with practical experience in teaching, teacher training, one or two heads of Training Colleges and a few men selected from Universities, secondary schools and primary schools. Donaldson felt that the committee's proceedings should be made public 'some months before the Minister decides on the changes that he is to propose' and that it 'should not be a Privy Council Committee'.[41] A fundamental prerequisite in each of the schemes seems to have been mutual respect and co-operation between the committee and the SED. Without the power to enforce the SED to act according to its wishes, or indeed even to pay it any attention, a consultative committee would have to hope the SED would be in agreement with its proposals, in which case its value would be doubtful.

In May 1908, James Leishman of Edinburgh School Board suggested that the SED should be moved from London to Edinburgh or, if this was unacceptable, that the creation of a Scottish Council of Education should be seriously considered.[42] The SED Secretary wrote a reply which, according to a note appended over three years later, was never sent. In the reply, in which Struthers totally ignored the suggestion to transfer the SED to Edinburgh, he explained how his position had changed regarding an advisory committee:

> Three years ago or perhaps even two years ago I should certainly have been strongly opposed to anything of the nature of a Council of Education, or even of a formal Consultative Committee. If such a Council or Committee had existed I am quite certain that many of the most useful reforms which I have had to propose would have been blocked.[43]

Struthers recognised that the situation was different for two reasons: the foundation of a new system had been laid and in the three years preceding 1908 a 'certain amount of friction and heat had been engendered by the possibly too rapid movements of the Department'.[44] However, while willing to consider proposals for an advisory body, 'even yet I see objections to such a body which, it seems to me, at present you do not fully realise'.

Four years later, Dr John Kerr, in his final speech as president of the Secondary Education Association in November 1912, argued for a Central Council on Education which Struthers assumed would be a non-statutorily established body to be set up as a form of organised pressure group of educationalists. Struthers' private letter to Kerr two days later was clear:

> A council of educational politicians – no: a Council such as you have indicated, bringing to a focus the opinion of earnest thinking men in the profession and have behind it the general support of the profession, – yes.[45]

The distinction between a formal, statutory body and a non-statutory body was noted in an unsigned SED minute in 1913,[46] as well as being evident in the different answers to the Parliamentary Question from James Hogge and another from Duncan Pirie asked three weeks later.[47] The First World War did not bring to an end demands for a consultative committee. Sir Edward Parrott MP had much justification in claiming in August 1917 that it was a 'day of committees'[48] though his inability to conceive that 'there can be any determined opposition' to a proposal to establish an advisory committee was soon removed when Sir Henry Craik rose in the same debate.[49] In 1917 the EIS's Education Reform Committee, consisting of representatives of the EIS, Secondary Education Association and the Class Teachers' Federation, proposed a National Education Council with representatives from the SED, local education authorities, universities, provincial committees, central institutions, teachers, and, if practicable, from chambers of commerce and trade unions. The committee wanted the Council to act as a statutory court of appeal in case of a teacher's dismissal by local authorities, to have powers regarding the admission and training of teachers and to act as a central examination board controlling the leaving certificate examination.[50] The reform committee envisaged the Scottish Secretary acting as chairman and the SED Secretary as its Vice Chairman and intended that meetings of the Council should be held in the office of the SED in Edinburgh. In effect, the Council amounted to a home rule Parliament for education with a functionally based membership.

The 1918 Education Act created an education council, but it was merely advisory. After the passage of the Act, Struthers commented on the legislation in a long letter to Lord Balfour of Burleigh.[51] Admitting to being 'personally not enamoured' by the new Advisory Council, Struthers felt that it could prove helpful if the right people were members and hoped that it would allay feelings about 'Departmental despotism', though the juxtaposition of his feelings and hopes suggest that Struthers saw the Council as being useful only as a screen behind which the SED could carry on its work unhindered.

The transfer to Edinburgh

In a debate in the Lords in 1884, Balfour of Burleigh had stated that he had 'very great doubts whether it was desirable for the government to allow such a large spending Department, such as the Education Department was becoming – indeed, had become – to have an Office away had from London'.[52] Within twenty years a campaign to have the SED sited in Edinburgh gained momentum. Demands for the transfer of the SED, and even the Scottish Office, to Edinburgh were, like calls for a consultative committee on education, symptomatic of the general dissatisfaction with central educational administration. Those MPs who were assiduous in pressing for the transfer were also those who had argued for a consultative committee on education and often the same who regularly and persistently raised the issue of Scottish home rule. Douglas and Jones' book (1903), backed by R.B. Haldane in its preface,[53] regarded a transfer of the SED to Edinburgh as desirable but admitted this to be 'superficial'. To make the Department less isolated could only be achieved by a 'radical change in the constitution of the Department, or, in other words, by establishing a National Council of Education'.[54] In 1903, the EIS argued that the central authority for education should be located in Edinburgh, though reform of local administration seems to have been a far more pressing matter for it.[55]

The reorganisation that took place in 1904, limited as it was, had the full support of both Sir Henry Craik and the Scottish Secretary, Graham Murray. In a letter sanctioning an Assistant Secretary of the SED to be based in Edinburgh, Chancellor of the Exchequer Austen Chamberlain informed Craik that he was,

> prepared to agree in principle to the changes which he [Scottish Secretary] has proposed with the object of securing that local representation of the Dept. in Edinburgh, to which both you and he attach so much importance and which you tell me is so generally desired in Scotland and by Scottish Members.[56]

Prior to this, the department's existence in Scotland included the Inspectorate, that most important component of the government of Scottish education, as well as the SED's accountant and architect. The Assistant Secretary was given a room in the Royal Scottish Museum some three-quarters of a mile away from the accountant whose office was in York Place. For over three years the central authority for education which existed in Edinburgh remained, as with Scottish administration in general, dispersed and unlikely to create conditions conducive to maximum administrative efficacy.

Those who argued for the transfer were highly critical of Edinburgh boards. Munro Ferguson asked the Scottish Secretary to institute an inquiry into the boards, proposing that consideration be given to amalgamating boards, while also maintaining that it 'would be a great advantage to have the Board of Education moved to Edinburgh as it would be to have the Board of Agriculture moved'.[57] This was an early espousal of a more consolidated central Scottish administration centred on Edinburgh. In the same debate, A.C. Morton, the Liberal MP for Sutherlandshire articulated the familiar criticisms of the Boards – lack of Parliamentary or Ministerial control and expenditure of vast sums of money without discussion. Morton's real objective was Scottish home rule, viewing each change in the administration of Scotland which he advocated as a step towards that end, however improbable the immediate effects appeared to be in reaching it.

During the course of 1907, consideration was given to moving some element of the SED to Edinburgh. Struthers, who was hostile to any major transfer throughout his Secretaryship, argued in a note in January 1907 that there was no section of work in London which could be transferred to Edinburgh with advantage.[58] A comment in the margin of this note presumably written by MacDonald, the Assistant Secretary in Edinburgh to whom the note was addressed, suggested that the section which might 'with least inconvenience and with the greatest public advantage, be brought to Edinburgh would be the Teachers' Section'. It can be surmised that administrative efficacy was not the essential reasoning behind the consideration of the transfer. In late 1907 permission to obtain premises in Edinburgh for the SED was given by the Treasury. The SED had sought 'headquarters well known and easily accessible, quite separate from any other public institution such as the Museum'.[59] Authorisation for the lease of the premises in Queen Street was given in December 1907.[60] The transfer involved staffing difficulties. The early months of 1908 saw Struthers negotiating inducements for a number of his Department. Struthers was only too well aware of his officials' desire to stay in London.

In his study of Struthers, Findlay noted that there was 'more than a suggestion in his [Struthers] correspondence with Craik over a proposed move to Perth in 1896 that he felt he would be leaving the social life of the capital for the rural backwoods' and the *Scotsman* had commented on Struthers' popularity with a wide circle when he was in Edinburgh.[61] It is therefore probably fair to suggest that Struthers also found life in London congenial and preferred not to return to the relative backwoods of Edinburgh and that, as in 1896, his social life was not unimportant in his judgement. Nevertheless, this cannot detract from the force of his arguments against the SED being based in Edinburgh. In a memorandum on the question in July 1909,[62] Struthers argued the case for the retention of the main body and work of the SED in Whitehall, though he accepted the then existing degree of dispersal which had been realised. Countering the frequently voiced criticism of the SED's lack of contact with Scottish educational interests, Struthers maintained that his meetings in Edinburgh, 'once a month at least, in addition to visits for special purposes', allowed the Secretary the opportunity to confer with the four Chief Inspectors and other sections of the Inspectorate enabling him to be kept 'very thoroughly informed as to the drift of opinion on educational questions, and the aspirations and grievances of School Boards in all the various districts of Scotland'.[63]

However, his most important argument for the retention of the Secretaryship in London concerned the relationship in London between the permanent official and the Minister:

> the demand for the removal of the headquarters of the Department
> to Edinburgh means, or ought to mean, the removal of the Secretary

for Scotland to Edinburgh. This, of course, is out of the question so long as we have one Parliament for the United Kingdom. His head-quarters must be in London, at all events during the time Parliament is sitting . . . The permanent residence of the Secretary of the Department in Edinburgh would mean a break in this intimate rela-tionship [with the Scottish Secretary], and I very much fear that it would mean one of two things; either, the Secretary in Edinburgh being forced to act upon his own responsibility, even more than at present, the Department would become in fact something of what it is wrongly said to be at present, namely, an autocracy exercising its powers and issuing its decrees in a semi-independent way without any adequate control by Ministers or by Parliament: or, what is equally probable, it would fall into lethargic condition feeling that the safest course, and the one which would cause least trouble in the absence of complete confidence between the executive officer of the Department and the political chief, and a full understanding of what is in the mind of the latter, would be to do nothing, or as little as pos-sible which would cause disturbance. Neither of these alternatives seems to be a satisfactory one.[64]

Supporters of the transfer found it difficult to counter the argument that if the Scottish Secretary and the Scottish Office remained based at Dover House then so too should the Secretary and staff of the SED. Pirie, the main Parliamentary supporter, seems to have accepted the validity of this argument in his response that the,

obvious answer is that at any rate during the months when Parliament is not sitting it is desirable that both these officials should be in Scotland. During the Session, on the other hand, the Secretary for Scotland would maintain contact just as he now does with the Local Government Board and the Fishery Board, or as he proposes to do with the Agricultural Department suggested to be established in Scotland under the Small Landholders Bill.[65]

Pirie's response to the suggestion that the SED's location in Edinburgh would make SED contact with Scottish MPs more difficult was that the Scottish MPs rarely met Struthers whose main business, claimed Pirie, was with school boards and other educational authorities. Pirie merely evaded Struthers' point that effective control of the SED would not be facilitated by a transfer to Edinburgh. Instead of explaining how to prevent an increase in Departmental powers, Pirie criticised the existing situation:

> to no one can this be more amusing than to the past and present holders of the office of Secretary to the Department, who must be fully alive to the thoroughly mythical character of that control.[66]

Pirie's response to the argument that the SED should be in close contact with the Treasury was that estimates were made once a year and that this would necessitate the Secretary's attendance at such time each year when expenditure levels were being set.

One consideration which Pirie stressed in Parliamentary Questions was the cost of SED officials travelling between Edinburgh and London.[67] This was also a matter which concerned the EIS who were obliged to rely on one individual to lobby on their behalf in London while a whole committee would often attend meetings in Edinburgh with SED officials.[68] There would, however, appear to have been more common ground between Pirie and Struthers than was publicly apparent. In his memorandum of 1909 on the subject, Struthers informed the Scottish Secretary that he had recently spoken to Pirie and,

> as I explained to him, and pressed strongly that the difference between what we had already done, and what they were asking for – very largely as a matter of sentiment – was so small that I ought to advise you to make some concession – a purely nominal one as he put it – to the extent of saying, for example, that what we had already done was all in the direction of what they were asking for, and that this policy will be steadily pursued, with the result that a complete transference might be effected in course of time.[69]

Struthers had become the defender of individual Ministerial responsibility:

> I don't mind what is done so long as that closeness of association and freedom of access between the executive officer of the Department and the responsible Minister, which I consider essential to sound administration, is not broken.[70]

Pirie was the main supporter of the Scottish view: 'There is no other instance of a nation having its education controlled by a Department situated out of the country.'[71] The Secretary for Scotland appears to have acted as the arbiter, with the Treasury's sanction, responding rather than initiating in a matter which did not require legislation. What happened, in the tradition of the development of Scottish central administration, was a gradual process of change founded on compromise rather than constitutional principle with administrative efficacy more an after-thought than a motive.

The Edinburgh office of the SED, set up in Queen Street in summer 1908, initially had a total of twenty-one civil servants. From the start there had been some spare capacity for expansion but by 1912, especially after transfers in 1910, overcrowding in Queen Street forced the SED to seek approval to secure additional premises.[72] The Office of Works approved the lease of a flat in premises adjoining the Queen Street offices in September 1912, to which the accountant's branch moved.[73] A table in a note of May 1912 compared the numbers of SED staff in Edinburgh in 1908 and 1912 (Table 4.2).[74]

Throughout the period from 1908 to the outbreak of war, as the Edinburgh office of the SED expanded, pressure was maintained in Parliament for further transfers. The extent of support from the Scottish backbenches was considerable. A petition organised by Pirie was signed by forty-one Scottish Liberal and Labour MPs and sent to the Scottish Secretary in June 1909.[75] A deputation was to meet Lord Pentland on 1 August but, ironically, the meeting was postponed owing to the absence of Struthers on business in Scotland.[76] In July 1912, another petition was sent to the Scottish Secretary advocating the transfer of the

Table 4.2 Numbers and ranks of SED Staff Based in Edinburgh, 1908 and 1912

	1908	1912
Assistant Secretary	1	1
Senior Clerk	—	1
Accountant and Assistant Accountant	2	2
Staff Clerks	2	4
Minor Staff Clerks	—	2
Second Division Clerks	5	16
Assistant Clerks	3	8
Boy Clerks	5	5
Typists	—	4
Messengers	1	3
H.M. Chief Inspectors	1	2
Architects	1	—
Total	21	48

Source: National Archives of Scotland, ED 7/3/6. Note to MacDonald from A.D.K., May, 1912.

Department to Edinburgh. On this occasion it stressed that MPs had 'satisfied themselves that the great majority of school boards desired the transfer'.[77] It was signed by forty-seven Scottish Liberal and Labour MPs, twenty-seven of whom had signed the earlier one in 1909. Backbench Liberals, on the whole, supported the transfer though in 1912 there were seven who had refused to sign.[78]

At a meeting with McKinnon Wood in July 1912, twenty-two Scottish Liberals heard the Scottish Secretary oppose the wholescale transfer of the SED, which would, he claimed, create an 'absentee autocracy'. He maintained that he wanted the central education authority to be in Edinburgh but only when a Scottish Minister for Education was responsible to a Scottish Parliament.[79] MPs were aware that home rule was unlikely under the Liberal Government. James Caldwell suggests others had publicly questioned the Government's commitment to Scottish home rule.[80]

Scottish Unionist MPs were overwhelmingly opposed to the transfer, with Sir Henry Craik leading the opposition. Craik's arguments were similar to those which Struthers stressed within the SED.[81] The Unionists, seeing themselves as the 'Constitutional Party', adopted the Whitehall view, though Harry Hope, Unionist MP for Bute, was critical of the dominance of the Inspectorate in the central guidance of Scottish education:

> I am not a Scottish Home Ruler, but I say, if the present administration of Scottish educational affairs under the Department here in London is the best that can be done, then bring it to Scotland.[82]

The prospect of creating the conditions for a Scottish legislature was a reason for Unionist opposition. In 1910, George Younger stated that the Scottish Secretary was right in refusing to transfer the Scottish Office to Edinburgh because this appeared to him 'to have been simply a Scottish Home Rule demonstration'.[83] The *Aberdeen Free Press* in July 1912 took a similar view and noted that prominent among supporters of the transfer were those who were involved in the proceedings of the Scottish National Committee, a Home Rule grouping, including Munro Ferguson, Sir Henry Dalziel, W.H. Cowan and D.V. Pirie.[84] Pirie had given the Unionists reason to associate the SED transfer to Edinburgh with home rule when he argued in the Commons on the Education (Scotland) Bill of 1908 that 'if they transferred the Education Board to Scotland, Home Rule would necessarily follow'.[85]

Struthers continued to base his office in Dover House and it was only after his retirement and George MacDonald succeeded him as SED

Secretary in January 1921 that the SED's senior official moved to Edinburgh. This occurred without a fanfare of petitions and Parliamentary debates and, indeed, without any official or formal warrant – the Civil Servant List continued to give the SED address as Dover House until after St Andrews House opened in 1939.

Having raised the issue of the transfer of the SED to Edinburgh it is not surprising that occasions arose when demands were made for the transfer of the Scottish Office. Munro Ferguson argued in 1910 that not only should the SED be transferred to Edinburgh but that Scottish administration should be modelled on Irish administration: 'All that is wanted here would be a small office for the convenience of the Secretary for Scotland and of the Scottish representatives.'[86] Though the boards already existed in Edinburgh, supporters of the transfer were not always keen to cite this in making their case. More than those who wanted the retention of the SED in London, the supporters of transfer were highly critical of the Edinburgh boards, seen as autocratic and Tory-dominated, even under Liberal Governments. The Housing, Town Planning, etc. Act in 1909 passed the central administration from the Scottish Office in London to the Local Government Board in Edinburgh. Notably, the Scottish member of the committee which considered the bill was Munro Ferguson who felt that he 'must see the Board reconstituted' before he would be 'disposed to submit the destinies either of the local authority or of the individual in Scotland to its fiat'.[87] From this it may be supposed that, for Munro Ferguson at least, transfer to Edinburgh was desirable but not to the boards.

The debate on the transfer of the SED was important in that it presaged the discussion which took place over a quarter of a century later with respect to the Scottish central administration generally. The SED transfer was a more open debate of the issues involved. There was also much more agreement later for a move, including the wholehearted support of Unionist MPs. The relationship between the Scottish Secretary and the SED after the transfer had been a major concern and particularly the role of the permanent head of the SED, which was paralleled in the debates on Gilmour concerning the position of the Permanent Under Secretary, as is discussed later. The general feeling of dissatisfaction with the administration was the environment in which the proposals for the transfer of both the SED and later the Scottish Office emerged.

The process of the SED transfer to Edinburgh permitted a concentration in larger offices of the educational administration of Scotland. The accountant's department, which had been geographically apart from the

Assistant Secretary's office in 1904, was moved in 1912 from the Queen Street office after further transfers made the Edinburgh office too small to concentrate the whole of the central administration in Edinburgh. Nevertheless the principle had been established that a department in Edinburgh should, when such an opportunity arose, be concentrated in one building.

The gradual transfer of the SED represented a major innovation in the territorial department. In April 1895, when MPs raised a petition from the Edinburgh Merchants' Association favouring the transfer of the headquarters of the Scottish Office to Edinburgh, the Liberal Scottish Secretary, Sir George Trevelyan had categorically refused to contemplate a move on the grounds that to 'carry on the business of Scotland in Parliament it is necessary that the headquarters of the Scottish Office should be in London'.[88] Within ten years the geographical proximity of Parliament, the Scottish Secretary and the Scottish central administration, which had seemed a fundamental principle underlying the Scottish Office for the first decade of its existence, began to crumble.

Conclusion

In his evidence to the Royal Commission on the Civil Service (the MacDonnell Commission), John Struthers stated that the SED was 'entirely independent' of the Scottish Office.[89] While the Scottish Secretary was also Vice President of the SED and thereby its political head, Struthers was clear that no officials of the Scottish Secretary 'pass judgement upon our papers or our doings'. The SED did differ from the boards in that it was structured like Whitehall departments with a Ministerial head, a permanent official and other subordinate officials. The other areas of Scottish central administration, with the exception of law and order, were governed by a system of boards which did not incorporate the 'English system of organisation on what I call the hierarchical system', which was the foundation of the SED, according to one Royal Commissioner.[90] Struthers preferred the 'English' system which allowed for a 'thorough-going responsibility which I think a Board weakens'.[91]

Notably, by 1914, educational administration had become much more similar to the Whitehall model than to the old Scottish board model. Career prospects in the SED, unlike the boards, were offered to Englishmen as well as to Scots: in fact, Struthers informed the Royal Commission in 1912 that he doubted whether the proportion of Scottish clerks in the SED was very large.[92] However, the Inspectorate, situated in Scotland, could be expected to differ from the personnel in the SED in Dover House. A problem arose for the department after the office in Edinburgh had been established but through time this problem disappeared. As Struthers informed the Royal Commission:

> many of the older men especially are averse to being removed down to Edinburgh, but we have made it a condition of all new appointments that an officer coming to the Office in London here must understand that he is liable to be removed to Edinburgh at any moment, so that our hand is getting increasingly free as to moving the staff to Edinburgh if it is thought expedient.[93]

Struthers' views on the location of the office in Edinburgh, the merits of the 'hierarchical' structure of SED, the demerits of the board system, and his opposition to any meaningful Educational Council for Scotland show that he very much accepted the Whitehall model.

Critics of the SED were sure of what they did not like but never very clear about an alternative. To some extent critics wanted to see something more clearly 'Scottish'. Underlying ideas to have the SED situated in Edinburgh and to establish an Educational Council seem to have been motivated by a vague desire for 'Scottish control of Scottish affairs', though this should not necessarily be seen as meaning legislative devolution. An interesting but ultimately unanswerable question is to what extent the establishment and development of the SED encouraged a feeling of Scottish distinctiveness, appeased this vague nationalism by assimilating it or, indeed, have any bearing on the perennially considered question of Scottish national identity. As Walker Connor has noted, nationalism 'appears to feed on adversity and denial . . . It also appears to feed on concessions'.[94]

5
Administering Agriculture, Health and the Highlands and Islands

As the state's reach extended into areas such as agriculture and health, the existence of separate machinery of government in these areas, especially extensive machinery dealing with Scottish education, created precedents. Scottish agriculture and health might otherwise have been assimilated, at least administratively, into English or British concerns. As the nascent liberal democratic interventionist state was emerging in the twentieth century, it would have a distinctly Scottish dimension. It was not, however, an entirely one-way phenomenon. In 1920, roads were removed from the ambit of the Scottish Office. A Ministry of Transport was created by legislation in 1919 and responsibilities relating to railways, canals, tramways, roads and bridges and harbours and piers were transferred by Order-in-Council the following year from the Scottish Secretary and Scottish Boards of Agriculture and Health. Some of these responsibilities were eventually re-transferred following the recommendations of the Royal Commission on Scottish Affairs (Balfour) in the mid-1950s. Nonetheless, for the most part, the traffic was one-way.

In a letter to A.J. Balfour following the General Election of January 1910, Austen Chamberlain wrote that the Conservatives' 'only chance of winning Scotland' was 'to change the issue on which Scotsmen vote. As long as it is the land, the landlords, and the rest of the Radical programme we shall be beaten.'[1] The issue of land had brought the Crofters Party[2] into being as a Parliamentary grouping in the year the Scottish Office was created and following crofter disturbances in 1886, A.J. Balfour argued that the functions of the Scottish Office should include law and order. The 'land question' was emotive and no more so than in the Highlands and Islands. Over time, while the Scottish central administration developed, a series of administrative and semi-judicial bodies emerged for the Highlands and Islands.

Piecemeal intervention by the state in agriculture, often to eradicate animal disease, had been a feature of nineteenth-century Britain. As in education, there were demands in the latter half of the century for a separate department with a ministerial head to take charge of agricultural affairs. This was finally conceded in 1889 with the passage of the Board of Agriculture Act. In theory, it consisted of a number of senior officers of state following the precedent of the Board of Trade but it never met and its powers were exercised by the President.[3] In a supply debate in March 1892, Munro Ferguson challenged A.J. Balfour, the Conservative leader in the Commons, on those responsible for Scottish agriculture on the Board of Agriculture.[4] Balfour rejected the basis of the question and stressed that the Board of Agriculture was 'not managed by a committee on which there are representatives, but it is managed by a single Minister, who is responsible directly to Parliament'.[5] Within only three years of its establishment, the Board was described as existing only in theory.

Scottish land reformers sought security of tenure of existing holdings and the creation of new holdings and hoped to establish a Scottish Board of Agriculture. Legislation for England and Wales allowed county councils to procure land. In 1903, Sheriff David Brand, the first chairman of the Crofters Commission, advocated a strengthening of the Crofters Commission rather than attempting to realise the aims through county councils.[6] Opponents' proposals to extend the system of smallholdings were designed to reduce the effectiveness of machinery intended for land settlement.[7]

Considerable differences between the Scottish counties and those south of the border made the proposal inappropriate. The rating system in Scotland involved greater variation between counties in respect to the average valuation and acreage per head of population. As an undated memorandum in the agricultural files states,

> In England the assessable rental per head of population in the administrative Counties varies from £3.4.0 to £8.6.0. In Scotland the corresponding range is from £1.7.0 to £12.3.0. Again, taking the acreage, the range in English Counties is from one-tenth of an acre per head to about 13 acres, with a general average for the whole of England of 2 acres per head. In Scotland, the corresponding range in individual counties is from 1 to 62 acres per head, with a general average for the whole country of 9 acres.[8]

An additional complexity in any proposed attempt to introduce a county-based system of land settlement was that the personal incidence of local rates was divided between the owner and occupier in Scotland while in England they fell only on occupiers. A table produced by the Scottish Office showed the financial difficulties which would result from a system based on counties without central subventions as the major source of finance (Table 5.1).

It was understandable that John Sinclair advocated a central board to administer the land settlement programme when he became Scottish Secretary. The return of the Liberals in 1906 gave Scotland one of the most radical Scottish Secretaries in the office's history. Sinclair had been tutored by Angus Sutherland, the crofter's son who became a Crofter MP in 1886. Sutherland's influence on the young Sinclair is unknown but as Scottish Secretary Sinclair set out to legislate for a scheme of landholding. The Small Landholders (Scotland) Act, 1911 – the 'Pentland Act' (Sinclair became Lord Pentland after moving to the Lords) – was a tribute to Sinclair's tenacity. Not only did he have the House of Lords to contend with, with its many landlords, he also had to face difficulties with his Cabinet colleagues.

Land legislation was also being proposed for England and in 1907, Carrington, President of the Board of Agriculture, had considered legislation for England and Wales 'with special clauses for Scotland' which Sinclair would see through the Commons and Carrington would see through the Lords. Carrington put this idea to Ripon, Lord Privy Seal and Liberal leader in the Lords, who agreed on the need for a Small Holdings Bill for England but wrote,

> I should strongly deprecate its being in Sinclair's hands or mixed up with his Scotch Bill in any way. His Bill of last year was based on the Crofters Act; we have no crofters in England; the cases of the two countries are quite distinct and ought to be kept so.[9]

The English and Welsh bill was 'an expression of moderate opinion largely as a result of Ripon's influence'[10] and successfully passed through the Lords with its main provisions intact. However, Sinclair's bill aimed to extend the provisions of the Crofters Act to the whole of Scotland and create new machinery in the form of a Land Court and Scottish Board of Agriculture. It was not merely the fact that the Lords were 'Mr Balfour's poodle', as Lloyd George suggested in another context, which led to the successive defeats of Sinclair's proposed land legislation. There was cross-party opposition to his proposals. Indeed, in the Lords, Ripon had difficulty finding speakers to support the bill and Sinclair's fellow cabinet members, Elgin and Tweedsmouth opposed the new legislation

Table 5.1 Comparison of Scottish and English/Welsh rates

	Population 1901	Land area (Actual)	Land area (Per head of population)	Assessable value, 1906 (Actual)	Assessable value, 1906 (Per head of population)	Produce Rate of 1 per £ of Assessable value
		Acres	Acres	£	£	£
I. England and Wales (administrative counties)	18,366,000	36,500,000	2.0	100,512,000	5.5	418,000
Consisting of (a) Urban areas	11,104,000	—	—	56,989,000 (57%)	—	—
(b) Rural areas	7,262,000	—	—	43,523,000 (43%)	—	—
II. Scotland (Landward area)	2,166,000	19,000,000	9.0	Owners: 15,587,000 Occupiers: 12,025,000	6.4	57,520
Consisting of (a) Urban areas	628,000	—	—	3,000,000 (20%)	—	—
(b) Rural areas	1,538,000	—	—	12,587,000 (80%)	—	—

Note: (1) The rate leviable by English County Councils under the Small Landholders Act, 1982, falls wholly upon occupiers. (2) The corresponding rate leviable by Scottish County Councils is divided equally between owners and occupiers. The owners as a body, bear 58% of the total rate, as the occupiers, owing chiefly to deductions under the Agricultural Rates Act, are assessed on a lower rental. (3) The figures given above as to land areas are approximations – a deduction having been made for the Metropolis and County Boroughs in England and for Royal and Parliamentary Burghs in Scotland, from the figures given for the whole of England and Wales and Scotland respectively in published returns.

Source: NAS AF 43/6 Item 9.

though Prime Minister Campbell-Bannerman had supported the measure. Tweedsmouth, First Lord of the Admiralty, publicly admitted his preference for the English and Welsh legislation in November 1907 in Perth while two months later Hamilton of Dalzell resigned as an official spokesman for the Scottish Office in the Lords.

In a confidential list of proposed legislation sent to the Prime Minister in February 1907, Sinclair placed the Small Landholders (Scotland) Bill at the top followed by the Education (Scotland) Bill and then nine others.[11] In the event, the Education (Scotland) Bill was given priority in 1908 and was passed into law. In September 1908 in a letter to the new Prime Minister, H.H. Asquith, Sinclair wrote of the general and near unanimous feeling in the party in Scotland, excepting dissenters such as Cathcart Watson, for his bill presented that year. This support, he maintained, was for the main provisions of the Bill and not for alternative schemes being spawned by opponents:

No purchase – either by tenant, or by State.
No English Bill – no County Councils.
No splitting up of Scotland, or separating Highlands from Lowlands.[12]

The party, wrote Sinclair, were 'perfectly reasonable and willing to wait for what is clearly unattainable at present, for they see and know that the Lords stand in the way of what they desire'.[13]

The most serious criticism of a Scottish Board of Agriculture, concerned the administration of the Diseases of Animals Acts.[14] Critics of the proposals may have exaggerated their fears but there seems to have been genuine concern at the prospect of a separate Scottish authority relaxing control of animal health regulations. With the flow of animals from Scotland to England this was a matter which concerned many agriculturalists. Opposition to this part of the original bill was expressed at the Annual General Meeting of the Scottish Chamber of Agriculture in October 1911. A resolution disapproving of the establishment of a separate Board of Agriculture for Scotland was passed by eighty-eight votes to forty-four. It criticised the lack of direct representation in the House of Commons other than an 'overburdened' Secretary for Scotland. It was felt that the separate administration of the Diseases of Animals Acts under such authority would result in 'enormous trouble'. They argued for the creation of a Scottish Department of the present Board, with fully staffed offices in Edinburgh, a chairman with a seat in the House of Commons, and assisted by a popularly elected consultative council composed of persons engaged in and connected with agriculture.[15]

More determined opposition came from Scottish landowners. The Scottish Land and Property Federation advised Lord Camperdown, who introduced an alternative bill, and organised opposition to Sinclair's proposals, particularly any attempt to introduce the compulsory purchase of land. Various 'Land and Property Defence Associations' were in communication with Conservative politicians either directly or through the Conservative Agent for Scotland at Westminster.[16]

The Commons rejected amendments to have the President of the Scottish Board of Agriculture and Fisheries made head of the Scottish Board rather than the Scottish Secretary,[17] as well as the removal of responsibility for diseases of animals and plants and adulteration of foodstuffs and fertilisers from the new bill.[18] The Lord Advocate, Alexander Ure had described the transfer of animal health to the Scottish Board as the 'central feature of the Bill' and stated that he would rather deprive the board of 'almost any other power' than the administration of the Contagious Diseases (Animals) legislation.[19] The compromise reached by Pentland re-inserted the clause to have the Scottish Secretary head of the Scottish Board while accepting the amendment to omit the administration of the Contagious Diseases (Animals) Act. Royal Assent was given three days later. Animal health was eventually transferred to the Scottish Office following the recommendations of the Royal Commission on Scottish Affairs, the Balfour Commission in 1955.

As Pentland had often argued, his attempts to introduce land reforms were motivated by the need to provide opportunities for Scots in Scotland; during the first decade of the twentieth century the Scottish population had grown by only 6.4 per cent, the lowest increase since 1861. Emigration had long been the response of government, a solution which was as defeatist as it was ineffective in securing greater opportunities for those who remained in Scotland. With the area of land devoted to sport increasing from 1.7 m acres in 1883 to nearly 3 m acres in 1908, Pentland's Act was expected to go some way in tackling the lack of opportunities. The Act, ultimately, failed to live up to expectations:

> Its funds were inadequate and – what was worse – its procedures, especially those regarding compensation claims, were woefully complex and slow as well as being notably generous to landowning and sheep farming objectors to its plans. Without the willing co-operation of the latter, therefore, the Act was clearly liable to prove a dead letter. And from the first it was clear that such co-operation was not forthcoming.[20]

One centrally placed critic of the Board's work was Jim Dunlop, one of four Sub-Commissioners in the Board of Agriculture for Scotland with responsibility for smallholdings. Dunlop was an advocate of Scottish home rule who believed that a Scottish Parliament would have passed a 'very different Act'. In a private communication in June 1920, he maintained that the legislation had been 'mutilated in the English House of Lords'.[21] As far as Dunlop was concerned, as he explained in a further letter to Muirhead, the 'lack of compulsory powers and the excessive compensation' were the principal reasons for the failure of the legislation to have much impact. The need for land settlement to be reviewed in London resulted in 'considerable delay and a large amount of unnecessary work'.[22]

The most enduring and important feature of the Act was the establishment of a separate Scottish central administration for agriculture in the shape of the Scottish Board of Agriculture and the Scottish Land Court, which together replaced the Crofters Commission and Congested Districts Board which had not administered the whole of Scotland. The three Commissioners of the Board of Agriculture were appointed in March 1912. Each of the three, Sir Patrick Wright (chairman), R.B. Grier and John D. Sutherland were undoubted experts in the field of agriculture;[23] but they were not administrators. Only eight months after the appointment of the Board, Lord MacDonnell, as chairman of the Royal Commission on the Civil Service, suggested to Sir James Dodds, Under Secretary for Scotland, that the Board of Agriculture for Scotland was 'practically a patronage Board'.[24] The Royal Commission urged that the 'system of boards should be reconsidered' and gave three reasons: the Boards provided inadequate responsibility for official action and advice; they weakened the distinction between the qualities and the methods of selection which are suitable for political and for permanent appointments; and they did not provide for the appointment of members who brought any special knowledge of administration to their charges.[25]

The Board had little success in developing distinctly Scottish policies. The lack of finance is one explanation. The finances of the Board were stringently controlled by the Treasury, far more so than was the case with the SED. An example taken from the volume of the Board of Agriculture/Treasury letters for 1912–16 exemplifies this. On 30 July, 1913, a letter was sent from T.L. Heath of the Treasury to the Board of Agriculture sanctioning expenditure for cleaning the rooms occupied by the Board in St Andrews Square in Edinburgh, giving Treasury approval for, the continued payment of similar charges as from the 1st April last, namely from 2/- to 2/6d. per week per room for cleaning (providing that the ordinary rate charged to other tenants is not exceeded) and 9d. per dozen for washing dusters and 1d. each for towels.[26] This had not been a general circular to all departments in the civil service but a reply to a letter five days before from the board. Between 30 January, 1912, before the Board had been properly established, and 29 July, 1914, the last note before the outbreak of war, the Treasury sent 256 letters authorising expenditure to the Board ranging from such details quoted above to the Board's Annual Estimates, averaging out at almost two letters each week.[27]

The special case of the Highlands and Islands

Much of the pressure for agricultural reform – as a result of poverty, emigration, lack of opportunities, and animosity towards landlords – had come from the Highlands and Islands. The Scottish Board of Agriculture grew out of the Congested Districts Board and the Crofters Commission. The extreme poverty of that part of Scotland gave rise to greater public health problems as well as lack of employment opportunities. The Royal Commission on Poor Laws and Relief of Distress (Scotland), reporting in 1909, commented that medical provision in the Highlands and Islands was deplorably insufficient and 'affects not only the physical well-being of paupers, but also that of the whole population'.[28] A committee was established to investigate the problems of medical provision in the Highlands and Islands, chaired by Sir John Dewar, MP for Inverness. The Committee reported in December 1912[29] and noted the high incidence of diseases and mortalities consequent on the 'grossly defective housing of the people' allied with blatantly inadequate medical provision: that such a condition of affairs as we found in Lewis should exist within twenty-four hours of Westminster is scarcely credible. Nor is it creditable from a national standpoint.'[30] The Committee recognised that the exceptional circumstances – social, economic and geographic – demanded 'exceptional treatment'.[31] In conclusion, they recommended that a 'special central authority and a special local authority' were required as well as substantial financial aid.[32]

In June 1913, MacKinnon Wood presented a memorandum to the cabinet on the subject.[33] In this, the Scottish Secretary expressed his opposition to Dewar's scheme which would have involved a number of new 'ad hoc hybrid authorities'. He felt the proposed new authorities would 'tend to become extravagant, irresponsible and slack in administration' and cited the Congested Districts Board as an authority similarly composed which was a 'failure in organisation'.[34] Predictably, he felt that the Treasury's proposed £42,000 for medical provision for the

Highlands and Islands ought to be the responsibility of the Scottish Secretary via the Local Government Board for Scotland, with an Advisory Committee of representatives from the Local Government Board, Insurance Commission, SED and Lunacy Board. Mackinnon Wood argued that under Dewar's proposals the 'Secretary for Scotland would be responsible to Parliament for an organisation over which he would have no real or effective control'.[35]

However, in a memorandum for the Cabinet, Masterman, the Financial Secretary to the Treasury, disagreed with Mackinnon Wood. He reported that the Cabinet Estimates Committee had approved a scheme for administering the grant recommended by the committee chaired by Dewar and, with the Scottish Secretary's agreement, the opinions of Scottish MPs had been sought on the matter. Scottish MPs had opposed the Local Government Board as the central authority because of its association with the poor law. It was suggested that large numbers of people in the Highlands and Islands preferred 'going without any medical attendance to accepting the pauper doctor'.[36] Masterman also cited the support of the Scottish Insurance Commissioners who maintained that if any single existing authority should be chosen to administer the Highlands and Islands Medical Fund then they ought to do so as they had inspectors independent of the Local Government Board and were not 'associated with any pauper taint' and they had direct responsibility for the medical health of at least one-seventh of the population.[37]

The Principal of Glasgow University, Sir Donald Macalister, who had given evidence to Dewar's Committee, told Masterman that administration by the Scottish Local Government Board alone would be 'fatal to the success of the scheme', a view which the Cabinet endorsed in accepting the Financial Secretary's case. The Scottish Secretary, with the support of John Burns, the President of the Local Government Board and Walter Runciman, President of the Board of Agriculture and Fisheries for England and Wales opposed the scheme preferring to vest the Scottish Local Government Board with responsibility. Support for the committee's recommendations came from the Chancellor of the Exchequer and the Lord Chancellor.[38]

The Highlands and Islands (Medical Service) Board was established with between five and nine members, one of whom had to be a woman. The chairman was a Crown appointment and its secretary appointed by the Scottish Secretary. Initially, it was to exist for two years with the possibility of extension. In fact, the Board existed only until 1919 when its functions were transferred to the Scottish Board of Health. In the intervening period, throughout the counties included in the Board's remit, posters appeared which informed the inhabitants that 'families and dependants of insured persons, uninsured persons of the cottar and crofter classes and their families and dependants, and others in like circumstances to whom the payment of the practitioner's ordinary fee for medical attendance would be an undue burden' would be eligible to receive medical attendance 'at modified fees'.[39] These posters set out the conditions and listed the practitioners in each of those districts and parishes who had agreed to participate in the scheme.

Three main reasons can be identified explaining why innovation occurred in respect to Highlands and Islands land, agriculture and health policies and administration that did not occur in Scotland as a whole. First, the exceptionally severe problems in the Crofting Counties, attested to in various inquiries, demanded action. Second, much disquiet, agitation and the determination of crofters and their elected representatives moved successive Governments to pay particular attention to and enact special legislation for the counties in the north and north-west of Scotland. Third, the Highlands and Islands could be treated as a special case because in terms of population, innovation was possible at not too high a cost.

The Scottish Board of Health

A number of events and influences explain the establishment of the Scottish Board of Health in 1919. The Boer War had highlighted the extent of unfitness and ill-health in the population. The Education (Scotland) Act, 1908 extended the scope of education to include physical welfare and the health of schoolchildren. A scheme of National Insurance established in 1911 had brought into being a separate Scottish Insurance Commission along with individual Commissions for England and Wales, and Ireland. The Highlands and Islands (Medical Service) Board marked an important acceptance of public responsibility for health in such exceptional cases of deprivation as those found in the crofting counties. The explanations for the establishment of the Scottish Board were applicable throughout Britain with the catalyst of the war being the most notable factor. Nevertheless, there were certain particularly Scottish aspects in the emergence of the consensus for greater central government involvement in health matters and these preceding institutions provided an important base.

Following the 1914–18 war in which Scots constituted a very high proportion of casualties, Scottish soldiers returned home with promises of 'homes fit for heroes' to a part of Britain in which housing standards had been condemned by a Royal Commission in 1917.[40] Contrasting sharply with a Royal Commission on the Housing of the Working

Classes in Scotland which had submitted a brief report in 1885,[41] the Commission of 1917 documented the extent of the appalling housing conditions in Scotland, investigated the reasons and suggested a need for 235,990 new houses before the 'housing conditions in Scotland could be regarded as satisfactory'.[42] Having defined its 'housing ideal' simply as the provision of a 'healthy, comfortable dwelling for every family in the land', the Commissioners in 1917 determined to keep this 'prominently before them' in writing their report.[43] The report testifies to the success of this simple aim. However, its proposals became obsolete in the rapidly changing circumstances after the war's end even if it were to be accepted that they could ever have succeeded in eradicating Scotland's housing problems.

The Royal Commission had been established after Scottish miners had campaigned for improved housing in mining areas around the turn of the century. A note to Scottish Secretary John Sinclair from his private secretary, H.M. Conacher in January 1909 warned that the Royal Commission on Mines, then sitting, had been considering evidence concerning the number of one-roomed cottages in miners villages, and as Conacher warned, 'I understand confidentially that the Commn. in their Report (now under consideration) will have something to say about this matter.'[44] Conacher was correct. Though the reference to housing in the report amounted to only a few lines in a substantial document, what was actually stated was unequivocal:

> Two of us took the opportunity, when in Scotland, to inspect some of these (single-roomed) cottages, and the conditions we found were extremely unsatisfactory, and in many cases the common privies, &c., in connection with these cottages were in a revoltingly dirty and insanitary condition. It is beyond the scope of this Commission to make any recommendations on this matter, but we wish to point the moral that for men and families living in such surroundings facilities for cleanliness are non-existent, and it is scarcely possible for men returning from the pit to wash themselves completely without a breach of the common decencies of life.[45]

John Sinclair, Scottish Secretary, directed the Local Government Board of Scotland to ask the County Medical Officers in mining counties to report on the housing conditions in their districts following the publication of the report and received a deputation from the Scottish Miners Federation on 19 January, 1909. That deputation, as another that met with the Scottish Secretary on 26 April, 1909, called for a committee of inquiry with a view to initiating necessary legislation. Continued calls for an inquiry came from J.H. Whitehouse, Liberal MP for the mining constituency of Mid Lanark in 1911, and Sinclair, by then Lord Pentland, agreed to this at a meeting with Scottish MPs representing mining districts on 20 November, 1911. However, the Royal Commission on Housing was only established on 30 October, 1912.

While recognising the peculiar nature of Scotland's housing problems, the Commission failed to make any radical proposals respecting the central administration. Its proposals concentrated rather on the local authorities. Housing had been a responsibility of the Scottish Local Government Board from 1909. The Royal Commission's recommended that the state should accept direct responsibility for the housing of the working classes in Scotland[46] and that the Local Government Board should ensure local authority compliance with its detailed recommendations,[47] focussed on the already existing Scottish central authority.

A Scottish tradition had grown up which gave the Scottish central administration a more centralist edge than its equivalent in England and Wales. An article by the President of the Scottish branch of the Incorporated Society of Medical Officers of Health in 1898 maintained that public health administration in Scotland differed from that of south of the border:

> While the Local Government Board in England had pursued a policy of masterly inactivity in relation to local authorities, the Scottish Board, inspired by the late Sir John Skelton, had exercised a very real supervision over the doings and defaults of the smaller local authorities. The Board was a strong Board. Its policy in public health affairs, as in matters of Poor Law administration, was one of centralization. It had a finger in the pie of every parochial local authority in Scotland. [48]

In 1909, the Royal Commission on the Poor Laws and Relief of Distress (Scotland) had recommended more direct powers of initiative and guidance for the Scottish central authority as well as an increased status for the Board.[49] Perhaps more important were the appointments to the Scottish Local Government Board, as Levitt noted,[50] which ensured that it developed an outlook positively favouring increased central intervention and which, through the activities and attitudes of these appointees, stimulated an awareness of health matters in Scotland and an appreciation of arguments for reforms in a Scottish context.

National Insurance enhanced the Scottish dimension in health administration before the First World War. Calls for 'special treatment' for

Scotland and Wales were made following Irish demands so that four National Commissions were established as well as a Joint Committee. This was initially thought by Sir Henry Bunbury to have 'finally wrecked the bill, splitting it up into four separate parts'.[51] Experience proved otherwise, as Bunbury acknowledged:

> In the atmosphere which prevailed, however, the Commissions for Scotland, Wales and Ireland possessed in their own countries an influence, and an authority, which nobody sitting in and operating from London could have hoped to exercise, even though it included representatives from those countries. Moreover, the 'Celts', as we called them, were in the first critical year a powerful influence against defeatism in London. ... It was, in my judgement not a necessary but a very successful experiment in applied home rule.[52]

In 1912, the Scottish Commission sought to increase its responsibilities. In February, John Jeffrey, Secretary of the Scottish Insurance Commission wrote to Braithwaite setting out the Scottish Commission's desire to deal with matters concerning medical benefit in Scotland[53] and in May 1916 wrote to the Treasury on behalf of the Scottish Commission, in respect to Treasury regulations under section 83 of the National Insurance Act referring to the Joint Committee's constitution, powers and duties. On the later occasion, Jeffrey argued in defence of the separate National Commissions, insisting that insured persons, employers and local officials tended to look towards their National Commission rather than the Joint Commission, and that the Joint Commission was less capable of taking local conditions into account in determining universally applied regulations, and used the classic argument for Scottish central administrative differentiation – that the 'national feeling in Scotland is strong that only by a separate administration can the Scottish position be properly met'.[54] Clearly, there already existed not only a background of support for further state activity in health-related matters but also strong support for Scottish central administration of such matters.

As part of the preparation for post-war reconstruction, the Machinery of Government Committee was established under the chairmanship of Viscount Haldane in July 1917. The Haldane Committee recommended the 'further concentration of health services under a Minister of Health'[55] but should be 'established to act in England and Wales only, leaving the separate systems already in operation in Scotland and Ireland for separate treatment'.[56] This proposal was adopted after the war but, as with the report generally, one important health matter on which the committee had deliberated was not taken up in the proposals. Early in the report, attention was drawn to the criticisms of the administrative boards by the Royal Commission on the Civil Service. Haldane agreed with the Royal Commission, maintaining that the system of boards was 'less effective in securing departments where full responsibility is definitely laid upon the Minister.'[57] Though this was heeded in the establishment of the new central authority for health in England and Wales in 1919, it was ignored in the establishment of the Scottish Board of Health.

The Royal Commission on the Civil Service sat from 1912 to 1915 under Lord MacDonnell and had considered the Scottish Local Government Board. The Vice President of the Board, Sir George MacCrae, gave evidence to the Commission in November 1912. In answer to one question, MacCrae gave his preference for a single head of the board as this would make clear where responsibility lay. He also thought there ought to be 'someone in Parliament directly responsible for the work of the Local Government Board' other than the Scottish Secretary.[58] The Commission's report appeared to agree with MacCrae. The boards were criticised on the grounds of the lack of direct responsibility as well as in respect to matters of patronage, and the Commissioners recommended that steps should be taken to 'substitute the organisation which prevails in the Scottish Office for the Board system as the normal form of organisation in the Edinburgh Departments'.[59]

The Haldane Committee had come under the remit of Christopher Addison who had been appointed as the Minister for Reconstruction by Lloyd George. Addison, who became the first Minister of Health, noted after meeting a deputation of Scottish MPs on reconstruction questions in June 1918 that the meeting had been 'intensely national in its feeling'.[60] Nine days later, the Minister for Reconstruction spent his morning at the Scottish Office with Robert Munro, the Scottish Secretary, receiving a deputation of Scottish Local Authorities discussing the Health Bill. In his diary, Addison commented on the deputation:

> I cannot say that they contributed much towards a solution of the Scottish difficulties, but it looks, on the whole, as if the best course will be to adopt Munro's suggestion and provide a special Scottish Board of Health.[61]

The Scottish Board of Health Bill was given a first reading in the Commons on 27 March, 1919. It set out to 'establish a Scottish Board of Health to exercise powers with respect to health and local government in Scotland, and for purposes connected therewith'.[62] At the second reading much of the debate was concerned with the position of the Ministerial head of the board, resembling discussions which had taken place in 1911 concerning the Scottish Board of Agriculture. Robert Munro maintained that the Scottish Secretary should be head of the Board and stressed that the Minister responsible should be a Cabinet Minister 'who will have the right to speak in the inner councils of the nation, and who will also be in close and intimate touch with the Treasury'.[63] Under the existing circumstances, as both Munro and Halford Mackinder stated, it was inconceivable that there could be two Ministers in the Cabinet representing Scottish interests.[64]

Those who argued for a separate Minister of Health in the debate, such as Liberal MPs Joseph Johnstone and Dr Donald Murray, were clear as to their reasons for not wanting the Scottish Secretary to have responsibility as Minister of Health. Murray called the Scottish Secretary a 'Jack of all Trades and a Master of None' but was vague on the practicalities of establishing a separate Scottish Minister for Health.[65] Sir John Hope, Unionist MP for Midlothian, sought to have the proposed Parliamentary Under Secretary as the 'real head of the Board of Health, not only under the supervision of the Secretary for Scotland, but that he should be the genuine working head responsible to Parliament'.[66] Hope pursued his idea during the report and third reading stages of the bill, urging the Scottish Secretary to assure him that the Under Secretary would be 'completely independent'.[67] This was an echo of the demands which had come from bodies outside Parliament including the Edinburgh Corporation, the Royal College of Surgeons of Edinburgh, the North British Pharmaceutical Society and the Scottish Conference of Friendly Approved Societies.[68] Each of these bodies demanded an 'independent' or 'separate' Scottish Board of Health but none were prepared to recognise the difficulties involved. At the second reading of the Scottish Board of Health Bill only the Unionist MP Halford Mackinder attacked the board system.

The creation of a Parliamentary Under-Secretary for Health for Scotland appointed by the Scottish Secretary under the 1919 Act, involved a weakening of the board system. One notable contribution to the debate was made by Walter Elliot who himself filled the office of Under Secretary for Scotland for much of the 1920s. Elliot, suggested that in Scotland the Under Secretary for Health would be seen as an Under-Secretary for Scotland and that the,

> ... enormously important duties that he has to discharge will not be
> efficiently discharged if in addition he has to act as an Under-Secretary

to the Secretary for Scotland in all the multifarious duties which the Secretary for Scotland has to carry out.[69]

Certainly, the first part of Elliot's prediction proved correct though he himself, no doubt, would have later challenged any suggestion that the duties of the Under Secretary for Scotland were not efficiently discharged. In 1926, a provision contained in the Secretaries of State Act had the effect of upgrading the status of the Parliamentary Under-Secretary to a Parliamentary Under Secretary of State, in conjunction with giving the office the wider remit which Elliot suggested would have already been assumed to exist by the Scottish people.

A maximum of six members, plus *ex officio* members – the Scottish Secretary (as President of the Board) and Scottish Under-Secretary (Vice President) – were to make up the board. The board had at all times to include two registered medical practitioners, one (or more) woman, and a member of the Faculty of Advocates or a law agent of not less than ten years' standing, but it was not, to the annoyance of Labour MP and future Scottish Secretary Willie Adamson, to have a representative of organised labour.[70] Deciding the constitution of the board inevitably led to special pleading. Medical bodies were dissatisfied that only two representatives of their profession would have a place on the board: the Royal College of Surgeons of Edinburgh urged the Lord Advocate at a meeting in March that at least one-third of the board should consist of registered medical practitioners. The North British Pharmaceutical Society wanted a qualified pharmacist to have a place on the board, while the Scottish Conference of Friendly Approved Societies disapproved of the proposal to have an advocate on the board. The Royal Faculty of Physicians and Surgeons of Glasgow had expressed their disgruntlement with the representation of the medical profession and called on the Scottish Secretary to take the opportunity of appointing representatives of the 'curative as well as the preventative sides of medicine' on the retirement of the former members of the Local Government Board who had been appointed to the Board of Health.[71]

Three years after the Act was passed, proposals were made to the Scottish Secretary by John Lamb, Permanent Under-Secretary at the Scottish Office that membership of the Board should be reduced from six to three. Partly as a response to the Geddes reports' demands for expenditure cuts and after the resignation of Dr J.C. McVail, one of its medical members, Lamb suggested that a bill should be introduced which did away with requirements for a second medical member and a legal member.[72] In response, Scottish Secretary Munro agreed that three members would be sufficient and directed Lamb to proceed with his proposals and produce a bill. Members of the board were divided.[73] One proposal upon which both Lamb and Munro were agreed was that it would be 'Parliamentarily impossible' to abolish the qualification that the board must include a woman.

Correspondence with the Treasury in April and May 1922 seemed to suggest that the Scottish Office was more determined to implement Geddes' recommendations: a letter from the Treasury stated that 'it looks as if it will be necessary, in order to be on the safe side, to provide that the Board shall consist of not more than four members',[74] to which the Scottish Office responded that Munro had a 'strong preference for a Board of three members against one of four'.[75] This may well have been explained not so much as Scottish Office enthusiasm to implement cuts but the determination of Robert Munro to reduce the role of the board. If correct, this would further confirm that the move against the boards came much more from within the Scottish central administration than from outside in the period following the war. One feature common to the Education (Scotland) Act, 1908 and the legislation establishing the Scottish Board of Agriculture was the establishment of machinery for consultation. This was in part a concession to the advocates of retaining the Boards. The Royal Commission on the Civil Service had endorsed the case for consultative and advisory bodies while firmly opposing the traditional board structure.[76]

Conclusion

The Scottish Board of Health was established in 1919 more easily than had been the Scottish Board of Agriculture seven years before. A common authority for forestry throughout Britain was established in 1919 despite the pleas of Scottish Secretary Robert Munro for a special Scottish forestry board in 1917,[77] demonstrating that Scotland would not always be treated as a separate unit. Separate Scottish health authorities already existed. The functions of the Scottish Local Government Board, Scottish Insurance Commissioners, the Lunacy Board and the SED pertaining to medical inspection and treatment of young persons could all be transferred to the Scottish Health Board without causing disruption in any British government department. The distinctively Scottish practices, the degree of centralisation and its basis in a separate Poor Law system added to the case for Scottish administrative distinctiveness. It is important to note that the establishment of the Scottish Board of Health was part of an overall scheme to rationalise the central administration of health in the United Kingdom. The debate on the Scottish bill concentrated on the peculiarly Scottish aspects of the government's proposals with the more general reasons for the legislation almost taken for granted. More general explanations had been stressed by Christopher Addison when he moved the second reading of the Ministry of Health Bill in February 1919. He noted that 'hundreds of thousands of men' had been discovered to be physically unfit according to the 'very moderate standard' required by the army and remarked on the consequences of such unfitness in terms of lost productive capacity. It was essential that health should not be left to the 'ill-defined and the combined responsibility of half-a-dozen different sets of people'.[78] But, nonetheless, this was a Scottish dimension to the arrangements.

Another reason for the ease of passage was that the opposition to the legislation was fairly muted. There were no contentious principles involved in the legislation, unlike the small landholding provisions in the Act of 1911. Moreover, the medical profession and others involved in health favoured a Scottish Ministry of Health. The agriculturalists' argument that the existence of two separate central authorities would make outbreaks of epidemics more likely and less controllable had no equivalent with respect to health, though logically it might have been expected. The cumulative development of a distinct Scottish dimension to public administration was going hand in hand with increasing central government intervention.

6
MacDonnell, the Boards and the 1928 Act

The Reorganisation of Offices (Scotland) Act, 1928 partially enacted the recommendations of the Royal Commission on the Civil Service (MacDonnell) and the Machinery of Government Committee (Haldane), each calling for Scottish administration to be modelled on Whitehall. But it was not until 1939 that the Scottish central administration was finally constituted on Whitehall lines with the dissolution of most of the remaining boards. The 1928 Act was passed fourteen years after the MacDonnell Commission and ten years after the Haldane Committee had issued reports. Bills were presented in 1923, 1924 and 1927 before an Act was passed in 1928; each bill had gone further than that of its predecessor towards a full implementation of a scheme consistent with the Whitehall model. The long wait was due to the lack of urgency attached to the measure, the desirability of which seemed to increase. Notably, the Act was passed at a convenient time when a large number of board members were about to retire and a year before a major overhaul of local government in Scotland. Nevertheless the case against the boards in Scotland had been assembled long before they were dismantled.

There were a series of Orders in Council, Select Committees and Commissions after the first effective challenge to the patronage system when Gladstone commissioned Sir Stafford Northcote and Sir Charles Trevelyan in 1853 to inquire into the organisation of the permanent civil service. This culminated in an Order in Council in January 1910 which had taken competitive examination to be the general rule for appointment to the civil service with such exceptions as Crown appointments and those included in Orders and Warrants made by the Treasury.[1] The Edinburgh boards, however, had been left relatively unaffected, though the office of the Scottish Secretary at Dover House conformed to the Whitehall model at the time of the MacDonnell Commission's inquiries.

MacDonnell classified the civil service under six headings: administrative and clerical group; executive group; professional and technical group; inspectorate; museums etc; and the subordinate service.[2] Functionally, the classification was perceived by the Royal Commission as constituting four main groups: general (administrative and clerical); executive; professional; and subordinate.[3] With such a frame of reference the Commissioners noted that Dover House employed officers of the administrative class, staff clerks drawn from the second division, second division clerks and a complement of assistant clerks and boy clerks as well as a staff of typists:

> All this is regular and we notice with satisfaction that there has been promotion from the Second Division to the Administrative Class, and that there is no room for the patronage except in respect of the recruitment of the few professional officers – inspectors whom the Secretary for Scotland appoints. There is no suggestion that this patronage has been improperly exercised, but the safeguards which we recommended would of course apply to these as to similar appointments.[4]

The safeguards referred to were those mentioned in an earlier chapter of the Commission's report dealing with 'Situations held direct from the Crown' in which it was recommended that the Minister should be required 'to lay, as soon as possible, before Parliament a minute stating the name, qualifications, and previous career of the person whom he has appointed or proposes to appoint'.[5]

A completely different situation existed with respect to the Edinburgh boards. The Scottish boards, as a distinctly Scottish system of central administration, were seen in Scotland as reflecting the existence of differences in social, educational, legal and local administrative matters from those in England and Wales. Allied to the belief that Scottish distinctiveness ought to be accommodated in a distinct form of central administration was one that Scotland's distance from London required some alternative method of central administration. Another explanation for the retention of the boards long after they had disappeared as the standard apparatus of government in London was that they came to be seen as a manifestation of Scottish national distinctiveness. It is unclear the extent to which the boards were permitted any autonomy of action in addition to that which senior permanent officials of departments were allowed, but from evidence given to the Royal Commission it would appear that the boards were not particularly independent, as implied in the debates in the late 1920s by many Labour MPs who attempted to portray the board system as the 'last vestige of independent government and nationhood'.[6]

Sir James Dodds, Scottish Office Permanent Under Secretary, in explaining the patronage system, stated that because the boards were geographically separated from their Minister then 'probably, the men at the head of those offices, have, even oftener than we have in London, to exercise considerable discretion. In London one can always go to one's minister and cover one's responsibility'.[7] While the peculiar characteristics of Scotland and its distance from London might justify the exercise of considerable discretion there seems to have been no good reason for the appointment of the boards by patronage. It was not as if the membership of the boards changed with each Government or that their members had any administrative qualifications. Neither were they in any sense representative of Scottish opinion. A claim which was made on behalf of the board members by Dodds was that they were 'university men generally of high standing of one of the Scottish universities',[8] whereas the class one persons at Dover House were 'not mainly men of Scotch birth'.[9]

Quite simply, the boards were perceived as being headed by Scots in Scotland. The Commission's report suggested that the 'local sympathy and knowledge' provided by the boards might be secured, 'partly by the natural tendency of Scottish officials to seek service in Scottish offices and partly by the creation in suitable cases of such unpaid Advisory Boards as that which exists in connection with the English Board of Education'.[10] Another possibility raised during the assembling of evidence, but not mentioned in the report, was that it might prove advantageous for the Civil Service Commissioners to have a more direct relationship with the offices in Scotland, including appointing a member of the Civil Service Commission to be specially involved with the Scottish side of the Commission's work.[11]

It had not been possible for the Commissioners to consider the Scottish administrative structure in Edinburgh in terms of the classification of the civil service which it had outlined earlier in its report. The Scottish Office kept no record of any kind of waiting list of applicants to positions on the boards and there was no formal objective procedure for determining who should be appointed to them. The procedure was therefore seen to be open to abuse and the Commissioners condemned patronage as a normal system of recruitment. Appointments by patronage, instead of a 'system purporting to open a career to talent', were an 'anachronism'; they were, 'disheartening and give colour to the suspicion that Governments may attach greater value to personal service to a particular Minister or to a political party than to lifelong efficient service to the State'.[12]

More specifically, the report instanced three major failings of the board system: it was 'less effective in securing responsibility for official action and advice than the system followed in the office of the Secretary for Scotland'; it must 'tend to weaken in some degree the important distinction between the qualities, and the methods of selection, which are suitable for political, and which are suitable for permanent, appointments'; and the 'higher business of administration is apparently sometimes performed by men who bring to it no special knowledge of the work'.[13] The Commissioners urged the Government to take advantage by employing officers of the administrative class in place of the boards. However, there was no indication of how insistent the Commission intended to be in its recommendations. It was merely stated that the time had come when the system of boards should be 'reconsidered'. When vacancies occurred in the 'higher staff' of the boards, it was suggested that it should be decided whether the post vacated was 'administrative' or 'professional or technical' and to fill the former from those entering the civil service following examination or by promotion, and to make appointments to the latter by the accepted method for professional positions.[14] From this, it seems that the Royal Commissioners intended that the boards should disappear gradually through the retirement or resignation of the individual members of the boards. If so, then the 1928 Act was introduced at an opportune moment when a very large proportion of board members were about to retire and generally conformed with the MacDonnell Commission's recommendations.

Sir James Dodds was the first class one Permanent Under Secretary at the Scottish Office, but there were no class one officers in Edinburgh. There had been no first division officer transferred to the Scottish Office at its foundation in 1885 though a second division clerk was promoted to the first division in 1888 and the following year Dodds entered the Scottish Office. 'He and I formed Class 1 in the department for some years,' Dodds remarked.[15] It was not until 1902 that a third class one entrant into the Scottish Office was to be listed in the report of the Civil Service Commissioners. In their 1903 report, P.J.G. Rose is listed as having come fourth in the general order of merit; four years later A.M. Smith, coming eighteenth in the Commission's examinations entered the Scottish Office; and after coming third in the general order of merit W.A.C. Goodchild joined the Scottish Office as reported in the 1910 report. In 1911, a year in which a very large number of class one officials were admitted to the home civil service, three were appointed to the Scottish Office – L.G.M. Glover, G.W. Milroy and P.R. Laird.[16] Of the six class one men appointed to the Scottish Office before the First

World War, three had come from Cambridge and three from Oxford; none had been educated at a Scottish university. The MacDonnell report had recognised the high proportion of graduates from Oxford and Cambridge universities amongst candidates for the civil service and the lack of candidates from Scottish universities and explained that, 'the tradition of the Civil Service as a career has not yet established itself (in Scotland), and there is a distinct preference for the learned professions, especially Medicine, Teaching, and Ministry'.[17] Another explanation for the few Scottish candidates may well have been the lack of opportunities in Scotland for ambitious potential recruits though it is important to remember that the boards were, in the main, mostly composed of Scottish university graduates. The fear that these boards might be replaced by Oxbridge administrators was to be a major consideration for MPs in debates in the 1920s.

Another feature of the Scottish central administration in 1912 was the absence of intermediate civil servants. In a question to Dodds, Lord MacDonnell suggested that a parallel was to be found in Ireland where the appointments below those made by patronage, with the exception of the Chief Secretary for Ireland's office, were organised on the second division basis:

> In other words, you in Scotland, and if I may anticipate, they in Ireland have not progressed far beyond the stage of the Playfair Commission which reorganised the second division. Then came the Ridley Commission, which confirmed the Playfair Commission's general expressions of approval of a higher division but did not carry them into effect. It would seem as if the policy of Civil Service Reform had been restricted to England and Wales, and that patronage was restricted as the means of filling the higher appointments in Scotland and in Ireland.[18]

If anything, MacDonnell had understated the position of the Scottish Boards; they had not even begun to challenge patronage by the outbreak of the First World War. The reform of Scottish central administration and the beginning of dismantling the boards came with the 1928 Act, seventy-five years after the Northcote–Trevelyan report, and the final abandonment of the board structure in Scotland was only achieved in 1939, sixty-five years following the establishment of Playfair Commission and twenty-nine years after the Order in Council of January 1910 in which competitive examination in appointments to the civil service was regarded as the general rule.

Sir James Dodds, Under Secretary at the Scottish Office, explained the continued existence of the boards in Edinburgh. 'It is historical', Dodds had stated, 'it has been the practice for a long time'.[19] 'The standard checks existed to ensure that patronage was not based on prejudice and favouritism, according to Dodds. The Board would be responsible to the Minister who, in turn, would be responsible to Parliament.'[20] The Under Secretary maintained that a system of competitive examinations would not prove feasible in making professional appointments which were often demanded by statute, because it was unlikely that any board member under the age of thirty would ever be appointed and it would be most unlikely to 'get professional people to compete at a mature age'.[21] Dodds' defence of the boards could easily be destroyed with reference to the then existing civil service provisions for such appointments.

Sir George MacCrae, Vice President of the Scottish Local Government Board, was asked by one Commissioner whether he was satisfied with the Local Government Board's method of administration. He preferred an administrative system with a 'single head' rather than divided responsibility as existed in the Local Government Board. There was a degree of delegation to the legal and medical members of the boards. MacCrae saw no great difficulty in a reorganisation which would give the 'higher work' of the board to a 'higher class of clerk instead of to the official members of the Board'.[22] It would be necessary, he felt, to 'follow the English precedent' and have a Minister directly responsible in Parliament for the board.[23]

The operation of the Local Government Board, as portrayed by MacCrae, suggested that it played a very limited role: indeed, it hardly ever met. On important matters, the normal practice was for the board's secretary to send a file to the medical member who would pass it on to the legal member who in turn would pass it on to the Vice President. Each would write a minute and any difference of opinion usually reconciled 'on paper'. It was not possible for two of the board to outvote a third. Whenever agreement could not be reached, the Scottish Secretary would be called upon to decide.[24] There were few fairly important questions which MacCrae felt should always to be decided by the board: these included appointments, such as medical, engineering and architectural inspectors. He explained that it was the members of the Board in Scotland who 'really see the people and know their qualifications'.[25] This was remarkable only in as much as MacCrae did not extend his logic to claim the board's prerogative over other important matters. If the board was best qualified in making appointments it remained unclear why it should not always be best qualified to deliberate on difficult and serious questions which might come before it. From the evidence given by Dodds it was also clear that the boards were not taking major initiatives or acting at all independently. The work done by the Edinburgh boards was supervisory and administrative, while clerical work was done by second division clerks in the offices in Edinburgh. In effect, as Dodds stated, 'The Edinburgh Boards take the place in Scotland of the higher division offices'.[26] It was not the work which was done by the boards which was to be criticised by the Commissioners but the method of choosing those who undertook this work.

Home rule demands and parliamentary dissatisfaction

Reforming central administration was unlikely to excite the public imagination. Despite the importance of the machinery of government there were few serious critiques of the way in which Scotland was governed. Home rule was more a slogan for winning votes than a considered alternative scheme for governing Scotland. Liberal support for Scottish home rule and home rule all round, if at all credible, was a consequence of the Irish question. Asquith was unenthusiastic in his reception to calls for Scottish Home Rule made by a deputation of Scottish Liberal MPs in May 1912 and had refused to make 'any specific pledge about a particular time' when a Scottish Parliament would be legislated for, which indicated at best that a low priority was attached to the idea.[27] Duncan Pirie, Aberdeen North's Liberal MP and ardent home ruler, suggested in Parliament, following the meeting with Asquith, that the Government's 'unwillingness or reluctance' to give information on the matter to the House was due to the 'divided opinion on the question in the Cabinet'.[28]

Illingworth, a Government whip, noted that the 'gist of the Scottish grievance to be that certain branches of administration which ought to be conducted at Edinburgh or elsewhere in Scotland are conducted in London, where officials are less in touch with Scottish opinion and less accessible to Scotchmen'.[29] Home rulers were invariably critics with a highly developed sense of the need to emphasise the distinctive Scottish aspects of public administration. Thus MPs existed who defended the board system in Scotland despite an antipathy to patronage. The converse was not true: supporters of the boards were not necessarily supporters of home rule. But where the relationship between home rule and administrative reform gained new significance, other than in the common, vague concerns about the preservation of Scottish distinctiveness, was with regard to the increased functions of the Scottish Office and the demise of the boards. During the first three decades of the twentieth century, the demise of the boards was thought to be a removal of one of the last vestiges of Scottish national distinctiveness, a system of Scottish government in Scotland.

Before the First World War, Scottish Liberals had been the principal standard bearers of Scottish home rule and after the war Scottish Labour MPs claimed that role. Debates in Parliament on the Government of Scotland Bills, supply debates and other discussions of the central administration saw Liberals arguing that the varied work of the Scottish Secretary and the lack of Parliamentary time necessitated home rule. In June 1911, Henry Watt MP stated that, 'There are sixteen departments over which the Secretary for Scotland is chief, and in discussing his salary we are not permitted to touch any of these sixteen departments.'[30] A debate on home rule in February 1912 heard Munro Ferguson criticising the Scottish Office: 'Its failure through twenty-five years is alone a strong reason in favour of Scottish national self-government'.[31] This future Scottish Secretary insisted that a distinctive set of administrative apparatus in Scotland was no substitute for a Parliament:

> Bureaucracy has no enthusiasm. It destroys it. Great reforms are carried by a living administration, are secured for the country through the dogged, persistent zeal of the representative individual whose place is found mainly under a free system of representative Government. That free system we have not got.[32]

However, Munro Ferguson's views seem to have changed by the time he became Scottish Secretary as he made no attempt to introduce a measure of home rule.

Scottish Unionists, vehement opponents of home rule, accepted the Scottish view of the central administration. During the years of Liberal ascendancy before the war, Unionists had no difficulty with the argument that the existing means of governing Scotland was inadequate. Sir George Younger's diagnosis was not dissimilar to that of Henry Watt but his remedy was very different. The Scottish Secretary was,

> four Cabinet Ministers rolled into one, he has sixteen departments of one kind or another under his charge. He has had another very important one added – namely, the Board of Agriculture, and it cannot be denied that his duties are very great. The answer to that is not that you want a Home Rule Parliament in Edinburgh, but that you want a reorganisation of the Scottish Office.[33]

Younger's reorganisation involved the appointment of Secretaries for the different departments responsible to the Commons under the control of the Scottish Secretary. The Unionists accepted the need for a Scottish dimension but were clearer than the Liberals that the Whitehall model had to prevail. Nevertheless the dissatisfaction with Scottish central administration was recognised and felt to require some kind of action. It is notable that the action in the form of Reorganisation of Offices bills was taken by Unionists. The Unionists were the reformers of the central administration: in part they were displaying their unionism, accepting the primacy of the Whitehall model and in part they may have been introducing reforms as a means of appeasing Scots and demonstrating that alternatives to home rule existed. Liberals who advocated home rule were critical of the boards. Munro Ferguson called for a departmental inquiry in 1906 to report on the modifications in the system of boards to secure efficiency, co-ordination and to keep them in 'closer touch with public opinion'.[34] Labour MPs were usually critical of the members of the boards but rarely, if ever, of the board structure itself. Labour MPs were the constitutional conservatives with reference to the boards though radical in their support for home rule. There was a remarkable degree of intellectual confusion on the issue of the government of Scotland in Labour and Liberal circles especially as compared with the Unionists.

The Parliamentary Under Secretaryship for Health for Scotland

During debates on the establishment of the Scottish Office it had been argued by many educationalists that Scotland required a Minister for Education as distinct from a Scottish Minister with varied duties. The Act of 1885 was passed for the appointment of a Secretary for Scotland and Vice President of the Scotch Education Department, thereby establishing, at least theoretically, a functional basis as well as the more general territorial basis for the department. However, in reality, there was no Scottish Education Minister as such. During debates prior to the formation of the Scottish Board of Agriculture there were calls for an Agriculture Minister distinct from the Scottish Secretary but these had come to nothing. When the Scottish Board of Health was established, an Under Secretary with responsibility for health in Scotland was included in its provisions. On that occasion, it was felt that health responsibilities increased the Scottish Office's remit to the extent that an additional Minister was required. What was unusual about the 1919 proposals was that the

Under Secretary would be functionally restricted. This was a rather perverse situation: education in Scotland was the responsibility of a Committee of the Privy Council which in Parliament was represented by the Committee's Vice President – the Scottish Secretary – who also had central responsibility for local authorities, lunacy, prisons, fisheries, and latterly, agriculture. Health was to be the responsibility of a board and in Parliament was charged to an Under Secretary and the Scottish Secretary.

At the beginning of the third decade of the twentieth century Scotland was being governed by an administrative medley of persons and governmental machinery without rational coherence. The establishment of the office of Under Secretary for Health for Scotland only confused matters further. In April 1919, along with a proposal to raise the status of the office of Scottish Secretary to that of Secretary of State, forty-seven Scottish MPs from all parties signed a memorial to the Prime Minister suggesting that there should be two Parliamentary Under Secretaries and that, 'subject to the general responsibility of the Secretary for Scotland, the three Ministers should divide among them the immediate responsibility for the several departments of the Scottish Office in such a way that each should have the supervision of a particular group of departments'.[35]

In 1923, Walter Elliot became Under Secretary for Health for Scotland with press speculation that the office would be extended to cover general Scottish administration and not limited to health.[36] Viscount Novar, formerly Liberal MP Munro Ferguson, had become Scottish Secretary following the fall of the coalition the previous year. Thus, as the rather hagiographical account of Elliot's life by the subject's friend stated, 'Walter's chief was in the Lords; and he had to answer for Scotland on topics which briefed a dozen English Ministers'.[37] Elliot became, in effect, Under Secretary for Scotland, if not in name. His ebullience and intellect could only have strengthened the case for the extension of the functions of the office. Contrary to what is sometimes suggested, Elliot's main achievements at the Scottish Office occurred during this period rather than during his brief period as Secretary of State in the 1930s.

The first Reorganisation of Offices (Scotland) Bill was introduced in July 1923 in the Lords and included provision for the 'appointment of a Parliamentary Under Secretary for Scotland and discontinuance of the Office of Parliamentary Under Secretary for Health'.[38] Proposals for an extended remit for the office were thus being considered only three years after the Act of 1919 had established the office of Under Secretary for Health for Scotland.[39] However, the 1923 bill did not proceed further. The following year, Lord Muir Mackenzie, who had served on the MacDonnell Commission, presented a bill. Once more the second clause dealt with the office of Parliamentary Under Secretary. At a meeting to discuss the Reorganisation Bill in late April 1924 this clause was not seen as contentious by those present, including the Lord Chancellor, Muir Mackenzie, the Lord Advocate and the Scottish Secretary.[40] The subsequent debate in the Lords confirmed that there was a general consensus in favour of that particular clause, but the bill, having proceeded through the Lords, was lost in the Commons.

Opposition to the clause, however, existed outside the Commons. In August 1923, the *British Medical Journal* joined with a number of bodies which questioned the desirability of abolishing the Scottish Board of Health, but unlike the others, the official organ of the British Medical Association went further. The *BMJ* defended the office of Parliamentary Under Secretary for Health for Scotland and argued that a Parliamentary Under Secretary for Scotland would be an 'official who will give only a portion of his time and attention to this most important duty'. The 'retrograde step' was regarded as a 'breach of faith'.[41] The views of the Standing Committee of Scottish Insured Women, also suggested that health should not be lost amongst the many concerns of Scottish central administration and stressed the case for retention of the Scottish Board of Health 'while not objecting to Clause 1 of the bill' to extend the scope of responsibilities of the Under Secretary.[42]

The development of the boards

For most of the period following the publication of the MacDonnell Commission up until the publication of the 1928 Act, its recommendations regarding Scotland were ignored. The establishment of the Scottish Board of Health indicated how little attention had been paid to the MacDonnell Report. There was no real intention to implement the recommendations before 1927. Both the Conservative measure of 1923 and the Labour proposals the next year were motivated primarily with reorganising the Register House Departments, especially following the vacancy in the office of Deputy Clerk Register caused by the death of Sir J. Patten Macdougall in 1919 and the resultant opportunity provided for reform. An influence on both bills was the economic mood following the Geddes reports and, with respect to the boards, it was this which had been the major influence. These bills were not so much attempts to reform Scottish central administration but set out to limit the size of the boards.

Later proposals in 1927 and 1928 were more serious attempts to reform the Scottish central administration. Economy was not central to their purpose but rather the partial implementation of the MacDonnell report's suggestions. Contrary to the suggestion made by one Labour MP, the Chancellor of the Exchequer was not the 'power behind the throne'.[43] Evidence that the proposal to abolish the board system was a Scottish Office initiative rather than an idea pressed on the Scottish Secretary by the Treasury exists in a letter from the Treasury of January 1927 commenting on an early draft of the reorganisation bill of that year, in which a Treasury Assistant Secretary writes that his department had 'no objection in principle to the proposal to abolish the board system'.[44] Support for reform had developed gradually in the Scottish Office and was then given Treasury approval.

There was support for the board structure in Scotland but even its defenders criticised particular boards weakening the case for retention. Unionists were critical of the amount spent by the Scottish Board of Agriculture and the number of officials employed by it, asking Parliamentary Questions in March, July and October 1921.[45] In January 1925, memoranda were written by the chairmen of the Scottish Boards of Health and Agriculture on the proposed establishment of Departments of Health and Agriculture. There was a marked difference in the two memoranda: Ewan MacPherson of the Health Board was defensive and clearly supported the retention of his board, while Robert Greig was more impartial. Greig accepted that it was 'unlikely that if Public Departments were being set up now in Scotland they would be set up as Boards'.[46] Towards the end of the piece, Greig listed advantages and disadvantages of the board system, but before this he had briefly described the operation of the Board of Agriculture in a manner which explains his more critical view of the boards than his counterpart in the Board of Health:

When the Board of Agriculture was constituted in 1912 it was not organised on the Board system. It did not meet as a Board. The Chairman took responsibility for all decisions after consultation with Heads of Departments and the Secretary. This method did not work well as the Board members had the undoubted right to put their views to the Secretary for Scotland and in some instances exercised this right. The result was that the Secretary for Scotland received the divided opinions, there was friction within the Board and work was delayed. During his period the Chairman of the Board reported directly to the Secretary for Scotland and not through his Under Secretary. In 1915 Mr McKinnon Wood [Scottish Secretary] instructed the Board to meet as a Board, to keep minutes and to report the decisions of the Board to London. At the same time the procedure in the

Scottish Office was altered and the submissions and reports to the Secretary for Scotland were made and continue to be made through the Permanent Under Secretary.[47]

One of the few bodies which came to the defence of the Scottish Board of Agriculture was the National Farmers Union of Scotland. The NFU(S) feared centralisation in Whitehall, but a civil service note remarked that the objection was based on a 'misunderstanding'.[48] Whatever attempts were made to convince the NFU that their fears were unfounded, the NFU persisted in defending the board. In March 1928, the General Secretary of the Scottish NFU sent a telegram to the Scottish Office reaffirming the unanimous opposition of his executive to the Reorganisation Bill and asked that the Board of Agriculture should be retained.[49] But the Scottish NFU was a lonely voice.

Opinion was much more evenly divided on the Scottish Board of Health. In his memorandum of January 1925, the chairman of the Scottish Board, Ewan MacPherson argued that the record of administration over the previous thirty years vindicated its existence.[50] MacPherson set out the case, as he saw it, for retaining the Scottish Board of Health:

It seems in other words that the collective wisdom of the Board upon any point of difficulty may be of more value to the Minister than that of any one individual. It further would appear that if the permanent Head is to keep in proper touch with this country, the former would have to spend the greater part of his time in London to the detriment of his administrative work there. The present system under which meetings of the Board are held every week at which all the more important questions are discussed and decided, Minutes of such meetings being sent to the Ministers, appears to be as good a method as can be devised of keeping them in touch with the general position in Scotland and is certainly well worth the two or three hours a week devoted to the meetings. It further enables every Member of the Board to keep in touch with the whole work of the Department. When the Under Secretary and the Secretary himself come to these meetings they gain a clearer insight into the conditions of Scotland than they could possibly attain by any amount of correspondence. It may be argued that the transaction of business by Committees of the Board subject to revision at the Board meetings, and subsequent approval by the President, involves a certain delay. In point of fact there is very little in this, as certainly no less time would be spent in consultations by the Head of a Department with his advisers before he can come to a decision. It may be confidently asserted that the record for expedition of the Board under the present system compares favourably with that of any Government Department in London.[51]

In its chairman, the Scottish Board of Health had a staunch defender. Also, it had supporters outside the central administration in Scotland. The Standing Committee of Scottish Insured Women in July 1924 wrote to James Stewart MP, Parliamentary Under Secretary for Health for Scotland, protesting against the terms of clause 2 which repealed the section of the Act of 1919 requiring the Board of Health to include a woman.[52] This organisation was amongst a list including fourteen local insurance committees, the Scottish National Housing and Town Planning Committee, Stirling Burgh Pharmaceutical Committee, the General Council of Panel Chemists (Scotland), the Scottish Conference of Friendly and Approved Societies and the 'North British' branch of the Pharmaceutical Society of Great Britain supporting the retention of the Board of Health. Once more the official view was that objections were based upon a 'mistaken apprehension that in future Health and Insurance work will be done in and controlled from London to a greater extent than at present'.[53]

MacPherson's views on the Board of Health were not shared by the permanent civil service. The *Civil Service Opinion* of November 1923 was critical of the 'evils' of the board system in an article on health administration in Scotland and maintained that there was no reason why the 'Health Department in Scotland should not be organised along the same lines as the Ministry of Health in England'.[54] A deputation from the Executive Officers' Association, an organisation representing the middle grade of the civil service, was received by James Stewart in April 1924 and William Boys, general secretary of the association, pointed out that the Reorganisation Bill did not go so far as the Royal Commission had recommended.[55] Boys explained that his Association had an interest in the grading of work in the Scottish Administration. In response to points made by Stewart, Boys sent the Under Secretary a proposed amendment to clause 1 of the bill to abolish the Scottish Board of Health. Under this amendment, the board was to consist of only two members, 'one of whom shall be the Secretary for Scotland, who shall be President of the Board, and the other shall be the Parliamentary Under Secretary, who shall be Vice President of the Board'.[56]

Two months later in February 1925, Boys again led a deputation which met Scottish Secretary Sir John Gilmour. Gilmour stated that he 'had not himself arrived at a decision but before long he would and he had no doubt that when the Bill was introduced it would be bound to have some minor alterations'.[57] Gilmour did in fact accept the views of the Association when the abolition of the Board of Health was included in the provisions of the bill presented in 1927. In reply to a Parliamentary Question in June 1925, Gilmour stated that there was no prospect for the introduction of a Reorganisation Bill that session;[58] the interest of the Scottish Secretary had turned instead towards the measure raising the status of the Scottish Office.

The earlier bills of 1923 and 1924 had only sought to reduce the size of the Board of Health but had not attempted to replace the board with a department. An existing membership 'not exceeding six' was provided for in the Act establishing the Board of Health. Four members were proposed in 1924. The Government wanted to take advantage of imminent retirements though it is notable that the opportunity to abolish the board through the retirement of all but one of its members over a period of five years was not taken advantage of in the bill presented in 1924. It was not that this possibility was not recognised – a note in 1924 detailed the particulars of each of the board members and remarked that three members were due to retire in three to five years[59] – but it would appear simply that the case for abolition had not then been established firmly.

The third clause of the 1924 bill made provision, similar to the bill of the previous year, for the Fishery chairman to hold office on civil service tenure, making him available for the ordinary pensionable position of a civil servant. However, there was no intention to abolish the Board itself though, as the former Labour Scottish Secretary, Willie Adamson pointed out in 1927,[60] this had been a proposal made by a Scottish Departmental Committee many years before as well as the Royal Commission on the Civil Service. In September 1914, Lord Pentland had appointed a committee under Angus Sutherland to inquire into and report on 'certain matters connected with the development of the Scottish Sea Fishing Industry, after visiting the various countries engaged in fishing in the North Sea'.[61] The Committee had recommended modifying the constitution of the Fishery Board for Scotland:

(a) by abolishing a nominated Board and entrusting the fishery administration in Scotland to a department with a permanent head (a member of the permanent Civil Service) acting under the instructions of the Secretary for Scotland, or (b) by making alternatively the Chairman a member of the permanent Civil Service, providing otherwise for the functions discharged by the Sheriff and the scientific member, leaving the other four members as at present.[62]

In April 1927, Walter Boys sent a letter to the Scottish Office calling for the Board to be fully included in the scheme of reorganisation.[63] Boys claimed that patronage appointments lingering on in Scotland were 'distasteful in most circles'. The basis of representation on the board required to be widened, according to Boys, to include branches of the industry then excluded such as wholesale and retail distributors but it would result in a much larger board which would be 'undesirable for practical reasons, and, in view of the many diverse interests concerned, a method of selection satisfactory to all parties would be a delicate and difficult matter'.[64] For these reasons, Boys felt that the arguments against the board system applied equally to the Fishery Board in particular.

The 1927 bill also set out to substitute the Prison Commissioners for Scotland with a Prisons Department for Scotland, though in his Cabinet Committee memorandum, the Scottish Secretary admitted that 'in this case the arguments for a change are perhaps not so strong. I should be prepared to exclude that Department if this should appear to be desirable in the course of the Bill's progress'.[65] This provision excited little attention in the debate in Parliament but as the bill was not proceeded with it made no difference. The inclusion of the Scottish Prison Commissioners in the scheme of the bill had been partly a result of the ages of the two full time Commissioners and partly due to the poor working relations between these individuals and with the Scottish Secretary.[66] A memorandum in 1928 on the Scottish Prison Commission remarked that the relations between the two Commissioners were 'not satisfactory' and also noted that the Commissioners had 'from time to time been reproved by the Secretary of State for failing to report to or consult him about important matters connected with their administration'.[67] As an example of the latter, the memorandum instanced the failure of the Commissioners to report on hunger the strike by Irish prisoners in Scottish prisons in 1925.

The Register House Departments

One matter which did arouse much interest was the administration of the public records, registers and rolls. It was a matter affecting the Scottish population as a whole and agitated a small but well-organised and vociferous section of the community. The records of Scotland included those relating to conveyancing, historical archives and general executry law. An office of Deputy Clerk Register had been established in 1806 by Royal Warrant to remedy deficiencies in the administration and control of the Scottish registers and records and over time the duties of this official were combined with those of the Registrar General for Scotland. By an Act of 1897 this arrangement was given legal authority; the office of Lord Clerk Register became an honorary one and the whole rights and duties regarding the public registers, records and roles of Scotland were given to the Deputy Clerk Register.

The 1924 bill proposed to abolish the office of Deputy Clerk Register, transferring the duties of that official to the Scottish Secretary. This resulted in a concerted campaign by Scottish lawyers' organisations opposed to the proposals. The Committee on Bills of the Society of Writers to His Majesty's Signet, a body of Scottish solicitors with the exclusive privilege of preparing Crown writs, presented a report on the bill in June 1924.[68] In it was contained the recommendation that 'there should be an official, such as Deputy Clerk Register, who would have control over the whole Registers and Records throughout Scotland with all necessary powers'.[69] The Committee of the Faculty of Advocates also issued a report on the bill in June 1924 and expressed their 'grave concern' respecting the 'efficiency of our registration system', fearing the concentration of the work of Register House being moved from Edinburgh to Dover House in London.[70] In the opinion of the Faculty of Advocates, the supervision and co-ordination of the registration system demanded the knowledge, experience and skills which the Scottish Secretary would not necessarily have. The problems which would arise of heads of each Register House Department having to seek Dover House sanction to act could be avoided 'under the superintendence of a real Head in daily attendance at his office in Edinburgh than by Departmental action in London in relation to separate Departments of the Register House not co-ordinated in any way'.[71]

In July 1924 the Council of the Society of Solicitors in the Supreme Courts of Scotland reported on the bill stating their interest to be solely concerned with the proposal to abolish the office of Deputy Clerk Register and the re-arrangement of officials in public registers, records and rolls of Scotland.[72] Once more a body of lawyers criticised clauses 4 and 12 of the bill transferring the 'practical control of the Register House Departments' to the Scottish Secretary's office in London as a 'retrogade' change which should be opposed.[73] On each of the occasions in the 1920s whenever discussion of the Register House Departments arose, these bodies offered informed criticisms in reports which would be sent to Scottish MPs and interested parties as well as the Scottish Office.

At a meeting in April 1924, officials anticipated opposition being concentrated on the clauses concerning the Register House Departments with the Lord Chancellor, Viscount Haldane fearing that the bill would not pass if it contained clause 4 abolishing the office of Deputy Clerk Register.[74] Haldane himself seems to have accepted much of the criticism of the clause when he stated at this meeting that he was afraid that the abolition of the office meant 'that there would be nobody to look after Scottish records efficiently'.[75] The case for the bill was then made by the Lord Advocate, Hugh MacMillan who admitted that initially he had been against abolishing an 'old and notable office'. However, he objected to the 'resuscitation' of the Deputy Clerk Register, an office which would either have to be filled by a 'superman' overseeing the gamut of responsibilities or else be a 'mere figurehead with a very limited ranged of individual power and not nearly enough work'.[76]

The 1927 bill intended a major reform of the Register House Departments with the office of the Deputy Clerk Register officially discontinued but a new office of Keeper of Registers and Records of Scotland was to be established. The Keeper of Registers and Records of Scotland marked a move towards centralised responsibility for Sasines, Records and Deeds offices, as Sir John Gilmour acknowledged in speaking at the second reading debate in March 1927.[77] This change probably arose from criticisms that the responsibility for Scottish registers, records and deeds would be concentrated in London. Such criticisms had been expressed by the various bodies representing legal opinion in Scotland and had also been voiced in the Lords at the second reading of the Reorganisation Bill in July 1924 by Lord Dunedin (formerly Andrew Graham Murray ex-Solicitor General, Lord Advocate and Scottish Secretary).[78]

The parties, responses

Out of the expansion of functions and responsibilities of the Scottish Office and the subsequent Royal Commission demands for reforms in the Scottish central administration, tenuous moves towards schemes for a rationalisation of the central administration were, as we have seen, emerging in the 1920s. Retention of the boards was incompatible with the Whitehall model. Legislative devolution for Scotland was never a serious prospect during this period but formed an important backdrop to the debate on the administration of Scotland. Home rule was never clearly defined. Scottish Labour and Liberal MPs supported home rule bills vehemently in principle but vaguely in detail and there was never the expert critique of the central administration which Irish Nationalists had demonstrated in respect to the administration of Ireland in the previous century. By the 1920s, home rule was a rhetorical answer to Scotland's problems.

The Unionists saw a reorganisation of the central administration as an alternative to a scheme of home rule and were in Government for most of the inter-war years. The 1927 bill set out to abolish the boards. The previous bills in 1923 and 1924 hardly began the process and only set out to limit the size of the Health Board and bring the Fishery Chairman into the permanent civil service and were concerned in the main with the reorganisation of Register House. In moving the second reading of the Reorganisation Bill in 1927, Sir John Gilmour described the intention of the provisions of the proposed legislation to replace the boards with,

> a system of Departments, following upon the lines both of the Education Department which we already have in Scotland and of those other great Departments of State which exist here in England such as the Department of Agriculture and the Ministry of Health.[79]

As a concession to Scottish opinion, Gilmour agreed that the measure did nothing to prevent the establishment or continued existence of advisory boards.[80] A further concession which was to be accepted later was an amendment supported by the Convention of Royal Burghs which set out to allay fears that the reorganisation of Scottish central administration would lead to the transfer of the offices from Edinburgh to London. The amendment was simply to add the words 'each situated in Edinburgh' after reference to the institution of departments replacing boards in clause 1.[81]

This concession to Scottish demands was an attempt to appease those who feared that the bill would, as Labour's spokesman suggested, 'subordinate Scottish administration to Whitehall to a far greater extent than has ever been the case, and to remove from Scotland practically the last vestige of independent Government and nationhood, and to have its centre in London'.[82] The Labour Opposition invoked Scottish national sentiment as much as the Scottish Home Rule Association in their stance against the Reorganisation bill. In 1924 it had been recognised by the members of the Government that 'there would be strong feeling in Scotland against the dropping of the Board system'.[83] The problem the Labour Government in 1924 identified with the bill it introduced that year was one which Labour played on three years later in opposition. Labour MPs were chided by Conservatives and Liberals for their conservatism in defending the nepotism of the board system.

Support for the boards also set them apart from the civil service staffs. A memorandum prepared for the resumption of the second reading debate written in October 1927 remarked that the Civil Service Confederation, representing the clerical staffs in government departments, had intimated their full support for reform and noted, 'It is understood that a Labour MP who endeavoured to obtain material for criticism at one of the Edinburgh Offices, received nothing but expressions of hope that he would facilitate the passage of the Bill'.[84]

During the second reading debate in 1927, James Brown, Labour MP for South Ayrshire stated 'We are conservatives' in response to a Liberal MP's criticism of Labour's position.[85] Despite pronouncements on home rule, Labour had no policy for reforming Scottish administration. Liberals accepted the 1927 Reorganisation Bill but claimed also to support home rule, though how serious their support was is doubtful. In reply to a question posed by the Scottish Home Rule Association at the 1924 General Election, Sinclair's secretary had replied that 'the present time is not favourable for the consideration of the question of a Scottish National Convention'.[86] With so little thought being devoted to questions of Scottish administration by their opponents, the Conservatives were left to devise a scheme to have the Scottish central administration conform with the Whitehall model. The only alternative was the status quo. By the late 1920s the Conservative scheme was slowly taking shape. Thus the Conservatives were to lead the way in the practical reform of the government of Scotland in the 1920s.

The 1928 Act

The debate surrounding the legislation which was finally passed reorganising the Scottish offices in the 1920s was well rehearsed. In the main, the bill presented in 1928 was the same as that of the previous year. There were only two minor alterations: at the end of clause 1(1) the words, 'The offices of the said Departments shall be situated in Edinburgh' were added and in clause 5(1) the words 'who shall receive out of moneys to be provided by Parliament such salary as the Treasury may fix' were added which provided for the payment of the new office of Keeper of Registers and Records of Scotland. These changes did not alter the substance of the proposals of the previous year. In introducing the Reorganisation Bill in February 1928,[87] Sir John Gilmour set out the Government's case. The efficiency and effectiveness of departments over boards, the desirability of the Secretary for Scotland having a single adviser at the head of a department in preference to a board, the inexpediency of retaining a system of patronage in Scotland while the accepted method of recruitment in Britain was that of public examination, were arguments which had all been heard in earlier Parliamentary debates. But one very important statement contained in Gilmour's speech was the intention, 'that we shall in course of time, when the claimant demands for economy shall have been overcome, centralize in Edinburgh under one roof all the Departments concerned with Scottish affairs'.[88] Lord Novar had once stated that 'Edinburgh is a rabbit warren of Departments'[89] in describing the Scottish central administration and this was an attempt to consolidate these warrens into one co-ordinated central body. The 1928 statement of intent was an important and clear enunciation of the Scottish Secretary's conception of how the central administration should develop.

Once more, the bill was limited in extent. Departments of Health, Agriculture and Prisons for Scotland were to be substituted for the Boards of Health and Agriculture and the Prison Commissioners for Scotland. Reforms were to be instituted in the Register House Departments which would result in a new post of Keeper of the Registers and Records of Scotland absorbing the office of Deputy Clerk Register with that of the Keeper of Sasines and the Keeper of Deeds. The Fishery Board was to remain largely unaffected except in that the chairman of the board was to become a civil servant. Gilmour justified the retention of the Fishery Board on the grounds that it had proved to be 'workable and of value',[90] but other factors were of importance. Apart from the chairman, the Fishery Board was unpaid and as the chairman was brought into the civil service under the terms of the legislation, the Fishery Board was more acceptable than the Health and Agriculture Boards simply because it appeared more like an advisory board than an administrative body. Nevertheless, the Association of Executive Officers and Other Civil Servants pressed for the inclusion of Fisheries in the scope of clause 1 of the bill. However the Association's criticisms may well have been the reason for its continued existence. The board's activities were limited to monthly meetings as the civil servants' union pointed out[91] suggesting that the role of the board was very limited.

Another argument employed by the Association was that statutory provision already existed for the appointment of advisory committees but, once more, practicalities tended to side with the boards as the memorandum stated:

> the existing statutory provisions for 'advisory bodies' are too cumbrous and complicated to be practicable; and if the Board were abolished it seems certain that provisions would have to be made for one or more

Advisory Councils on different lines. This would be a matter of extreme difficulty to settle to the satisfaction of all parties interested.[92]

In essence, the Fishery Board could continue because the implications of its abolition would have been more troublesome than its retention would have been. A feature of the legislation ignored in the Parliamentary debates was the unusual constitutional status of the departments. Sub-clause 5 of the first clause defined a department as a 'body corporate' with an official seal and stated that 'a department,[93] "may sue and be sued in the name by which it is referred to in the first subsection of this section, and may for all purposes be described by that name, and service on the Department of all legal proceedings and notices shall be effected by service on the Secretary of the Department".' The departments were conceived as distinct entities, separate from the Minister to whom they were responsible. Because of this, the Scottish constitutional lawyer, W.I.R. Fraser described the departments as 'constitutional freaks' and maintained that this 'contravened the constitutional principle that a department and its Minister are indistinguishable'.[94] The unique position of the departments had been thought necessary, as a civil servant's note on amendments remarked:

> This, though in a way anomalous, is clearly a practical necessity. It lends point, incidentally, to the description of the Secretary of State as in reality a Prime Minister for Scotland (holding all the available portfolios himself !).[95]

The 1939 Reorganisation Act was to remove the anomaly and brought the Scottish Departments of Health, Agriculture and Prisons fully into accord with British constitutional practice.

The 1928 Act was very much a movement towards, the Whitehall model of central administration. The tendencies of the reforms, such as instituting departments as distinct constitutional entities, could only help maintain an impression of a very distinct administrative structure in Scotland. Tom Johnston, Labour MP for Dundee, questioned the Government's 'urgency' in his opposition to the measure.[96] As the Bill was presented fourteen years after the Royal Commission had recommended major reforms in the Scottish central administration and as the reforms had been discussed and considered over the preceding five year, accusations of acting hastily had little credibility. The explanation for the timing of the bill was given by the Duke of Sutherland, Paymaster-General, when he stated at second reading that in the Boards of Health,

Agriculture and Prison Commissioners 'there have recently been or will shortly be no fewer than six retirements of Board members representing two-thirds of the paid personnel of these Boards'.[97] The opportunity offered by the retirement of these board members was one unlikely to occur again for some time.

Apathy and opposition

The bill was not regarded as directly relevant to unemployment or housing conditions. Administration was not a subject which excited many Parliamentarians and far less the general public; far more importance was attached to the policies a Government would implement rather than how they were to be implemented. Even in the Scottish Office itself, the reorganisation bill did not seem to have been accorded the priority status by the civil servants which Gilmour attached to it. Sir William Murrie, who was to become Permanent Under Secretary of State at the Scottish Office (1959 to 1964), joined the staff of Dover House as a young civil servant in 1927 and recollects the work done in the late 1920s on local government reform and legislation concerning rates but does not recall any great importance being attached to the reorganisation bill.[98] While this can partly be explained by Murrie's interest in local rather than central administration at the time, it is notable that the issue, with consequent opportunities for the permanent civil service, seems to have excited little interest.

This perception of the Reorganisation Bill caused problems for the Government. In April 1928 the Scottish Secretary sent letters to Scottish Unionist MPs pointing out that attendance at the Scottish Grand Committee that session had seldom constituted a 'bare quorum and at no time has the Government been in a position to move the closure'. In the letter, Gilmour recognised that the Reorganisation Bill was 'not one of great interest' to some MPs though it was designed to improve the machinery of government in Scotland and warned that 'if neglected by our party now will inevitably strengthen the demand for Home Rule'.[99] The Scottish Secretary ended his letter urging his colleagues to make every effort to attend the next meeting of the committee. Two months previously, Gilmour had urged Scottish Unionist whip, F.C. Thomson MP to reassure his own party that the abolition of the boards would not lead to 'further centralisation in London and further bureaucracy'.[100] A mixture of worries about the effects of an unpopular aspect and the relative unimportance of the bill caused the Government problems with its own backbenchers.

Strong feelings were vented in Parliament that the Government was undermining Scottish institutions but the strength of feeling implied by the language was probably more likely to have been only the standard form of exaggerated rhetoric from the Clydesiders. Noel Skelton, Unionist MP for Perth, was as obstinate, though more informed, in his defence of the boards. Skelton admitted that he knew 'intimately many of the heads'[101] of the boards. Over a period of thirty-one years his father, Sir John Skelton had successively been secretary and chairman of the Board of Supervision and chairman of the Local Government Board. Skelton maintained that the board system 'unquestionably gives to Scotland a certain degree of administrative Home Rule'[102] and he feared that by diminishing the aspects of 'administrative individuality which Scotland possesses' the Government would be taking 'one more step towards bringing above the horizon the question of Scottish Home Rule'[103] which he strongly opposed.

Sidney Webb MP distanced himself from many of his Labour colleagues by favouring a permanent civil service but warned against the failure to provide for a body 'upon which will be found various professional officers and civil servants who are there solely because of their professional qualifications'.[104] One of the most interesting contributions to the second reading debate came from Sir Archibald Sinclair, Liberal MP who became Secretary of State three years later. Sinclair maintained that the question of Scottish administration could be approached from two standpoints: one being that of administrative efficiency and economy and the other being national sentiment.[105] However, Sinclair did not automatically defend the boards in the name of national sentiment, as did Scottish Labour MPs but viewed them as,

> the creatures of Whitehall. ... If you look into the present situation not only do you find these boards are no protection for Scottish nationality, and they can give us no security from interference from Whitehall, but that the Department is actually the freest departmental organisation.[106]

For Sinclair, only home rule provided a satisfactory solution though, when given the chance as Scottish Secretary, he made no effort to establish a Scottish Parliament.

Conclusion

The 1928 Act was passed with further reforms in the future in mind and represented the first major attempt to adopt the Whitehall model. The weakness of the opposition's case lay in defence of the boards. Furthermore, the reforms of 1928 were not seen by opponents, or supporters of the Government for that matter, as being of sufficient importance to merit other than perfunctory attention. The Government was being portrayed by the opposition as having little regard for Scottish national traditions and institutions. In particular, local government reform, with the abolition of the parishes as units of local government, was cited as an example of the Unionists' contempt for Scotland by the Labour Party. Indeed, P.J. Blair, political secretary of the Scottish Unionists' whip's office in Edinburgh, noted in a piece written to Gilmour following the defeat of the Conservative Government in 1929 that the Local Government Act of that year 'probably was the cause of losing a considerable number of votes'.[107] Allied to the unpopularity of the Local Government measure, the Reorganisation Act of 1928 could only have added to the belief that the Unionists were contemptuous of Scottish institutions as their opponents forcefully argued.

The Reorganisation Act had only begun the process of change. Only one month after the legislation received the Royal Assent a memorandum was written by P.R. Laird, an Assistant Secretary in the Scottish Office, surveying the Scottish central administration after the Act, which considered means of devolving work then done at Dover House to the departments in Edinburgh and attempted to envisage the implications of further changes. Some lessons appear to have been learnt or so future developments would suggest. It would be better to gain wider acceptance for any future major reform in the central administration rather than having to face opposition, however deficient it was. Ensuring that further proposals were portrayed as far as possible as measures which did not neglect the Scottish dimension of central administration would be important. By laying stress on those parts of future proposals which provided for anything distinctively Scottish, the Government could avoid the charge that they were anglicising Scottish administration. The 1928 Act was flawed in that it failed to go so far as the MacDonnell Commission had demanded. The General Board of Control for Scotland administering the 'Lunacy Acts' and the Fishery Board for Scotland continued to exist until 1939. The anomaly of the independent existence of the three new departments established under the Act would also require to be reviewed within a decade.

7
The Reorganisation Debate and Gilmour

The Reorganisation of Offices (Scotland) Act was the most important measure to influence the development of Scottish central administration after the establishment of the Scottish Office in 1885 until the creation of the Scottish Parliament in 1999. Unlike the reorganisation legislation eleven years before, the 1939 Act had all-party support in Parliament and was preceded by a committee of enquiry, the Gilmour Committee. Dissatisfaction with the general economic and social conditions in Scotland lay in the background to the proposed reforms. Of importance was the dominant part played by permanent officials in these reforms. Their submissions to Gilmour, unsurprisingly, were far more detailed and informed than were those of the politicians. Further, an internal Scottish Office committee, headed by Sir Horace Hamilton, Permanent Under Secretary of State, considered the Gilmour report and effectively produced the blueprint for the Scottish Office structure and procedures which emerged. Ignorance of the existence of the Scottish Office, not to mention its workings, probably ensured that the debates were not of a public nature with MPs even displaying little knowledge of the Scottish central administration. Some questions, such as where the main location of the Office should be in Edinburgh and the means by which co-ordination of the work of the various departments, had been raised in earlier discussions of the educational administration (see Chapter 4). However, it was only in the 1930s when the nature of the Scottish Office was being considered in a fairly comprehensive way that anything approaching answers began to emerge. Prior to 1939, the development of Scottish central administration had been haphazard, reacting to pressures with little thought as to the impact on the overall framework of the machinery of government in Scotland.

The opportunity to reorganise was linked to the construction of a new building intended to house the Scottish Departments under one roof but by the time St Andrews House was completed the number of officials had grown so that the new building proved too small to house them all. What was created in 1939 was a co-ordinated department headed by a single Cabinet Minister responsible for a plethora of functions organised internally like other Whitehall departments, though nomenclature, location and the linking of responsibilities and a more diverse career structure set the Scottish Office apart.

Wellsprings of discontent

In his study of Scottish home rule, Arthur Turner included a chapter entitled the 'Wellsprings of Discontent'.[1] Sceptical of the benefits of home rule, Turner stressed the economic and social conditions which had afflicted Scotland during the inter-war years as explanations for nationalist and home rule activities. These wellsprings of discontent were also of consequence in the debate on the central administration of Scotland prior to 1939. Broadly, the Scottish grievances that fuelled the pressure for change, whether for legislative or administrative change, fell into four kinds. Dissatisfaction with the economic and social situation in Scotland was the most widely perceived of these grievances. There also existed a belief that Scottish affairs were neglected in Parliament, a grievance that, as we have seen, had been voiced persistently from before the foundation of the Scottish Office. Dissatisfaction with the efficacy of the machinery of government was another matter. This was obviously of most concern to the permanent officials. Finally, a common grievance which added to the protests coming from Scotland was the feeling that Scotland was simply ignored in Whitehall.

Parliamentary time devoted to Scottish affairs was an important factor, as discussed in Chapter 3, contributing to unrest behind the emergence of the Scottish Office in 1885. The establishment of the Scottish Grand Committee was partly a consequence of Scottish Liberal pressure at the turn of the century when Liberals were still the dominant force in Scotland but also a concession to Scottish national sentiment. In a book written in 1930 supporting the newly formed National Party of Scotland, Andrew Dewar Gibb described the Scottish Grand Committee as a 'mere debating society with no power to pass legislation (or refuse legislation) for Scotland over and above what its members may be able to secure in a full sitting of the House'.[2] By the 1930s, the Committee was being portrayed as an insult to Scotland. The sensibilities of the Scottish Members must have seemed delicate to English Members. Scotland's representatives wanted special treatment for Scotland and some would disrupt ceremony and tradition whenever they deemed Scotland's special position was being threatened or insulted. An example of this occurred in February 1933 when Clydesider Davie Kirkwood, in his inimitable style, attempted to move the adjournment of the Scottish Grand Committee because an English Member had been appointed to chair it.[3]

The issue that excited most concern in Parliament was the time devoted to Scottish affairs. J. Henderson Stewart, National Liberal Member, raised the issue frequently during the late 1930s. In July 1937, he attempted to raise the issue in an Adjournment debate but the motion was not reached and instead a series of exchanges followed in the press. Secretary of State Walter Elliot disagreed with Henderson Stewart's suggestion that the Scottish Grand Committee should undertake a close detailed inquiry of every item of expenditure because this would be 'different in scope from that in the case of the corresponding English Estimates'.[4] The extra work which Henderson Stewart's suggestion would have entailed was felt by Elliot to make it difficult for Scottish Ministers to leave London and might diminish Scottish Members opportunities for taking part in the general business of Parliament. Another proposal which Henderson Stewart put forward was that a special annual conference of Scottish Members might be convened in the new government building in Edinburgh. Elliot's response was only as vague as the proposal itself; the idea would raise 'wide constitutional issues on which consultation in other quarters would be necessary in due course'.[5]

Henderson Stewart maintained that time to debate Scottish issues was severely limited and pointed to the number of subjects of 'vital concern to Scotland' which were passed over by Parliament without any discussion and those new regulations made 'without any opportunity being offered to Scottish Members to examine them'.[6] The Government responded by publishing the number of hours of Parliamentary time devoted to Scottish Supply and 'other Scottish business' over a number of years. According to Scottish Office calculations, the amount of time devoted to supply in the years from 1929 to 1939 inclusive totalled 154 hours 37 minutes, averaging 14 hours 3 minutes each year, while the time devoted to 'other Scottish business', though it is unclear how this was calculated, totalled 383 hours 13 minutes, averaging 34 hours 50 minutes for each year.[7] There was great variety from year to year, particularly respecting 'other Scottish business' and it was hardly surprising that the Scottish Office's published figures should begin in 1929 when 94 hours 35 minutes were devoted to 'other Scottish business', largely due to the major local government legislation that year. When this is set beside the 7 hours 10 minutes for 1932, an idea of the variation over the years can be seen. The extent of 'other business' would depend on the amount of Scottish legislation being passed. Time given to Scottish Supply debates might have been expected to have been more uniform over time though even this varied from 22 hours 45 minutes in 1931 to 9 hours 2 minutes in 1933. The pressures on the Parliamentary timetable were both considerable and unpredictable. While Lord Advocate Cooper maintained that complaints concerning Parliamentary time were an 'imaginary grievance'[8] it was well voiced by home rulers and their opponents.

The economic and social grievances of Scotland in the inter-war years were those of a depressed, peripheral part of the United Kingdom. Unemployment, emigration, poor housing, appalling ill-health all served to fuel discontent in Scotland. It was from these years that many of the most potent myths of the deprivation of the industrial west of Scotland owe their origins. It was hardly surprising, therefore, that successive Scottish Secretaries viewed their role in cabinet as being advocates of increased government assistance for Scotland. In November 1937, Walter Elliot had a memorandum prepared for the Cabinet by the Scottish departments. Surveying his first year at the Scottish Office, Elliot concluded that the administrative proposals contained in the Gilmour Report 'will not in themselves dispose of the problems upon whose solution a general improvement in Scottish social and economic conditions depends'.[9] Elliot was aware of the discontent and suggested that a cabinet committee should look at the 'Scottish problem as a whole'.[10] The Scottish Secretary rather ominously gave warning:

Recently Scotland – largely, I think because of the unsatisfactory conditions mentioned in my Cabinet Memorandum – has become increasingly conscious of itself and of the need for a material and spiritual revival on a national scale.[11]

Elliot's case for a programme of additional state assistance in Scotland was rejected by the Chancellor of the Exchequer John Simon. In reply to Elliot's plea, Simon responded

I feel quite certain that it would be impossible to apply a special stimulus to Scotland without arousing demands from the rest of the

United Kingdom for corresponding treatment. In fact we should see the reverse of the familiar process under which England initiates a series of social schemes and Scotland demands that a proportion of the expenditure contemplated should be applied to her needs.[12]

Elliot had cited the feeling of dissatisfaction in Scotland which was giving rise to proposals for 'various constitutional reforms, such as the increased use of the Scottish Grand Committee'.[13] This made no impression on the Chancellor of the Exchequer who persisted in basing his argument on the grounds that differentiation could not be made between one part of the state and another.[14] What emerges from this episode is Elliot's belief that the discontent was rooted in the relative social and economic deprivation of Scotland. The recognition that Scotland was a distinct entity, as the existence of a Scottish Minister and Scottish central administration suggested, must have implied to many Scots that distinctly Scottish solutions, even if these were costly, were justified. The existence of the Scottish Office seems to have helped focus economic and social problems in a Scottish context.

Another aspect of the dissatisfaction with Scotland's position concerned public expenditure. During the years from the late nineteenth century until the creation of the Irish Free State, successive British Governments had published the national accounts of the constituent nations making up the United Kingdom. The intention had been to demonstrate that Ireland, far from being economically raped by mainland Britain, was being subsidised. In demonstrating this, Scotland was shown to have been a net contributor to the Exchequer. In the early 1930s, the expressions of dissatisfaction coming from Scotland prompted a similar response. In December 1932, the Treasury issued a white paper which gave the figures for revenue and expenditure for Scotland for 1931–32. According to the white paper, Scotland contributed 5.6 per cent towards the cost of Imperial Services while England and Wales provided the balance of 94.4 per cent.[15] Scotland remained a net contributor to Imperial Services though not to the extent of earlier times. Some debate occurred following the publication of the figures but doubtless few opinions were changed (see Chapter 8 for a detailed discussion).

Scottish discontent may have been fairly general and failed to focus on any single alternative. Home rule was more seriously talked about but the home rulers failed to make progress in elections. Lecturers in Greek, Professors of Law and Scottish novelists and poets seemed to dominate the Nationalist scene – colourful but irrelevant to the social and economic problems afflicting Scotland.[16] Nevertheless, the discontent, however, disparate and unchannelled, existed and gave cause for concern. The Scottish Office may have been evidence of Scotland's unique status in the system of government but it was also seen to have failed to tackle the problems afflicting the nation.

This background of discontent had fed into the process of changing the administrative structure directly and indirectly. The greater these economic and social problems were, the more challenging was the workload of the departments. The responsibilities of the Scottish departments were at the cutting edge of public policy affected by high levels of unemployment and social disadvantage. The Scottish Secretary may have had no direct responsibility for the Scottish economy but he was expected to 'speak for Scotland' and did have very real responsibility for services designed to alleviate these problems. Indirectly, the background had an impact in that it fed into a sense that something was wrong and change was needed. The scope for doing anything substantial was largely limited to alterations in administrative arrangements and symbolic change. Taken together, the changes which were brought about in the late 1930s were probably as much as could have been done within the powers of the Scottish Secretary.

Administrative considerations

Scottish local government, as Scottish central government, had developed in a fairly haphazard manner. W.E. Whyte, one of the leading authorities of Scottish local government, remarked upon developments in an address in February 1926:

> It may be said that, as a rule, local and central government have in recent years developed along similar lines, although each has grown up in its own way and without at first much reference to each other.[17]

Again, the 1928 Reorganisation Act was followed the next year by a major reform in Scottish local government but these Acts were not linked. The Scottish Local Government Act was a consequence of reforms, particularly respecting rates, that had originated in England as well as the need, which Whyte had suggested in 1926, for a major overhaul of local government machinery as a consequence of its piecemeal development. Following the enactment of the local government legislation in 1929, the case for a reform of the central administration to provide for the comprehensive streamlining of Scottish government was strengthened.

Though the divisions within the newly created Department of Health had been reorganised in 1928, this was not sufficient to satisfy the civil servants that optimum efficacy had been achieved. In November 1928, John Lamb, Secretary of the Scottish Department of Health, proposed the creation of four divisions within the new Department in the event of the Local Government Bill being passed:[18] health services, housing and general sanitation, health insurance and pensions, and public assistance and general local government divisions were to be created in addition to an accounts department. The main problem was with the location of the divisions. While most of the work was done in offices in Princes Street, Edinburgh, other work was concentrated in two other Edinburgh offices, not to mention Dover House in London. Similarly, the Department of Agriculture for Scotland, had three offices in Edinburgh and the SED was located in a number of sites in Scotland. The problems increased with the growing responsibilities and staff of the Scottish offices at the time.

Ensuring that London and Edinburgh were kept in constant touch with each other caused many problems. Willie Adamson in January 1930 commented on this matter 'of real difficulty in these hustling times, and even with all the facilities there are for quick transport and communications, for the Secretary of State for Scotland to keep fully in touch with his advisers in Edinburgh on the urgent problems that arise from day to day'.[19] Five years later, Godfrey Collins, in a major speech in his constituency, also stressed this problem:

It is easy in London, in these days of rapid communication, to be kept informed of what is happening in Scotland. But it is not so easy to keep in touch with the spirit, the heart of Scotland, and if the Government of Scotland is to be successfully conducted, it can only be done by those who, through personal experience, are familiar with the desires of Scotland and the atmosphere in which its people are living, and who have the opportunities of discussing with its local authorities and its citizens.[20]

Both Adamson and Collins recognised that more work would have to be done in Edinburgh. Adamson suggested that the Scottish Office should take 'more and more the character of an Embassy or Liaison Office between Scotland on the one hand and Parliament and the other Departments of State on the other'.[21] The erection of a new government building in Edinburgh was seen by both as offering prospects for administrative improvements.

Co-ordination in Edinburgh

The idea of having a central site for all the Edinburgh offices dated as far back as October 1923. The Scottish Secretary Viscount Novar had conducted an inquiry with a view to the possibility of accommodating all the government offices in Edinburgh in a central site and had requested the addresses and numbers of the Scottish and UK Departments in the city.[22] The following year, Sir John Gilmour also considered the matter. In December, he received a letter which offered a site in the West End of Edinburgh for the erection of a central government building (see Table 7.1).[23] Two months later, in February 1925, the Scottish Office was attempting to calculate the probable financial savings in centralising the Edinburgh offices. However, nothing came of this early idea though the matter seems to have remained in the background as a policy to be pursued when the time was right. The time only became right when pressures, both administrative and political made it so.

The pressure for a central building grew. An undated memorandum, probably from late 1933, listed reasons for erecting such a building.[24] The unsatisfactory accommodation of certain departments which had been a source of complaint for a decade was noted. About thirty buildings in Edinburgh housed some twenty departments or branches of departments that were the responsibility of the Secretary of State, with the Department of Health housed in seven buildings. Public opinion was noted to be pressing for a new building. Economies of over £3000 were to be expected immediately with more savings expected with the centralization of departments and reorganisation of staffing arrangements which would be possible in a single building.

Apart from centralising the offices under one roof, consideration was given to transferring work to Edinburgh from Dover House. This had normally been proposed in conjunction with the idea of centralising the Scottish central administration though it was less widely accepted. In September 1932, P.R. Laird, a Scottish Office Assistant Secretary, wrote a memorandum on the 'possibility of extending devolution'.[25] Laird examined in detail the different types of relationship between the Scottish Office and the other Scottish departments prior to the Reorganisation Act. He considered the extent to which more work could be done in Scotland and related this to questions of staffing and recruitment and the distribution of work amongst departments. Laird noted the very different types of relationship between the Scottish Office and the departments. Laird thought that more clearly defined and standardised relationships would greatly improve the workings of the machinery

Table 7.1 Edinburgh offices, addresses and staff, 1923

Departments Scottish Departments	Address	No. of staff
Register House Offices	H.M. New General Register House	
Accountant of Court		c.20
Chancery Office		3
Court of Session Clerks		53
Deeds Office		c. 38
Great Seal Office		2
Lyon Office		2
Record Office		c.13
Registrar General's Office		41 (excl. 5 District Examiners)
Sasines Office		c.195
Signet Office		4
Messengers		11
Bookbinders		5
Parliament Square Offices		
Chancery – Sheriff Court Office	2, Parliament Square	3
Commissary Office		c.19
Crown Office	9, Parliament Square	8
Justiciary Office	2, Parliament Square	6
Secretary for Scotland and Lord Advocate Chambers	6, Parliament Square	4 (incl. Parliamentary Counsel)
Other Offices		
Board of Agriculture	29, St Andrews Square and York Buildings, Queen Street	314 (incl. Inspectorate and Surveying Staff)
General Board of Control	25, Palmerston Place	24
Fishery Board	101, George Street	30 (Head Office staff)

Table 7.1 (Continued)

Scottish Board of Health	121a, Princes Street, 125, George Street and Grassmarket	521 (incl. Insurance inspectorate 51 and other surveyors and inspectorate 26)
Prison Commission	11, Rutland Square	29
Scottish Education Department	14, Queen Street	72
Scottish Land Court	1, Grosvenor Crescent	c.22
		1,439
Branches of UK Departments		
Customs and Excise, Collectors Office	12 and 14, Waterloo Place	10
Exchequer	1, Parliament Square	23
Forestry Commission	25, Drumsheugh Gardens	28
General Post Office		?
Geological Survey	33, George Square	c.15
Inland Revenue	Waterloo Place	c. 205
Ministry of Labour		
Employment Department (exchanges excluded)	44, Drumsheugh Gardens	c.160
Finance, etc.		70
Commissioners of Northern Lighthouses	84, George Street	15
Ministry of Pensions (Area Office excluded)		
Regional Headquarters	122, George Street	416
Pensions Issue Office	Pilton Huts, Inverleith	352
Stationery Office	23 and 25, Forth Street	c.11
Woods and Forests		
Crown Receiver	H.M. General Register House	1
Office of Works	4 and 5, Drumsheugh Gardens	14
	Excluding General Post Office	1,320

Source: NAS, HH 45/51.

of government. His comment on the most complex and unclear of these relationships was striking: 'As for the Board of Agriculture for Scotland, it is only by a miracle that it works at all.'[26] His solution was that more work should be done in Edinburgh. Whether work ought to be done in London or Edinburgh could be judged by simple criteria:

> Broadly, the test to be applied will be the convenience of proximity to the Edinburgh Departments, local authorities, and the Scottish public, as against convenience of proximity to Ministers, Parliament and London Departments; and for the moment I must proceed on the footing that there is no *branch* of General Headquarters in London.[27]

Using such criteria, Laird accepted that the functions which could be exercised in Edinburgh 'do not appear to be very numerous'. The most important matters to be listed concerned local government and the administration of justice. In this functional analysis, Laird seems to have been intent on clarifying relationships rather than concentrating more responsibilities in Edinburgh. However, any proposal to devolve work to Edinburgh was bound to be limited by the lack of an Edinburgh branch of the Scottish Office, as distinct from the various offices of the departments in the city. Such responsibilities as those for elections were not regarded by Laird as likely to fit in with the work of the existing Scottish departments with offices in Edinburgh. The 'missing link' was a Scottish Home Department which could be 'partly a direct administrator, partly General Headquarters and liaison' in Edinburgh.

The London office of the Secretary of State was seen by Laird as needing to include the Minister's principal adviser who would be concerned with the whole field of administration plus three or four officers of high status, probably three private secretaries and a small clerical and typing staff. The daily routine work of Dover House should be moved north with some co-ordination work, liaison with other Whitehall departments, Parliamentary work and cabinet business remaining the prerogative of the London office.

Laird saw two possible courses. Either another Scottish Department of Home Affairs should be established with miscellaneous statutory powers along with local government responsibilities or a fresh attempt to set up a branch of the Scottish Office in Edinburgh should be made. The major problem with the former proposal was that the departments brought into being in 1928 were defined in law as corporate entities and thus could act only in their own name and not that of the Secretary of State. A new department would require to be legislated for to be able to co-ordinate the work of the existing departments. This problem had not been recognised when the 1928 Act was drafted. An Edinburgh branch of the Scottish Office therefore appeared more feasible and required to be staffed by an officer, as Laird mentioned, of 'no less status than the heads of the principal Edinburgh Departments, who would be entitled to sign official letters, as is done in London, in the name of the Secretary of State'.[28]

There were problems in both possible courses advanced by Laird. An office of the Secretary of State in Edinburgh would be seen as superior to the others. In Laird's words, ' ... it does not fit into the theory of planets revolving round a central sun, since one of the planets would be a bit of the sun hanging loose!'[29] Furthermore, friction between the London and Edinburgh offices might ensue and duplication of work would be likely. The required *modus operandi* would have to involve both the relief of departmental work without the loss of authority on the part of the Secretary of State's office in London while encouraging a co-ordinating and liaising role without usurping the role of the departments in Edinburgh. One proposal certain to be met with hostility was that of standardising the relationships of each of the departments with the office of Secretary of State. Laird pre-empted the opposition of the department least likely to agree: 'This means that the Scottish Education Department must in future be solely in Edinburgh, and their affairs within the scope of General Headquarters work.'[30]

Laird envisaged the admission of recruits to the Scottish departments in Edinburgh who would be able to transfer between the departments and, after some years, suitable candidates would be drafted to London for service as private secretaries and would normally return to Edinburgh on promotion. A Scottish civil service would seem to have been in the making with Laird's proposals. In essence, Laird's proposals went beyond the partial reforms of the past and were concerned primarily with effective administration. Some form of machinery had to exist in Scotland whether to appease Scottish sentiment or to maintain necessary direct contact. For probably the first time since the Scottish Office's establishment, a comprehensive analysis of the variety of bodies was conducted attempting to rationalise, standardise and improve the system of central administration in Scotland. Administrative efficacy was very much to the fore in the document with Laird ignoring SED sensibilities and departmental distinctiveness. However, in framing his proposals under the heading of 'extending devolution', Laird had incorporated a Scottish dimension. In his intention to allow for greater departmental work in Edinburgh, he could not be accused on centralising responsibilities in London. That his scheme proposed to go so far in this direction might, earlier in the century, have been construed as challenging the Whitehall conception of the government of Scotland, as indeed the proposals to site the SED in Edinburgh twenty years before (see Chapter four). By 1928, this was not the case. Laird was obviously setting out to improve the machinery of government and not only to appease national sentiment which was an aim fully in accord with the Whitehall model. In all, the proposals seemed on paper to combine the need for a strong Scottish dimension and a Whitehall model more harmoniously than the existing arrangements allowed. Laird's proposals were not likely to be taken up by the Government at that time. However, as the 1939 Act and the preceding discussion demonstrated, Laird's ideas were influential and were eventually largely those which were to be put into effect. One problem with his memorandum was that his proposals included ambitious ideas requiring legislation. The memorandum seems to have begun as a modest attempt to rationalise the existing administrative arrangements but developed into a blueprint for a major overhaul of the machinery of Scottish government.

Four years later home rule agitation gave Laird's proposals added relevance. Noel Skelton, Parliamentary Under Secretary of State, had been discussing home rule questions and suggested that Laird should 'further explore the question of administrative devolution!'[31] The result was a second, shorter memorandum with the bolder title, 'Administrative Devolution'. In this paper, written in November 1932, Laird took into account the decision of the Secretary of State to press actively for central government buildings in Edinburgh which he maintained, 'strengthens the case for a proposal of a far-reaching character to which other considerations have led me and which was not considered in my previous memorandum'.[32]

Laird went beyond his earlier proposals. He rejected the idea of transferring the Secretary of State's powers and duties to the existing Edinburgh departments as this would involve another separation of the Minister and his department and viewed the 1928 Act as having effectively perpetuated the board system 'in so far as it did not weld the Secretary of State into one entity with his machinery'. In this later memorandum, Laird's proposals were summed up in one of its paragraphs:

> The clean method of overcoming all the difficulties is to make one fold as there is one shepherd, by a general transfer of the powers and duties of departments to the Secretary of State, so that all the departments concerned would be in effect 'The Scottish Office' or 'The Department

of the Secretary of State for Scotland'. Under such a scheme the Minister could make whatever arrangements for departmental organisation might be best suited to times and circumstances. Any branch of work could be undertaken in London or Edinburgh according to requirements, and all official letters, whether from London or Edinburgh, would go in the name of the Secretary of State.[33]

The advantages accruing from these proposals were greater flexibility of staffing arrangements, greater economy following the pooling of common services and bringing together cognate subjects then dealt with in different departments. Also, they would permit the relief of the London office of much detailed work allowing the staff in Dover House to concentrate more on Parliamentary and intra-Whitehall work. Laird anticipated that his ideas would be attacked for proposing a huge, unwieldy, heterogeneous department but noted that 'if the objection is a serious one, it is equally an objection to the wideness of the jurisdiction of the Secretary of State'.[34] In considering whether any functions of British or English departments ought to be transferred to the Secretary of State, Laird concluded that any such proposal would strengthen the case for his scheme. This was based on his belief that those matters which then seemed most likely to be transferred – administration of the Aliens Act, appointment of Justices of the Peace, responsibility for piers and harbours, steamer service contracts and the establishment of a separate Office of Works for Scotland – all seemed to be best placed under the Secretary of State's jurisdiction rather than any individual department.

In his memorandum, Laird distinguished between his far-reaching proposals requiring legislation and the short-term expedients which could be put into effect by Ministerial fiat. The latter included creating two divisions within the Department of Health: one division would be responsible for health and the other for local government with as much of the work of the local government division done in Edinburgh. It was this proposal which was first put into effect though in time Laird's other ideas can be seen to have been the foundation on which the modern Scottish Office was based.

Another civil servant, F.O. Stewart, a Principal in Dover House, responded to Laird's proposals.[35] Stewart noted three main criticisms of the structure suggested by his colleague. There was the possibility that conflicting decisions might be issued simultaneously by the London and Edinburgh offices. The fear that with all the 'real work' being done in Edinburgh then the 'London Satellites would become easy prey for Treasury economists' was dismissed by Laird as highly unlikely. This fear was probably based on Stewart's misapprehension that the London officials were to be 'really glorified personal assistants of the Secretary of State'. Laird's memorandum made clear that the London office would be doing exceptionally important work which, in terms of policy-making and relations with the rest of Whitehall and Parliament, might be construed as giving it greater standing than the Edinburgh offices. The third criticism was that differences of opinion might well lead to 'constant bickering' with the Secretary of State being frequently called on to overrule either an Edinburgh or London official. This, Stewart felt, would lead to the eventual demise of one set of officials – an eventuality which he believed would also result from constant agreement between London and Edinburgh. However, such fears and expectations failed to appreciate fully Laird's proposals which ultimately accepted the supremacy of London but intended to devolve as much administrative work as possible. Conflict was as likely to arise between or within departments in Edinburgh or amongst individuals in London as between Edinburgh and London.

Predictably, the SED opposed the proposals. The following year, McKechnie, SED Secretary, wrote to Sir Godfrey Collins concerning housing SED staff in the new Edinburgh offices. Apart from that work which would have to be retained in Dover House – financial, legal and Parliamentary business – there was a 'real advantage in keeping in London certain parts of the Department's activities which can be dealt with as conveniently there as in Edinburgh'.[36] The SED Secretary also defended his department's 'independence', opposing any move to subordinate the SED to 'another Department of State'. McKechnie reminded the Secretary of State that legislation would in any event be required.

The basis for a major overhaul of the Scottish central administration was being laid within the Scottish Office. With a new government building planned for some future date to accommodate the various Edinburgh offices, any plan to overhaul the central administration would be bound to be postponed until such a building was ready in order to take advantage of the possibilities for co-operation and pooling of resources. However, in the intervening period, Laird's proposal to establish an Edinburgh branch of the Scottish Office was brought about. In January 1935, an Edinburgh branch with a staff of twenty was opened under David Milne, then an Assistant Secretary in the Scottish Office and later to become Permanent Under Secretary. In reply to a Parliamentary Question the previous year, Sir Godfrey Collins told the House that 93 per cent of staff of Scottish departments (1542 individuals) were located in Scotland while only 7 per cent (117) were in London and that he had,

> ... made arrangements that a branch of the Scottish Office should be established in Edinburgh at as early a date as possible for the transaction of such business as can be conveniently carried on there, including in particular work connected with local authority administration in its various aspects.[37]

Additionally, Collins indicated his intention to transfer SED officials at the earliest possible date. The office was opened in Drumsheugh Gardens in Edinburgh's New Town. By this transfer and that of certain officials of the SED later that year, the number based in London was reduced to 66, so that 96.2 per cent of all officials of the Scottish departments were then based in Scotland. At the official opening in February 1935, Collins made it clear that this branch was only a beginning:

> If we are to reap the full benefit from concentration of all the big Scottish Departments in one large modern building it will be necessary to undertake some comprehensive review of all our Scottish administrative arrangements, including the important question of our representation in London. I visualise the Scottish Office in London developing into a centre for responsible representatives and liaison officers from each of the Departments – an advanced headquarters thrown forward from our new base upon the Calton Hill.[38]

Establishing the Gilmour Committee

As with previous reforms the gestation period between the idea's initial proposal and its eventual realization was fairly lengthy. In the debate on the King's Speech in November 1932 John Buchan complained about the neglect of Scottish affairs which he maintained explained Nationalist activities in Scotland.[39] Sir Godfrey Collins at that time had also recognised the existence of discontent and felt that the remedy was to be found in centralising the work of the Edinburgh departments and endeavouring to transfer as much work as possible to Edinburgh.

Following the general election in Autumn 1935, R.N. Duke, a senior Scottish Office civil servant wrote a memorandum on how to 'reap the full benefit from concentration of all the big Scottish Departments in one building' by 'some comprehensive review of all our Scottish administrative arrangements'.[40] Duke's memorandum suggested terms of reference for a committee to investigate Scottish central administration which were essentially those to which the Gilmour Committee eventually worked. In November 1935, on Collins' suggestion, Treasury sanction was sought for the establishment of such a committee and by June the following year the membership was agreed on.

Sir Archibald Sinclair (Scottish Secretary 1931–32) was Duke's first choice as chairman followed by Lord Alness (Scottish Secretary 1916–22). The committee he proposed included Sir John Lamb (Permanent Under Secretary 1921–33), John Erskine (Manager of the Commercial Bank of Scotland) and a Treasury official. In the event, Sir John Gilmour was appointed chairman. Gilmour had been Scottish Secretary from 1924–29, during which time the office had been upgraded from Secretary for Scotland to Secretary of State for Scotland. This had been a superficial change though at the time the press and the Unionist Party had made great play of it. Gilmour had been recommended as chairman by the King's and Lord Treasurer's Remembrancer and had been supported by Sir James Rae of the Treasury, who also served on the committee.[41] Representatives of the Labour and Liberal Parties were thought to be desirable. Sir Robert Hamilton from the Liberals and Tom Johnston from Labour were chosen on the agreement of their respective party leaders. Additionally, Lord Fleming, a former Solicitor-General and Senator of the College of Justice was appointed along with Professor Alexander Gray, former senior civil servant and economist and G.A. Steel, general manager and director of the British Aluminium Company. John Aglen of the Edinburgh branch of the Scottish Office was appointed secretary. The inclusion of politicians was an attempt to achieve consensus around the committee's recommendations. Tom Johnston, noted home ruler, accepted a place on the committee on condition that meetings took place in London so that his Parliamentary duties would not be neglected.[42] Johnston's position on the committee proved to be important in ensuring a degree of cross party consensus.

Initially, Collins had hoped to announce the appointment of the committee at the end of July 1936 with the inquiry beginning in October but this plan was postponed. In the letter to Sir John Gilmour inviting him to accept the chairmanship, Collins indicated that the committee would regulate its own proceedings and that he did not anticipate that its work 'should be at all protracted, or that any very large number of witnesses should require to be heard'.[43] However, Collins never made the formal announcement establishing the inquiry. He died just before the new

Parliamentary Session in Autumn 1936 and it was left to his successor, Walter Elliot to make the announcement. Collins had done more than any Scottish Secretary to move as much work of the Scottish Office to Edinburgh and to prepare for the reorganisation but his death robbed him of recognition for his efforts. Sir William Murie, who was later to serve as Permanent Under Secretary from 1959–64, was Collins' private secretary and has suggested that as a member of the publishing family, Collins was an astute businessman and manager who brought these talents to his tenure at the Scottish Office.[44] Elliot has frequently been given credit for the initiative of his predecessor.

Elliot had to go through the process of inviting the committee to serve once more but this did not prove to be a major setback. One interesting comment which emerged from this second round of invitations came from Professor Gray who reflected on the terms of reference,

behind the innocuous phraseology of the terms of reference, the Scottish Office has hidden away a bevy of hornet's nests. My preliminary consideration suggests that for a person of a logical mind, there are only three possible solutions of the Scottish problem:

(i)   Home Rule
(ii) Complete absorption and anglicisation
(iii) Such a speeding up in the air service as will enable the S. of S., Jeffrey, Peck, Highton, Laird etc to be each, separately and collectively, simultaneously in London and Edinburgh. On the whole I am inclined to the third solution, as being the least revolutionary.[45]

The committee's remit was fairly straightforward,

to enquire into and report upon the duties of the Scottish Office, Scottish Education Department, Departments of Health and Agriculture for Scotland, and other Scottish Administrative Departments under the control of the Secretary of State for Scotland, the distribution of those duties between Departments, the position of the Departments in relation to each other and to the Secretary of State, and the arrangement under which liaison is maintained between Edinburgh and London, in the conduct of public business; and to recommend what changes, if any (whether legislative or otherwise) should be made, keeping in view the prospective concentration of Departments in one building in Edinburgh.[46]

A fairly narrow interpretation was adopted by the committee. At the committee's first meeting it was agreed that the scope did not include consideration of home rule. Notably, Tom Johnston was absent from this meeting. Thirteen meetings were held taking evidence from each of the Scottish Departments concerned, from the local authority organisations, English/British Ministries and from other Associations and individuals connected in some way with the work of the Scottish central administration. The issues considered by the committee largely revolved around two concerns – the division of work between Edinburgh and London and the extent to which co-ordination of work within the Scottish central administration could permit Departmental independence. Allied questions included the centralisation of the legal work of the Departments, establishing advisory councils, the positions of the General Board of Control and the Fishery Board. The generally accepted view, Scottish Education Department apart, was that as much work should be done in Edinburgh as possible; this seems to have been tacitly accepted by the committee as well as by those giving evidence.

The Permanent Under Secretary

The role of the Permanent Under Secretary appears to have been crucial in determining the nature of the reorganised offices. First, this official's relations with the Departments was believed to reflect the extent to which the Scottish Office was to become a homogeneous or, at least, well co-ordinated administrative entity. Second, the geographical location of the Permanent Under Secretary, either with the Departments in Edinburgh or with the Minister in Dover House, may be seen as really about where power or at least final responsibility would lie. A memorandum written by Sir John Jeffrey, the incumbent Permanent Under Secretary, was the most important evidence received by the committee. Jeffrey envisaged a new office of the Secretary of State for Scotland as a 'confederation of four large Departments under the leadership of the Permanent Under Secretary of State and Deputy Under Secretary of State'.[47] This was not to be such a dramatic departure from the existing state of affairs in that it would depend largely upon 'the maintenance of the importance of the individual Departments, and of their heads'. However, with the help of a Deputy, the Permanent Under Secretary was to act as head of the civil service in relation to all Scottish Departments, 'to give inspiration and leadership to the Departments: to co-ordinate their activities: and to act as right-hand adviser, over the whole field of Scottish administration, to the Secretary of State'.[48] Jeffrey foresaw closer relations between the Departments and not just through the geographical proximity offered by St Andrews House:

> The interests of the Office as a whole will take the place of departmental interests. Duties will from time to time be distributed, or re-distributed, to Departments in the light of what is best for Scottish administration generally. Transfers of personnel between one Department and another will be made whenever such transfers are desirable in the interests of the service as a whole. The rigidity of the present departmental boundaries will be relaxed. The Departments will work as members of a team represented by the Office, and in various respects it may be desirable, on grounds of efficiency as well as economy, for particular duties to be performed by one Department on behalf of others.[49]

He advocated the stationing of the Permanent Under Secretary of State in London but that his Deputy should co-ordinate the work of the Department in Edinburgh. However, he did recognise arguments for having the Deputy in London also:

> It is in London that Government decisions on questions of high policy have to be taken; and if the Deputy Under Secretary of State is effectively to assist, and when necessary to take the place of, the Permanent Under Secretary, it may be better that he should be stationed in London.[50]

This would also have avoided the Deputy encroaching upon the authority and responsibilities of the Departments. It was logical to have a Permanent Under Secretary with an overall responsibility for all Departments under the proposed new Scottish Office. It was hoped that it would prevent the Secretary of State receiving conflicting advice from different Departments. As Ministerial adviser, chief of staff and co-ordinator of policies, the Permanent Under Secretary's role would be crucial.

Not all officials favoured this course. John Highton of the Department of Health told the committee that 'something would be lost if the Under Secretary of State were made responsible for Departments under the Secretary of State'.[51] Predictably, George MacDonald, head of the SED from 1922–29, was opposed to the establishment of what he described as a 'Super-Under-Secretary'. He maintained that such an official could not possibly acquire the knowledge and expertise of four Departments and would 'seriously detract from the personal respect which the heads of

Departments ought to be able to enjoy in the eyes of the general public'. This would make service in the Scottish Departments 'less and less attractive to men of outstanding ability'.[52] MacDonald viewed the role of the 'Super-Under-Secretary' as being one of two unattractive alternatives:

> Either he would become a mere pillar-box, into which the Departmental Heads would drop their opinions – in which case he would be a useless luxury – or he would surround himself with a small army of subordinates to 'devil' for him, not only perpetuating but intensifying the most unsatisfactory features of the present regime.[53]

These views were expressed by MacDonald both in a lengthy memorandum to the committee and in his spoken evidence. MacDonald's successor as head of the SED, Sir William McKechnie also asked that the 'dignity, independence and usefulness of the Heads of the Departments should not be impaired by the super-imposition of an Under-Secretary'.[54] In turn, the serving head of the SED Sir James Peck, viewed the office of Permanent Under Secretary with some suspicion but, perhaps because of his position, he was less antagonistic towards the idea than were his predecessors. Sir Arthur Rose also regarded the idea of a Permanent Under Secretary with some suspicion[55] and Sir John Lamb, who had served as Scottish Office Permanent Under Secretary from 1921–33, was careful in his support for a Permanent Under Secretary and suggested that the official should be the 'essence of tact and should not meddle with ordinary Departmental affairs'.[56] On the other hand, R.N. Duke of the Scottish Office felt that the Permanent Under Secretary should not merely be a 'super private secretary'.[57] One of the clearest statements concerning the position of the Permanent Under Secretary came from Lord Advocate Cooper in his oral evidence before the committee. Cooper recognised the dangers of the office becoming a bottleneck or a 'mere embassy of four separate Departments in Edinburgh'. Though envisaging the official to be senior to the Departmental heads, Cooper viewed the Permanent Under Secretary as having three roles: head of the Scottish administration, co-ordinator of policy and adviser to the Secretary of State.[58]

Few desired to see the Scottish Office consolidated in the manner advocated by Patrick Laird, head of the Department of Agriculture from 1934–53. In his evidence to the committee Laird had argued for 'one big Office' under a Permanent Under Secretary of State assisted by a Deputy Under Secretary of State and probably three Assistant Under Secretaries.

He suggested, as an example, that a branch for 'Milk' could be set up which would allow for greater 'co-ordination, initiative and drive' than would be obtained from leaving the work in the hands of four Departments.[59] Not only were all the other Departmental heads against such a scheme but so too was former Secretary of State Sir Archibald Sinclair and the Society of Civil Servants (Executive, Directing and Analogous Grades).[60] Sinclair had particular doubts about education under the new Permanent Under Secretary's responsibilities. Education was certainly the greatest obstacle in the way of Laird's scheme but it was not the only one and support for 'one big Office' seems to have been confined to Laird.

In the event, the committee opted for what was the most pragmatic solution. A Permanent Under Secretary was thought necessary to co-ordinate and advise while a degree of Departmental independence was retained. The Gilmour Committee emphatically stated its opposition to any intrusion into the work and responsibilities of the Departmental heads by the Permanent Under Secretary and envisaged the normal station of the top official to be in London 'at the Minister's right hand'.[61] A functional organisation within the territorial Office was the aim of the committee. The Permanent Under Secretary would provide co-ordination and the Departmental Secretaries functionally responsible. Notably, the reforms did not involve the concentration of the accounting officer's role in the person of the Permanent Under Secretary but allowed for the continuation of the practice of separate accounting officers for each Department. The role of the Permanent Under Secretary highlighted the basic questions which the committee set out to consider.

London–Edinburgh liaison

An obvious matter on the committee's agenda was liaison between London and Edinburgh. Once more the most important comments were to be found in the memorandum by Sir John Jeffrey. Not only did this paper outline the complexity of Dover House relations with the Scottish Departments and local authorities, it drew out the disadvantages of the arrangements described and suggested a future basis for improved liaison. Jeffrey noted that though London had to remain the centre where government decisions would be taken and administrative and legislative action would be initiated, the Departments should be located in Edinburgh. He recommended that the relations between Edinburgh and the Minister ought to be 'regularised and unified'.[62] While advocating this, the Permanent Under Secretary still wanted each Department to be responsible for its own liaison work in London. The chief London representative of each Department, whose work would include advising the Minister, would have to be of at least Assistant Secretary rank. Jeffrey suggested the possibility of having the deputy head of each Department stationed in London but was clear in his belief that the Departmental head would have to be based in Edinburgh. The temporary transfer of additional staff to London at times of pressure was recognised by Jeffrey.

The Gilmour Committee agreed that staff with the sole responsibility for liaison should be stationed in London and noted that 'mechanised appliances' would be of much benefit including a rented private telephone wire between Dover House and the new government building in Edinburgh and the installation of a teleprinter circuit. Nevertheless, the committee pointed out that a liaison officer divorced from departmental responsibility and day-to-day administration 'cannot discuss questions with officers of another Department in quite the same way as the officer, in Scotland, who is dealing with the subject and who is familiar with all the details of the work'. The liaison officer, they remarked, would be a 'second best', but he would be a 'necessary "second best"'.[63] The logistical problems of separating the Minister from the bulk of his officials over a distance of 400 miles was a major problem which technological advances could diminish but never obviate.

Boards and advisory councils

As mentioned earlier, not all Boards had disappeared under the Reorganisation of Offices (Scotland) Act of 1928. Gilmour heard evidence on the question of the remaining boards. Lord Alness, who as Robert Munro had been Scottish Secretary from 1916–22, and Sir Archibald Sinclair, Scottish Secretary in 1931–32, favoured retaining the Boards. Alness thought that the board system was satisfactory and disputed any suggestion that the boards had autonomy from the Scottish Secretary.[64] The more common view was that of the Lord Advocate who argued that the Scottish Boards should be absorbed into the larger Departments. The General Board of Control, responsible for the administration of mental health in Scotland, defended itself in a submission to Gilmour and suggested that closer association with the Scottish Office might be possible but was against becoming a branch of the Health Department.[65] Local authorities voiced criticisms of the Board of Control, as did the Lord Advocate. The former wanted mental health to be included under the Department of Health's remit. The Lord Advocate was critical of the Board's outlook and felt that consolidation and revision of the lunacy laws was long overdue and that that this would have happened before had the Board of Control been 'less insular, if it had had wider vision and a stronger staff'.[66] The Committee on Scottish Health Services, the Cathcart Committee, had been set up by Sir Godfrey Collins to review health services in Scotland and recommend changes in policy and organisation for the promotion of efficiency and economy.[67] In 1936, Cathcart had recommended 'linking up measures for the diagnosis and treatment of mental and nervous disorders with the corresponding measures for physical conditions'.[68] In order to achieve this, Cathcart had accepted the evidence of local authorities and medical officers of health and proposed that the administrative functions of the General Board of Control for Scotland should be transferred to the Department of Health.[69] The Gilmour Committee decided to recommend the continued existence of the Board because a 'separate body with independent judicial functions is necessary to protect the interests of the insane',[70] in preference to Cathcart's proposal that the Sheriff be given these semi-judicial powers, while recommending the removal of its administrative functions.

The Fishery Board was also examined by the Gilmour Committee. George Hogarth, chairman of the Board, thought it best to change the Board into a Department but opposed a merger with the Department of Agriculture as there was 'no community of interest' between fishing and agriculture.[71] The abolition of the Fishery Board seems to have been more readily acceptable than was the case with the General Board of Control. Though the Scottish Herring Producers' Association favoured retaining the Board, as did other bodies representative of sections of the industry, no strong case for retention was made beyond the industry. Debate on the administration of fishing centred around whether there should be a merger with the Department of Agriculture or whether a separate Fisheries Department should be established. Those most disposed towards the Fisheries Board were least inclined to the idea of a merger with the Department of Agriculture. Those involved in fishing wanted to safeguard their interests and feared that this relatively small industry might be submerged in the Department of Agriculture. Gilmour decided to recommend that a Fisheries division should be established within the Scottish Home Department. It was hoped that this would satisfy those who opposed Boards *per se* while satisfying those who wanted Fisheries to be treated separately. It was a rather strange choice as Fisheries probably had less in common with other functions of the Home Department than it would have had with the Agriculture Department.

In his written evidence to the committee, Sir John Jeffrey had tentatively suggested that the Secretary of State might consider appointing non-statutory councils for matters then administered by the Board of Control and Fisheries Board.[72] When he came to give his oral evidence, Jeffrey's views had hardened; he felt that legislation should make it obligatory for the Secretary of State to appoint advisory councils.[73] Advisory councils were considered to offer an official means by which educational, agricultural, fishing and other interests could express their opinions and offer advice to the Government. They had been seen as an alternative to the Boards. With the movement towards a more professional administration the case for advisory councils was therefore increased. However dubious the boards' claims that they were some kind of Scottish self-government, the development towards a more Whitehall system required some public affirmation that the Scottish dimension in the central administration was not being totally neglected. The advisory boards were to help fulfil this.

Gilmour's recommendations

The report of the Committee on Scottish Administration was published in October 1937. It offered the first comprehensive official analysis of the Scottish central administration as well as a blueprint for reform. The anomalous situation of the statutorily autonomous Departments was to end. Likewise, but more of a break with tradition and challenge to official pride, Gilmour recommended the demise of the Committee of the Privy Council for Education in Scotland with the SED taking its place alongside the other Departments as part of the Scottish Office. The Department of Agriculture, Scottish Education Department, Department of Health and Scottish Home Department were to be established, each headed by a Secretary based in Edinburgh with liaison work done in London where a Permanent Under Secretary would be situated. Common services for typing and messengers but not for technical and professional staff were recommended. The Prisons Department and a Fisheries Division were to be placed within the Scottish Home Department and the Registrar General was to serve in the Department of Health. The General Board of Control was to continue in existence but with its administrative duties discharged by the Department of Health leaving the Board to perform semi-judicial functions protecting the rights of patients.

Each of the seven members of the committee felt able to put their signature to these recommendations though in addenda two members placed on record their dissatisfaction with some aspects of the report. Alexander Gray, who had also served on the Cathcart Committee, felt that the Board of Control should be abolished with the Sheriff given its semi-judicial functions. Tom Johnston's note was of dubious relevance, though he effectively admitted this in his opening sentence. Johnston recommended extending the work of the Scottish Grand Committee and allowing it to meet in Edinburgh. Johnston was the one committee member regarded as likely to have caused problems and perhaps to have issued a minority report. Following the Labour opposition to the 1928 reorganisation legislation it was felt necessary to approach this major reform of Scottish central administration by gaining broad consensus. Gilmour regarded the agreement as a considerable achievement. In a letter to Walter Elliot shortly before the publication of the report, Gilmour stated that the avoidance of a minority report was 'possibly due in some measure to the fact that Tom Johnston is not going on in Parliament'.[74] Johnston, of course, remained in Parliament during the war and served as Secretary of State when he attempted to implement the recommendation contained in his note of dissent.

The Hamilton Committee

Even before the publication of the Gilmour report an inter-departmental committee composed of representatives of the various Scottish departments began to meet. This committee, under the chairmanship of newly appointed Scottish Office Permanent Under Secretary, Sir Horace Hamilton went through the report paragraph by paragraph and made its own recommendations. The committee was the final filter through which ideas on the reform of Scottish central administration passed before they took shape in a bill. As the Parliamentary debates were perfunctory and superficial, the Hamilton Committee was also, in effect, the final filter before the ideas were passed into legislation. The inter-departmental committee consisted of Hamilton, W.S. Douglas, R.N. Duke, Patrick Laird, J.W. Peck and P.J.G. Rose. The committee simply considered whether recommendations should be accepted, modified or rejected. As was to be expected, it broadly agreed with Gilmour. Evidence was once more heard from some of the various bodies that had supplied Gilmour with their views. Many of the same arguments were repeated and largely with the same effect.

Hamilton himself submitted a memorandum on the future of his own office in which he stated that it was clear from discussions that 'by far the most difficult question for decision is the future of the office now known as the Permanent Under Secretaryship of State'.[75] This was to be reflected in the inter-departmental committee's (unpublished) report in December 1937. In his note, Sir Horace suggested that Gilmour had been overcautious in his endeavour to avoid creating an official who would impinge on the work of the Departmental Secretaries. Gilmour had thereby gone 'too far in the direction of depriving the Permanent Secretary of any sort or kind of authority'.[76] In particular, Hamilton was scathing about Gilmour's statement that the Permanent Secretary's position should be that of a 'permanent personal assistant to the Minister'.[77] According to Hamilton, this was the definition not of his office or anything like it but that of a principal private secretary: 'I fail to see that he can be more than a super-Private Secretary and I am not very clear about the "super".'[78] He recommended that co-ordination affecting more than one Department, matters requiring the personal attention of the Secretary of State and those which gave rise to a difference of opinion between Departments should be the responsibility of the Permanent Under Secretary. Additionally, he wanted to retain the title of Permanent Under Secretary of State rather than Gilmour's proposed designation, Permanent Secretary of State. However, the committee was not inclined to be any more specific with respect to the functions of the Permanent Under Secretary than Gilmour had been. A vaguer approach was proposed leaving the relationship between the senior official and the departmental heads to develop by mutual agreement and through experience. The Hamilton Committee did recognise the need for creating a headquarters staff though it accepted the danger of this becoming a rival to the departments.

In no real sense did the Hamilton Committee propose to increase the powers or responsibilities of the Permanent Under Secretary beyond that proposed by Gilmour, apart from the detail, suggested by Sir James Rae of the Treasury, that the Permanent Under Secretary should have more assistance.[79] Hamilton had written an influential memorandum on penumbra and co-ordination for the committee. In this he noted that Gilmour had failed to discuss how the Permanent Under Secretary was to cope with work arising out of 'penumbral' subjects, whether by means of his own staff or the staff of the Departments.[80] For this reason he advocated greater assistance for the Permanent Under Secretary. Hamilton also considered the SED's plea to continue working from London. Peck, SED Secretary, stressed the importance of Treasury contacts and listed nineteen committees and other bodies in London on which the SED was represented.[81] Despite his inclusion on the Hamilton Committee, the memorandum he submitted failed to impress the committee as a whole.

The administration of fisheries matters was also debated. The Fisheries Board had met and discussed the Gilmour report in November 1937 and from that meeting had sent Hamilton its views. While reluctantly accepting the abolition of the Board, they dissented from Gilmour's recommendation that a Fisheries division of the Scottish Home Department should replace the Board. The Board favoured an independent Fisheries Department[82] but the committee agreed with Gilmour on this matter. Discussions were also held concerning the General Board of Control which were very similar to those heard when Gilmour was taking evidence. The position of the head of the reconstituted Board was raised. Under Gilmour's proposals the Board was to be headed by a full-time paid chairman but the Board stressed its support for an unpaid chairman.[83] Hamilton discovered through informal discussions that this was the main concern of the Board but his committee agreed with Gilmour.

N.F. McNicoll, who was responsible for collecting and recording information at Dover House, noted the importance of this function in a memorandum to the committee. McNicoll had linked this with the need for adequate public relations machinery and argued that the information service was 'one of the main weaknesses of Government organisation in Scotland'.[84] Each of the main Departments submitted statements on the subject. None had separate sections dealing with public relations. In early 1938 it was agreed that a single press officer should be appointed for the Scottish Departments.[85] On the suggestion of the editor of the *Glasgow Herald*, a journalist called W.M. Ballantyne was appointed. Ironically, this appointment was itself controversial. The National Union of Journalists expressed dismay at the method of appointment when it became known that the editors of the *Glasgow Herald* and the *Scotsman* had been asked to make recommendations and that no effort had been made to advertise the position.[86]

Gilmour had taken evidence from Whitehall Departments. The crucial department was the Treasury. A Treasury official, Sir James Rae, had sat on the Gilmour Committee. Prior to the establishment of the committee, Rae had informed Treasury head Warren Fisher that he should welcome the enquiry, 'I have long felt that much of the present work of the Scottish Office should be performed in Edinburgh and that, in general, all that is required in London is something which has more resemblance to a Ministerial Private office with adequate capacity for liaison work.' This would, he believed, 'kill the idiotic "Home Rule for Scotland" movement'. Fisher agreed and responded that by asking Rae to serve on the committee.[87] After the Hamilton Committee had reported, Rae signalled his support for the proposals to Fisher. The Treasury had no strong view on minor differences between Gilmour and Hamilton but tended to support the civil servants. Treasury involvement in the process from the outset to the end of the Gilmour enquiry had been supportive and ensured that the recommendations were implemented. Other Whitehall departments were consulted but for the most part provided evidence rather than opinion. The Privy Council's views on the abolition of the long defunct Committee of Council on Education in Scotland were sought by Walter Elliot. The Privy Council clearly had no corporate opinion and sought the advice of the Lord Advocate whose only concern was that the formal abolition of the Committee might end future Lord Advocate's *ex officio* Privy Council membership.[88] In fact, this did not happen. Notably, the one department that counted – the Treasury – had been involved from start to finish.

The new government building in Edinburgh

As Prime Minister, Ramsay MacDonald had taken an active interest in the proposals for a new building in Edinburgh for the Scottish departments. In June 1933, MacDonald had suggested that a 'biggish central area' be chosen to site a building of the 'Scottish domestic type'. The Prime Minister thought that though this might be expensive it would be worthwhile, especially given that 'every bankrupt country in Europe can find money for such a worthy undertaking'.[89] MacDonald's support was, no doubt, valued by the Secretaries of State who set out to make the case for a new building.

What aroused most public controversy was the choice of architect and even the composition of the committee to choose the architect. Public outcry at the *Scotsman*'s disclosure of the 'jam factory' had ensured that the design was to be offered to an architect beyond government employment. In the event Thomas Tait was chosen. The site of the building was less controversial than the choice of architect, or more accurately, the means of choosing the architect. Calton Jail had ceased being used as such from March 1925 and the site of the jail met with general approval. The Royal Fine Art Commission of Scotland approved the selection of the site in July 1933.[90] Though the decision was effectively taken that year, Collins and Ormsby-Gore had to reiterate the case a year later in order to get a final decision to go ahead with the project. Collins brought forward the familiar arguments concerning the difficulties of having a number of buildings house the Scottish departments and noted the savings of centralisation. He also maintained that the new building provided the opportunity for a general reorganisation of all the Scottish departments. Additionally, the new building would be a 'manifest sign of the administration of Scottish affairs in Scotland'.[91]

Though the intention had always been to house all government offices in the new building, problems arose with the increase of around 200 in the staff of the departments, especially in Health and Agriculture. By the time the new building opened in 1939, it was too small to house all of the departments. In September 1934 before the accommodation problems were recognised, the Prisons Department had volunteered to remain outside the proposed new building feeling that the large number of 'undesirable characters, ex-convicts, ex-prisoners and ex-criminal lunatics' who called on the office might 'spoil its amenities'.[92] In fact, the Prisons Department disappeared under the Gilmour proposals, becoming a division of the new Scottish Home Department and was housed in St Andrews House.

A complete reallocation of space had to be undertaken towards the end of 1937 as it became increasingly obvious that insuperable problems had emerged. Much to the annoyance of the Department of Health, it was proposed to house the Insurance staff outside the new building. Health, more than any other department, had suffered from the dispersal of offices in Edinburgh but had to accept this.

The outbreak of war meant that the official opening of St Andrews House had to be postponed. The possibility of war had been a consideration which had been taken into account. The dangers of air attacks in the centrally housed Scottish administration was not thought by the Home Office's Air Raid Precaution Department to be very great. In January 1938, in reply to queries, the Home Office had stated, 'Edinburgh is not particularly high on the vulnerable list, although of course, it is on the way to Glasgow.'[93] The newly housed Scottish Office began work in unusual circumstances.

Conclusion

The Scottish central administration had traditionally been different from the rest of British central administration. Where Scotland did not impinge on the work of other Whitehall departments there was little interest in London in what went on north of the border. Apart from the Treasury, concerned with expenditure, the influence of the English Departments at this stage in the development of the Scottish Office, or indeed at earlier or later stages, was negligible. Within Scotland, various bodies that were closely associated with the offices gave evidence to

Gilmour. However, despite the importance of these proposed reforms there appears to have been little public debate. The Gilmour report had a 'neat and workmanlike air' according to the *Glasgow Herald* while its east coast rival thought it to be a 'business-like document'.[94] When the Scottish Liberal Federation debated the question in October 1937 the Duke of Montrose described the report as providing little other than a 'game of musical chairs for the boys of the Scottish Office'.[95] Administrative reform may have been the issue but, publicly, home rule was being debated. Addressing a Scottish Unionist Association political school shortly after Gilmour's publication, Walter Elliot indicated his support for the report but dwelt mainly with proposals being put forward by the Liberal National MP, James Henderson Stewart for the Scottish Grand Committee to examine the Scottish Estimates.

One of the most comprehensive and important reforms of the machinery of government in Scotland was hardly remarked upon in Scotland. Not only was the most informed debate taking place within the central administration but the only serious discussion of the reforms took place there. Even Parliament proved obstinate in its refusal to debate the administration of Scottish central administration seriously. Parliamentary committee reform, home rule and sundry items on the long list of Scottish grievances were to dominate the second reading debate. Anyone who imagined that administrative devolution could be separated from political devolution should have realised that this was only possible for civil servants. Civil servants were, necessarily, the most influential body of people who determined the structure of the reformed Scottish central administration. From Patrick Laird's memorandum in 1928, the most important evidence to the Gilmour Committee came from civil servants. The Hamilton Committee, publicly unheard of, was composed entirely of civil servants and it was, of course, civil servants who drafted the legislation. None of this is surprising. The detailed knowledge of the workings and the failings of the existing organisation was held by the permanent staff. Few Members of Parliament and few people outside the Scottish administration knew much about the machinery of Scottish government. Few seemed to care either.

The 1939 reforms created the modern Scottish Office. Though the internal organisation was to change on a number of occasions subsequently, the Act of 1939 allowed this to happen without the need for legislation. The quasi-federal structure of the Office remained intact with the Permanent Under Secretary of State in the pivotal central position working closely with the Secretary of State and with the Departments acting with some measure of autonomy below him.

By concentrating its case on the consolidation of Scottish central administration and portraying the changes as involving a transfer to Edinburgh from London and having established an all-party committee of inquiry, the Government had learned lessons from the 1928 episode. At committee stage amendments were usually of a technical nature and the Act received the Royal Assent in May 1939. St Andrews House opened its doors as the symbol of the consolidation later that year. The intended fanfare at the opening by the King had to be cancelled because of the outbreak of war and the building proved to be too small to house all the Scottish office civil servants whose numbers had grown since the initial conception of turning the site of the old Calton gaol into the centre of Scottish central administration.

8
The Origins and Development of the Goschen Formula

Introduction

The development of central government finance might have been expected to integrate Scotland into England. In fact, Scotland was treated as a distinct administrative entity for many aspects of public finance. Arguing for resources 'for Scotland' became an inevitable consequence that underlined the idea of a Scottish fiscal community. Of course, this did not involve Scotland having any financial autonomy but it played an important part in the development of twentieth-century Scottish politics. Amongst the grievances of the Scottish Rights Association, founded in 1853, was the perceived inequitable distribution of public funds between Scotland, Ireland and England and Wales. A pamphlet produced that year, taking the form of a letter to Scottish MPs, surveyed Parliamentary Papers and concluded that,

> during fifty years, from the year 1801 to the year 1851, – that lavish expenditure as regards England and Ireland, and extreme niggardliness as regards Scotland, are characteristic of the entire period.[1]

The charges in the letter were never answered because, as Ferguson has noted, in many instances they were self-evident truths culled from Parliamentary papers. Though the Crimean War diverted public attention, the issue of Scotland's share of public expenditure and contributions to the Exchequer never really left the public agenda.[2] It may have rarely if ever attracted the attention of the wider public but many Scots maintained an interest.

One of the most interesting aspects has been the use of formulae to determine territorial shares of public expenditure. The Goschen formula, whereby Scotland received 11/80ths of England's share of public expenditure, is referred to in most works on Scottish government, though little is said beyond stating the proportions involved. But the history and development of Goschen's application tell us a great deal about Scotland's position within the United Kingdom. Unravelling it is no easy task. Apart from the complexities of public finance involved, much mythology surrounds its application. This may explain why the practical application of Goschen is 'astonishingly badly documented'.[3] It has been assumed to have been based on Scotland's share of population.[4] Others have linked it to Scotland's contribution to the Treasury in 1888.[5] A former Scottish Office Permanent Secretary wrote of Goschen's original application being applied to the Education (Scotland) Act of 1918.[6] A volume in the New History of Scotland series suggested that the Goschen formula was adopted in 1886.[7] Confusion concerning Goschen today is understandable given the inconsistency of its use as a means of determining national shares of public expenditure and because it became an important yardstick by which politicians measured how favourably Scotland was treated.

The focus of most debate in the period up to the First World War was on educational finance. Education was the main responsibility of the Scottish Secretary from the establishment of the Office in 1885 and represented by far the largest item of public expenditure under his responsibility. The debates between the SED and Treasury on this subject were often long and difficult. The suspicion and contempt that some officials in each department held for the other was evident. Lord Salisbury found cause for concern with the 'Treasury mind' and mentioned specific incidences of bad relations with spending departments to Goschen, his Chancellor of the Exchequer, including relations with the Scottish Office.[8] Maynard Keynes reportedly remarked that the Treasury of 1920 was 'half-way between Heaven and the Scottish Education Department'.[9] Long after Sir Henry Craik, SED Secretary from 1885–1904, had left the civil service and entered Parliament as a Unionist MP, he antagonised the Treasury and provoked an exchange between the head of the Treasury and the Prime Minister. In February and March 1926, Craik tabled Parliamentary Questions concerning Sir Warren Fisher's standing as senior Treasury official. This elicited a note from Fisher to Prime Minister Baldwin explaining the background:

> Sir H. Craik was himself a Civil Servant from 1870 to 1904, during the last nineteen years of the period being Secretary to the Scottish Education Department. He conceived that position as one of great

importance and the contemporary Treasury (unfortunately) never seems to have disguised its view that neither Sir Henry nor his post was of any particular importance.

Hence an abiding resentment on his part in particular against the Treasury and in general against the Service.[10]

Relations were poor from the start.

Origins of Goschen: the Local Taxation Accounts

In 1888, Chancellor of the Exchequer Joachim Goschen attempted to simplify and separate imperial and local finance. Grants-in-aid to local authorities had developed over the years up to the 1880s for various purposes and different grants were paid to different authorities. To a large extent, the grant-in-aid as a form of rates relief, and most notably in relief of agricultural rates, had been a response, particularly from 1847 to 1875, to English demands. The growth in 'Imperial subventions' to local authorities was noted in a report on local taxation prepared by John Skelton, Vice President of the Board of Supervision, in 1895 for the Secretary for Scotland.[11]

Goschen decided to introduce Local Taxation Accounts for Ireland, Scotland and England and Wales. Into these accounts would go certain 'assigned revenues', taxes or duties which would be assigned for local purposes. These assigned revenues were not to be paid directly by the tax payer to the local authorities but via the Exchequer through the Local Taxation Accounts held at the Bank of England. Certain licences – for selling alcohol, dealing in game, for dogs, killing game, guns, pawnbroking, horses and mules, armorial bearings, male servants, hawkers and other inconsequential paraphenalia – would be paid into the Accounts.[12] Scotland received its own licence duties. Probate duty (later known as estate duty) was also to contribute to the Local Taxation Accounts, particularly because it was felt that personalty (represented by people), and not just realty (represented by rates), ought to make some contribution to local finances. In the first year, Goschen intended that one-third of probate duty should go to the Local Taxation Accounts and that this would be raised thereafter to two-thirds of the duty. Probate duty was abolished by the Finance Act of 1894 and a corresponding sum granted out of the estate duty was derived from personal property.[13]

This would, then, determine the sum to be paid into the Local Taxation Accounts as a whole but it did not answer how much should be allocated to each Account – for Scotland, Ireland and England and

Wales. On previous occasions when sums had been allocated to England and Wales and an equivalent amount was awarded to Scotland there had been no fixed principle or formula involved. On this occasion, the proportions of probate duty to be allocated was to be on the basis of what became known as the Goschen equivalent or Goschen formula with 80 per cent to England and Wales, 11 per cent to Scotland and 9 per cent to Ireland. As noted, attributing the formula's origins to a population basis has now become almost standard but population was clearly not the measure used. Had population been used, Ireland's share would have exceeded Scotland's (Table 8.1).

Neither was it based on the sum raised in each of the constituent nations of the UK. In his budget speech, Goschen explained that by 'handing back to the countries the proportion of the probate duty which they pay, Ireland would come off very badly indeed'[14] with Ireland receiving only 5 per cent of probate duty, Scotland 10 per cent and England and Wales 85 per cent. Instead, the Chancellor decided to,

> give each country a share of it in proportion to the general contributions of that country to the Exchequer. On this principle, England will be entitled to 80 per cent, Scotland to 11 per cent, and Ireland to 9 per cent. This division is, if anything, a little too favourable to Ireland, as its contributions are in reality only 8.7%; but I have felt obliged to give the benefit of the doubt to the poorer country.[15]

Thus the Goschen formula was born. Its origins lay in an attempt to separate imperial and local expenditure which was to last only a short period. But the formula itself was to have a far longer history. It lingered on into the second half of the twentieth century.

Table 8.1   Population of United Kingdom by constituent nation

	1881 population	%	1891 population	%
England and Wales	25,974,000	74.5	29,002,000	76.8
Scotland	3,736,000	10.7	4,026,000	10.7
Ireland	5,175,000	14.8	4,705,000	12.5
Total	34,885,000	100	37,733,000	100

Source: Final Report of Royal Commission on Local Taxation (Scotland) 1902, C.1067, ch. III, p. 15.

The attempt to provide local government with some form of entirely self-supporting financial basis was bound to fail. As K.B. Smellie states in his history of local government,

> Looking back, it is difficult to see how it could ever have been thought that the growth of the proceeds of certain national taxes, however wisely chosen, would keep pace with the cost of the new services with which local authorities were to be charged. There could be no simple correlation between the cost of services which in the public interest should be locally administered and the proceeds of particular taxes. Moreover, the greater range and subtlety of public finance made it necessary for the Chancellor of the Exchequer to retain every instrument and tool of his craft.[16]

But what was established was a formula to be used in certain cases when some equivalent sum required to be allocated to Scotland after a decision had been made to allocate an amount to England and Wales. This was the unintended consequence of Goschen's attempt to identify a tax that would be used for local purposes.

In his budget speech, Goschen willingly acknowledged the distinctive use to which Scotland could put its share of probate duty. Though legislation would be required to determine how the Local Taxation (Scotland) Account funds should be distributed, this, as far as the Chancellor was concerned, would be 'settled by the Secretary for Scotland and his advisers, according to the general views of Scottish ratepayers'.[17] Aberdeen North's Liberal Member, Dr Hunter argued that the Scottish share should be used for the relief of school fees rather than for rates relief and thus provide free education in Scotland.[18] Initially, the Scottish Secretary, Lord Lothian had no intention of having the Local Taxation Account revenues used for Scottish education[19] but the partial use of the Local Taxation (Scotland) Account to relieve school fees took statutory form in the Local Government (Scotland) Act, 1889.[20] An SED minute of August 1889 established a system of grants to school boards for the relief of fees of pupils below standard IV and for partial remission of fees in standards IV and V. Alexander Morgan credited the 1889 Act with having 'ultimately led to free elementary education.'[21] Perhaps credit should go to the assistance provided by the pressure for rates relief in England, and particularly the pressure of English farmers for agricultural relief, and to Goschen's failed attempt to separate Imperial and local finance. The assigned revenues 'withered away, and the new grants flourished like a green bay tree'[22] but the

Goschen formula had provided the basis for a ratio which was to have some importance in the determination of aspects of Scottish public expenditure beyond the first half of the twentieth century.

Further application and non-application of Goschen

Further grants followed as Goschen's intention to separate Local and Imperial taxation receded from sight. In a paper delivered to the Glasgow Philosophical Society in 1899, Sheriff W.C. Smith of Ross, Cromarty and Sutherland outlined grants that had been provided from 1889 with the legislation which authorised them:

Local Government Act, 1889
Local Taxation Account (Customs and Excise) Act, 1890
Education and Local Taxation Account Act, 1892
Agricultural Rates Act, 1896
Taxation Account Act, 1898.[23]

Money was to be distributed under the Local Taxation (Customs and Excise) Act, 1890,[24] provided by the Customs and Inland Revenue Act, 1890.[25] Certain customs and excise duties – known as 'whisky money' – were divided between England and Wales, Scotland and Ireland. Under the Customs and Inland Revenue Act, 1890 this revenue was to be 'divided between England, Scotland, Ireland in the same proportions, and be paid to the same local taxation accounts ... as the one-half of the proceeds of the probate duties applicable to local purposes is now by law divided, paid, and ascertained'[26] that is using the Goschen formula. The residue of this grant could be used for technical education after certain deductions were made which were not the same on either side of the border. In the case of England and Wales the deduction amounted to a fixed sum of £300,000 for police superannuation while in Scotland the deductions amounted to £95,000 in addition to a variable charge for the purpose of the Contagious Diseases (Animals) Act, 1890.

Fluctuations in the amount produced each year by Customs and Excise duties and, in the Scottish case, uncertainty as to the amount available for purposes of technical education due to the variable charge relating to the public health legislation, caused the Scottish Education Department to complain to the Treasury.[27] In an SED memorandum in November 1897 it was pointed out that these fluctuations and uncertainties had resulted in the residue for purposes of rates relief or technical education varying between £38,262 in 1895–96 and £58,423 in

1891–92. Though one educational historian claimed that the greater part of the residue was used by Scottish local authorities to develop technical education, with one-third going to rates relief,[28] there was disquiet in the SED concerning the extent to which Scottish burghs were failing to use the money for technical education on the grounds that the amount was too small to be of practical use.[29]

In the memorandum it showed that the total customs and excise duties received by England/Wales and Scotland conformed to a ratio of 80:11 in 1894–95 but after a reduction by less than one-third from the English/Welsh figure and a reduction of over two-thirds from the Scottish figure, the residues for the two funds produced a ratio of 80:4.2.[30] Further sums were paid to Scottish education by Acts of Parliament over the period up to 1908 when consolidating legislation established the Education (Scotland) Grant. In 1891, a fee grant of 10s. per child was provided in England and Wales. The following year the Education and Local Taxation Account (Scotland) Act, 1892 was passed. At the time a fee grant of 12s. per child already existed in Scotland, which was provided for out of a number of sources,[31] but it would not have been politic to exclude Scotland from any equivalent grant. The SED argued that Scotland ought to receive an equivalent to that paid to England and Wales calculated in the same manner, that is 10s. per child in Scotland.[32] As school attendance was proportionately lower in England and Wales this would have been to Scotland's advantage but instead the Goschen proportions were used. Repeated protests from the SED failed to change the basis of calculation with the Treasury re-affirming the arrangement of allocations based on the Goschen equivalent in a letter of 17 January, 1894.[33] While the SED continued to argue for the same capitation basis as in England and Wales, school attendance there rose with the progress towards free education. This gradually eroded the disadvantage for Scotland of the Goschen formula in this case.

In 1895, Sir Henry Craik, SED Secretary criticised the application of the Goschen formula:

> After three years experience it can hardly be maintained by anyone that it is either just and reasonable in principle or convenient in practice. It is plain that the grant in Scotland ought to be regulated by the attendance in Scottish schools. This would enable an Estimate to be made in the usual way, and no complaint could possibly be made that it is either unjust or unduly favourable to one country or the other.[34]

The SED provided figures showing how Scotland was losing out on the Goschen basis (Table 8.2).

In a letter to the SED Secretary two years later, R.W. Hanbury, Financial Secretary to the Treasury, confirmed these figures but noted that later years suggested that the capitation basis had not been bad for Scotland (Table 8.3).

Hanbury's figure of the amount voted in 1895–96 of £301,469, however, was exaggerated as it included £4,125 voted the following year. In 1896, the SED was therefore inclined towards a Treasury proposal[35] to,

> submit to Parliament in the Estimates for 1896/7 grants for Scotland and for Ireland respectively based on the same lines as in England, viz: an allowance of 10/- a head for each Scholar in average attendance during the year, in each of these countries.[36]

The SED recalled that the 11/80 fraction had been fixed 'not by the desire of their Department but by the decision of the Treasury'.[37] The Treasury's conversion to the capitation basis was due to potential financial savings though, from the SED's perspective, the new basis was more relevant to Scottish needs. An added complication concerned the supplementary estimates which had been made for the English and Welsh grants but which had no equivalent for Scotland or Ireland. During the

Table 8.2   Goschen losses, 1892–94

	Account voted	10/- on average attendance	Loss
1892–93	£265,000	£277,555	£12,555
1893–94	£272,660	£284,678	£12,018

Source: NAS, ED 7/5/17 Draft of note to Treasury sent to Vice President for approval by Craik, 2/3/95.

Table 8.3   Goschen loss/gain, 1894–96

	Account voted	10/- on average attendance	Loss/gain
1894–95	£286,000	£291,761	£5761 loss
1895–96	£301,469	£295,004	£6465 gain

Source: NAS, ED7/5/17 Letter from R.W. Hanbury MP to SED Secretary, 12 March 1897.

course of 1896 the SED argued that the Treasury ought to make amends for the loss. According to the SED, Scotland had lost out by £34,265 from 1892–93, calculated as 11/80 of the total supplementary estimates to 1895–96 of £249,200 which England and Wales had received. The Department proposed that,

> an understanding should be arrived at that if in any year, the sums at their disposal should not be sufficient to maintain the fee commuta-tion at its present rate, they should be empowered to submit a Supplementary Estimate until the sum stated above (£34,265) is exhausted.[38]

As the SED argued for the Scottish equivalent of the English and Welsh supplementary grants, it warned the Treasury that pressure was being exerted in Parliament. Questions asked by J.H.C. Hozier, James Caldwell and W. Thorburn[39] revealed differences between the SED and the Treasury concerning the supplementary estimates. The Lord Advocate, Sir Charles Pearson told the Commons that the SED had communicated with the Treasury on the matter, even stating that the SED had,

> repeatedly pressed upon the attention of the Treasury the claim which arises on behalf of Scotland in respect of the supplementary fee grants to England during the financial years 1892–93.[40]

A letter from R.W. Hanbury, Financial Secretary to the Treasury, in April 1896 partially conceded the point raised by the Scottish MPs and the SED.[41] However, by only admitting the claim of the SED for a propor-tionate share of the English and Welsh supplementary fee grant for 1895–96 but not for the preceding years, the Treasury failed to resolve the matter. The following day Craik wrote a letter for the Vice President's signature questioning the Treasury's logic of restricting the amount due to the SED to the financial year 1895–96. Agreement was only reached in March 1897 when the Treasury conceded that,

> if in any year the sums at the disposal of your Department should not be sufficient to maintain the Fee Commutation at its present rate, Their Lordships of the Committee may submit a Supplementary Estimate until this sum of £23,875 is exhausted.[42]

The sum of £23,875 had been calculated from the total amount which Scotland would have received had the capitation method of calculation operated from 1892–93 minus that amount which was actually voted rather than £34,265 claimed by the SED using Goschen. The SED accepted this compromise though the Treasury, as Craik pointed out to Scottish Secretary Balfour of Burleigh, had 'antedated' the 10s. system,[43] and that the 11/80 principle would have meant that the arrears due to Scotland came to £28,796 that is £4921 more than the Treasury were finally willing to admit. However he suggested that compromise be reached and Balfour of Burleigh accepted the view that 'it would be expedient to accept the concession which the Treasury have made'.[44] Scotland received a larger proportion of education expenditure than a *per capita* basis would have allowed. In an adjournment debate in March 1891, the Liberal MP for Caithness, Dr Gavin Clark had recited a list of 'very inadequate grants given to Scotland for various purposes, as compared with those given to England and Ireland',[45] but had to concede that this was not true of education.[46]

Further legislation enhanced the state's contribution to education before consolidating legislation was passed in 1908. In 1897, bills presented to aid English and Welsh education again raised the question of how to determine the equivalent amount for Scotland. Balfour of Burleigh, in a memorandum of April 1897, calculated that the total additional grant to England and Wales would probably be over £710,000 but noted that the 11/80 principle had been abandoned with regard to the fee grant and stated that he did 'not desire to press for its revival in regard to the new Grant'.[47] He proposed a basis aimed at 'an equitable adjustment rather than an exactly defined amount' which he argued would 'inevitably provoke and prolong discussion'.[48]

One major problem for Balfour was that though the 11/80 principle had been abandoned for calculating the fee grant it had been adopted in the Agricultural Rates Act, 1896 to determine the amount Scotland was to receive to correspond with the sum paid towards agricultural rates relief for England and Wales.[49] An annual grant from the Exchequer equal to half of the amount raised in respect of agricultural land in England and Wales in 1895 was provided for by the Agricultural Rates Act, 1896. The Government did not accept that such a measure of grant should be applied to Scotland. Instead, 11/80 of the sum allocated for England and Wales was distributed under the Agricultural Rates, Congested District, and Burghs Land Tax Relief (Scotland) Act, 1896.[50] Though this money was not allocated for educational purposes the use of the 11/80 fraction exemplified the Treasury's willingness to remain flexible in determining the method of allocating a grant to Scotland corresponding to any made for England and Wales.

Once more, in 1902, developments in England and Wales increased the Scottish educational budget. Under the English Education Act of that year, additional grants from the Exchequer were given to England and Wales and some form of corresponding grant was thereby due to Scotland. In a note to the Scottish Secretary, Craik suggested that the sum should be applied to 'certain temporary objects'[51] until such time as a comprehensive Scottish Education Bill could be presented. Legislation allocating imperial funds to Scottish education, largely following new developments in England and Wales, had resulted in considerable incoherence in the development of Scottish central funding, even without taking account of the complexities of local authority financing and the voluntary sector of endowments and trusts which had semi-official status. After a number of failed attempts, a consolidating Act bringing together various central subventions was passed in 1908.

In calculating the amount due to Scotland by adopting a replication of the English and Welsh principles embodied in the Education Act of 1902, Balfour of Burleigh made a claim to the Treasury for £229,700 and accepted that 'such grants to each country should not be regulated by any fixed proportion such as 11/80ths' but should be regulated 'upon the application, not of a fixed proportion, but of uniform principles'.[52] However, Chancellor of the Exchequer Ritchie was not inclined to accept this. The English and Welsh grant, maintained Ritchie, had been determined by 'considerations wholly apart from the scheme for its allocation to the individual authorities. That scheme was adapted to fit the amount of the grant; the amount of the grant was in no way dependent or consequent upon the scheme of allocation'.[53] Other reasons for the scheme's inapplicability to Scotland were given by Ritchie. In England, all public elementary schools, including voluntary schools, were being put under a new authority thus imposing a substantial new charge but in Scotland there was no proposal to alter the status of voluntary schools. Ritchie also noted that Balfour of Burleigh did not propose to apply the scheme of allocation in its entirety to Scotland. The age up to which scholars in public elementary schools in Scotland counted for grants differed from that in England. Finally, Ritchie pointed out that a similar grant would have to be made to Ireland and while the English scheme was 'inapplicable to Scotland, it is, if possible, still more inapplicable to Ireland.'[54]

Ritchie's alternative was to base the allocation on population and he cited the Royal Commission on Local Taxation (Table 8.4) in support of such a method. Its final report on Scotland had been chaired by Balfour of Burleigh and had stated, with regard to the Goschen formula, that 'in

Table 8.4 Local Taxation (Scotland) Account, Financial Year ending 31 March 1901

PAYMENTS INTO:

I. Probate and Licence Duties

	£
1. 11/100 of probate (or estate) duty grant	300,091
2. Proceeds of licences	30,533
	670,624

II. Customs and Excise Duties

	£
1. 11/100 of proceeds of certain duties	350,395
2. 11/100 of proceeds of certain customs	24,053
	174,448

PAYMENTS OUT OF:

I. Probate and Licence Duties

	£
1. Relief of rates in Highlands and Islands	10,000
2. Cost of roads	35,000
3. Cost of police pay, &c.	155,000
4. Poor law medical relief	20,000
5. Pauper lunatics	£90,000
Additional	25,000
	115,500
6. Secondary education	60,000
7. Universities of Scotland	30,000
8. Parish councils, &c (relief rates)	50,000
9. Cattle pleuro-pneumonia account	3,000
10. Counties, burghs, &c., relief of rates	146,933
11. Balance – relief school fees	45,191
	670,624

II. Customs and Excise Duties

	£
1. Police superannuation	40,000
2. Relief of school fees	40,000
3. Medical officers and sanitary inspectors	15,000

III. Estate Duty		*III. Estate Duty*	
11/80 of grant to England under Agricultural Rates Act, 1896	182,499		
		4. Counties, burghs, &c. (relief if rates or technical education)	79,448
			174,448
		1. Burgh land tax relief	7,990
		2. Congested districts in Highland and Islands	15,000
		3. County and parish council's relief of agricultural occupiers	159,627
			182,617
IV. Consolidated Fund		*IV. Consolidated Fund*	
Additional grant towards relief of agricultural rates	97,626	1. Additional contribution in relief of agricultural rates	20,000
		2. Additional contribution to cost of pay and clothing of police	25,000
		3. Marine superintendence	15,000
		4. Residue to secondary or technical education	37,795
			97,795

The receipts and expenditure under headings iv and v do not correspond due to some misunderstandings with the Treasury. The total receipts were £1,125,197; the total payments £1,125,484.

Source: Mabel Atkinson, Local Government in Scotland 1904, p. 342.

view of the complexity and obscurity of the calculations made in 1888, we consider that the populations of the two countries constitute a better and simpler measure of their respective claims'.[55] The Commissioners' desire that the 'payments to the Scottish Local Taxation Account should bear to the payments to the English Account, that proportion which the population of Scotland bears to that of England'[56] meant, using the figures from the Preliminary Report of the 1901 Census,[57] that Scotland would receive 13.78 per cent of that amount given to England, three-hundredths of a percentage point more than would have been allocated had Goschen been adopted.

An SED official, replying to queries from Craik, told him that the Scottish education grant would have been £1,364,185 that is £43,527 less than was actually voted had a population basis been adopted.[58] The official had used different figures from those quoted above – his calculations were based on population figures of 32,526,075 for England and Wales and 4,472,103 for Scotland. Even had the above figures from the preliminary census return been used Scotland would have been worse off had a population basis been adopted – by £3555. Balfour, therefore, argued against the population basis and challenged the Treasury's argument that the English system of allocations would be inappropriate, while admitting that certain modifications would be required. However Ritchie insisted that the population basis of calculation be adhered to 'for fixing the initial amount of the Grant to Scotland' and that this amount would work out to a,

> certain sum (say X) per annum per child under the age of 15 in average attendance. I am willing to agree to this rate of X per annum per child under the age of 15 in average attendance being stereotyped and given for future years, so that the total amount of the Grant to Scotland would vary precisely in proportion to the number of such children.[59]

By this stage the debate had gone on into February 1903 and the Treasury was becoming increasingly exasperated with, as they saw it, the SED's obstinacy. The SED's estimate for 1903–04 remained the only outstanding estimate to be agreed that year due to differences over the new equivalent grant.[60] Agreement was finally reached at the beginning of March. The General Aid Grant for Scotland, corresponding to that provided for England and Wales under the Education Act of 1902, amounted to £186,000, calculated on the population basis from the £1,352,000 allocated south of the border, plus £26,000 guaranteed in

1897 by the Chancellor of the Exchequer in order to maintain the fee grant in Scotland at 12s. a head. The total sum of £212,000 divided among 640,543, the number of children under 15 years old in average attendance in primary schools, gave a figure of 6s.$7\frac{1}{2}$d. per child.[61] Agreement between the SED and Treasury had been reached, 'In future years the General Aid Grant will be the said sum of 6s.$7\frac{1}{2}$d. multiplied by the number of children under 15 years of age attendance.'[62] The Grant in Aid to Scotland approximated 11/80 of that provided for England and Wales. The population basis happened to be the same as that which the Goschen principle would have provided and a *per capita* amount was determined from the initial calculation of the grant which was to be used in the future.

Consolidating educational finance

Much of the controversy that surrounded Goschen throughout its existence focussed on its application to education. Scotland's educational heritage has proved rich in controversy and mythology, particularly as compared with England. This was also the case regarding educational finance. Expenditure on public education was the largest single item in the estimates under the responsibility of the Scottish Secretary in the period up to the First World War. The Scottish public expenditure estimates for the year ending 31 March, 1914 amounted to just under £2,500,000.[63]

The head of the English Board of Education, Selby-Bigge remarked that until 1902 there was a 'system of grants, but no system of finance' for education.[64] This applied equally to Scotland where there was little coherence in central–local relations regarding educational finance until 1908. In a memorandum prepared for a cabinet meeting in March 1908, the SED reminded cabinet ministers that the Education (Scotland) Bill was the sixth such bill presented to Parliament over an eight-year period. Three reasons lay behind these attempts: first, there was a desire to consolidate the existing legislation, particularly concerning finance; second, it was argued by the SED that expenditure on education had risen faster than grants leaving an exceptionally heavy burden on ratepayers; and third, a desire to widen the scope of education to include physical education and welfare was felt desirable. Inevitably, additional grants given or promised in England were a cause for claims by the SED.[65] In a note to the Treasury in October 1906, the SED expressed the desire to have the 'educational needs of Scotland as a *whole* considered in view of the additional subventions now given to or to be given to

England'.[66] Increased expenditure on public education over the preceding decade had resulted from two causes outwith the school boards' control, on whom the burden had largely fallen. The Education (Scotland) Act, 1901 had made it the duty of 'every parent to provide efficient elementary education in reading, writing, and arithmetic for his children who are between five and fourteen years of age'.[67] By thus raising the school-leaving age, despite the fairly liberal interpretation of exceptions permitted, considerable financial outlay was required for additional teachers as well as for accommodation. Demands for reductions in the size of classes and increased salaries for teachers also put pressure on finance.

The SED hoped to establish a comprehensive reform of the system of finance and to introduce coherence based on established principles in place of the 'constantly recurring questions of "equivalent" grants for special objects'.[68] To this end, they argued that the sum allocated should be related to population. The SED's reasons for favouring a population rather than average attendance basis was understandable. Scotland's population was 13.75 per cent of that for England and Wales and the number of pupils in average attendance in 1902 was 13.32 per cent of those in England and Wales.[69] An amount per head would therefore be provided that would be the same throughout Britain and this, the SED demanded, should be fixed for a five-year period. This annual sum would cover national charges such as teacher training and inspection with the remainder distributed amongst the local education authorities (Table 8.5).

Though the 1908 Act did not replace the parish with larger areas for the local administration of elementary education as the SED had desired, county education committees were established to administer grants available for secondary, technical education and bursaries. The newly constituted system of grants was made to these local bodies from the consolidated central fund, the Education (Scotland) Fund. The Fund brought together grants provided in legislation from 1890 for 'higher education' which at that time meant post-primary education.[70] In addition to the five subventions consolidated in the fund was a further sum to be 'voted by Parliament' for that year as a general aid grant for education in Scotland.[71] At the Bill's second reading in the Lords, the Scottish Secretary Balfour of Burleigh estimated that this latter subsection, the general aid grant, would amount to at least £250,000 which, with other grants, would amount in total to 'at least £500,000 a year'.[72] As ever, the SED attempted to convince the Treasury that Scotland had particular needs. Amongst their arguments, they claimed that Scottish

Table 8.5 Comparison of grants for Scottish and English and Welsh Education, 1901–02

Grants	England/Wales £	Scotland £	Scottish Grant as % of England and Wales
Annual	5,220,230	779,525	14.9
Fee	2,430,321	322,702	13.3
Blind, deaf etc.	33,703	3,325	9.9
Necessitous Schools Boards	217,500	48,600	22.3
District Organisation	760	–	25.8
Highlands and Islands	–	1,200	–
Training Colleges	231,883	59,875	25.8
Total	8,759,597	1,227,527	14.0
Average Attendance	4,846,635	645,404	13.3
Average grant per scholar	1.15.6s. $1\frac{3}{4}$ d.	1.18s.$0\frac{1}{2}$ d.	

Source: NAS, ED7/5/7.

ratepayers were particularly overburdened. This was rejected by the Treasury in a letter in January 1908 replying to a claim for an addition of £48,000 from the SED of December 1907.[73]

The Act of 1908 consolidated the system of subventions but failed to provide an agreed rationale for the allocation of grants to Scotland, Ireland, England and Wales. The next year Struthers noted that a call for relief of rates in England would, if acceded to, be followed by demands for an equivalent grant for Scotland:

> But what I wd. urge upon the Government very strongly is that no further grants shd. be promised to England without a comprehensive enquiry into the question as affecting all the three countries and within any one country as to the relief that might be brought to the more heavily burdened localities if the aid at present given were distributed more in accordance with the comparative needs of the several communities.[74]

Struthers had good reason in arguing that Scottish considerations ought to be taken into account by the President of the Board of Education in the formulation of new measures, just as the SED was expected to take account of and inform the Board of new proposals. However, a confidential memorandum initialled by Walter Runciman, President of the Board of Education, in December 1909, on the 'Need for an Increase of Exchequer Grants in Aid of Elementary Education'[75] failed completely to mention the proposals' implications for other parts of the United Kingdom.

One proposal with support in Scotland was that the Exchequer contribution towards education should consist of a definite proportion of the approved expenditure of each year. This was largely a consequence of the increased burden on rates. At the annual congress of the EIS in April 1911, D.M. Wilson, chairman of Lanarkshire Secondary Education Committee stated that, overall, from 1894–95 grants had increased by about 30 per cent and rates by 108 per cent and cited areas where the disparity in the increased contributions from grants and rates was even greater.[76] A table of figures compiled by the SED suggested that Wilson had grossly exaggerated (Table 8.6). The SED claimed that the increase in grants from 1894–95 was 70.3 per cent rather than Wilson's figure of 30 per cent but the SED figure included local taxation money that was not wholly devoted to educational purposes. Even accepting the SED figures, the proportional increase in grants amounted to only 68.3 per cent of the proportional increase in rate according to the official figures.[77] The

Table 8.6 Comparison of figures used by Mr D.M. Wilson at Oban EIS Congress on 18 April, 1911 with those of Accountant's Report for 1908–09. Selective examples from table

	Figure given by Mr Wilson %	Figure given in Accountant's Report, 1908–09 %
Increase in school rates since 1894–95:		
Average for parishes	56.9	56.9
Average for Burghs	62.4	62.4
Govan	90.6	77.8
Glasgow	94.4	88.9
Increase in grants since 1894–95	30	70.3
Increase in rates since 1894–95	108	103
Increase in grants since 1894–95 Glasgow	30	50.5
Increase in rates 1894–95 Glasgow	262.6	138.7
Proportion of maintenance met by grants, 1894–95	67.9	70.4
Proportion of maintenance expenditure met by grants 1908–09	59.7	60.9
Proportion of maintenance expenditure met by rates, 1894–95	25.9	24.5
Proportion of maintenance expenditure met by rates, 1908–09	36.4	33.9

Source: NAS, ED 7/5/22.

Treasury and the SED were opposed to allocating a set proportion of all expenditure on education each year to local authorities as this would oblige it to finance schemes that they might not agree with or might regard as extravagant.

The 1908 Act was described as 'not one Act but several Acts rolled into one'.[78] One important and contentious issue was that of teachers' superannuation. The superannuation scheme for teachers had led to increased demands for state support. Scotland, unlike England and Wales, was expected to introduce a scheme by 1 April, 1912. As the date for the full implementation of the scheme drew nearer pressure increased for Treasury assistance. On 11 January, 1912 a meeting of larger school boards, secondary education committees and the School

Boards' Association was held in Edinburgh and resolved to approach the Treasury. Scottish MPs also requested a meeting with Lloyd George, the Chancellor of the Exchequer. In June 1912, a deputation of Scottish MPs pointed out that school boards in Scotland opposed the establishment of a superannuation scheme unless it was supported by Exchequer aid. Lloyd George replied that in making a grant to Scotland he had to take into consideration what the effect of imperial aid for superannuation in England would be, 'the sum which might be a comparatively small figure if it were confined to Scotland, when multiplied by 10 becomes a very considerable sum'.[79] Conversely, any initiative in England and Wales would not be greatly affected by provoking similar demands in Scotland because of their relative sizes. It was this imbalance in the relations between the SED and the Board of Education that led Munro Ferguson, a future Scottish Secretary, to argue at the meeting with Lloyd George that,

> Scotland is simply tied to the tail of England, and she is denied all initiative. She becomes a dumping ground for some equivalent grant when expenditure is undertaken in England for some purpose which in Scotland is practically uncalled for.[80]

McKinnon Wood, the Scottish Secretary and Sir John Struthers of the SED privately agreed with the Scottish MPs who met Lloyd George. However, publicly the department had to be seen to agree with the Chancellor and thereby face harsh criticism from Scottish MPs such as Munro Ferguson. It seems unlikely that the Scottish MPs did not realise that the SED was constantly arguing with the Treasury but the SED was an easy target. Many of its most outspoken critics were home rulers. The SED's reputation for 'despotism' provided the basis on which prejudices against the department could develop and which home rulers could exploit to the full by suggesting that not only was the SED failing to represent Scottish educational interests but it accepted the Treasury position on every occasion. The SED was attacked by Scottish MPs for failing Scottish education while within Whitehall it was seen by the Treasury as a parochial, institutionalised special interest.

Munro Ferguson was wrong to suggest that the SED was failing to defend Scottish educational interests. Following an address by Henry Keith to Lanarkshire Teachers' Association on 'Scottish Educational Finance' in May 1912 in which this prominent local authority official argued for greater state aid for education,[81] a debate began in which Sir Walter Menzies, Liberal MP for South Lanark attacked Keith in letters to the press arguing that the 'School Boards in Scotland have no shadow of a claim upon the Imperial Treasury for increased grants'.[82] Keith contacted Sir John Struthers about Menzies' letter seeking information. In his reply to Keith's request, Struthers insisted that his letter should be treated as strictly confidential and that any statement Keith made using information supplied by the SED had to be 'on your authority and that I [Struthers] am not to be referred to'.[83] The ensuing debate in the *Scotsman* and *Glasgow Herald*, was between two well informed but irreconcilable viewpoints, mirroring the debate between the Treasury and SED.[84]

The Treasury focussed on the total education grants received by Scotland compared with those for England and Wales while the SED noted the deficiency in the increase in Treasury support for education compared with the increased contributions paid by rates over the preceding fifteen years. But what was most notable about the discussion was not the positions adopted by the protagonists but the manner in which it was publicly conducted. The SED passed on figures and information to a local authority administrator. The Scottish Liberal's complaints about the SED's handling of Scottish education must have exasperated the SED as it struggled to gain more resources from the Treasury but at least provided the background of discontent helpful for the department in making its case.

The Education (Scotland) Act, 1918

The next major attempt to rationalise central government educational finance came in the Education (Scotland) Act, 1918.[85] Scotland was to receive 11/80 of additional Treasury grants for education in England and Wales except so far as these referred to departmental administration, superannuation of teachers, or services for which Scotland already received an equivalent. The base year adopted for calculation was that of 1913–14. It was more than just good fortune that enabled the SED to win 1913–14 as the base year. The Treasury had argued that a more appropriate base would have been that of 1911–12 because after that date Scotland had gained an annual addition of £25,000 fixed contribution set in a Treasury letter in March 1912 under provisions for a superannuation grant in the Education (Scotland), 1908.[86] The Treasury's objection was that though they did not doubt the justice of the SED's case, it had been intended that England and Wales would receive £200,000 annually for similar purposes, but this had not occurred. Therefore they argued that 1911–12, the year preceding the first £25,000 contribution to Scotland, should be adopted as the standard year.[87]

During November and December 1917, the SED and Treasury discussed the matter and 11/80 was accepted by both parties but the standard year was not agreed. Struthers informed Armitrage-Smith, an Assistant Secretary at the Treasury, that the Scottish Secretary was 'very averse in any case to a departure from the principle of the "standard year" [i.e. 1913–14] which he is inclined to regard as fundamental' in response to suggestions that 1911–12 be adopted.[88] Stanley Baldwin, then Financial Secretary to the Treasury, wrote to Munro the following day guaranteeing that Scotland would receive 11/80 of the English and Welsh provision for superannuation of teachers but refused to agree to proposals that would 'give Scotland more'.[89] On December 17, in a manner certain to provoke Treasury anger, the SED published their draft bill that was still the subject of such unreconciled discussion. This was the very day that Armitrage-Smith and Struthers had passed their opposing views to each other. Baldwin's indignation was evident in his very formal letter:

> My Lords [of the Treasury] do not conceive that the Lords of the Committee of Council on Education in Scotland were cognisant of this proceeding which appears to be somewhat lacking in courtesy to this Board.[90]

Attempting to minimise the breach of procedure, and with less formality, Munro insisted that no discourtesy had been intended and maintained that the cabinet had agreed on December 13 to his proposal to put the bill before the Scottish people at the earliest date. Munro would introduce the bill in the Commons the following week.[91] Baldwin sought assurances that Government amendments would be moved but the Bill presented to the Commons on December 17 did not differ fundamentally regarding finance from the Act that was finally passed. In brief exchanges at second reading, there was no intervention when the Scottish Secretary outlined the financial provisions so much in dispute.[92] What had been clause 23 of the original bill defined the standard year as the year ended the 'thirty-first day of March nineteen hundred and fourteen'. The standard year of 1913–14 had been won by the SED.

Just how advantageous to Scotland the 1918 Act was depends on the perspective adopted but the SED's assiduous work in defending the Goschen formula in the inter-war period testifies to its view of Goschen's benefits. The SED in the early 1920s sought means of presenting the figures to suggest that Scotland was not being favourably treated. This was necessary because of the calls for public expenditure cuts made by the Treasury. On the other hand, the SED had problems in Scotland where

Goschen was frequently presented as disadvantageous to Scotland. A familiar dilemma faced the SED. It could not boast of any gains in Scotland for fear of provoking a Treasury or Board of Education backlash. No sooner had the SED finished tackling the potential threat posed by the Treasury than they were doing battle with its critics in Scotland.

A paper prepared in Scotland in 1923 by R.T. Hawkins, private secretary to SED Secretary George MacDonald, presented two different pictures of how Scotland was faring under the Goschen formula arrangements (Table 8.7).[93] The higher Scottish figure in 1913–14 in Table 8.8 was due to three causes. First, Scotland had a higher grant-earning capacity at the time owing to its greater activity in many educational fields. Second, a comparatively larger amount of Local Taxation money was devoted to education in Scotland which England and Wales used for other purposes. Third, until the 1918 Act, Scotland was saved the kind of burden of denominational schools whereas in England such schools were forming a heavy rate charge. The lower Scottish figure for 1920–21 was caused by the earlier effect of improved teachers' the salaries in Scotland as well as matters relating to the transition to the new system. By 1921–22, the system had become more settled. Taking the figures from the 1921 census, a rough calculation was made of expenditure per head of population (Table 8.9). On this basis, Scotland appeared to be doing very well though it should be noted that Scotland's school population was proportionately

Table 8.7   Percentage which receipts from Exchequer bear to total in various years, prepared by SED including Local Taxation monies, 11 April 1923

	England and Wales	Scotland
1913–14	47.0	55.3
1920–21	57.4	54.3
1921–22	56.5	59.9

Table 8.8   Percentage which receipts from Exchequer bear to total in various years, prepared by SED excluding Local Taxation Monies, 11 April, 1923

	England and Wales	Scotland
1913–14	44.1	50.5
1920–21	56.0	51.3
1921–22	55.2	57.3

Table 8.9   Expenditure per head of population from public funds using 1921 census

	England and Wales £	Scotland
1913–14	0.806	0.959
1921–22	2.065	2.507

Source: NAS, SOE 6/1/26.

larger than that in England and Wales. The author of the paper concluded that it could safely be said that Scotland in 1921–22 and 1922–23 was gaining a 'slightly better proportion of expenditure than England was receiving in aid of its educational expenditure'. However, he was concerned that a further fall in English expenditure might wipe out Scotland's advantage.[94]

Comparisons of Treasury contributions to education north and south of the border are only one measure of whether Scotland had grounds for complaint or reason to be pleased. Such a measure ignores the extent to which Scottish resources could meet Scotland's needs; if Scotland was much poorer and had a large school population there would be a case for a greater Treasury contribution. Another paper prepared by Hawkins in 1926 detailed figures and arguments demonstrating that set out to show that Scotland had no grounds for complaint respecting educational finance (Table 8.10).

Scotland lagged behind England in terms of the numbers of teachers and Scottish teachers were required to have better qualifications. The Scottish standard year figure of £2,306,835 was £454,578 above the 11/80 proportion of the English and Welsh base. Though Scotland had few grounds for complaint regarding the standard year figure, the advantages decreased as legislation for England and Wales further reduced the gap in educational provision on either side of the border. Problems for the SED arose in the course of time when the standard year became, as the Goschen formula fraction before, the manner of determining how fair the Treasury was in allocating expenditure. The proportion,

Scottish Standard Year Grants: English & Welsh Standard Year Grants

was bound to be larger than the proportion,

Scottish Grants from Early 1920s: English & Welsh Grants from the early 1920s

Table 8.10   Note marked 'confidential' initialled R.T.H. (Hawkins), 23/3/26

	England	Scotland	Scottish figure as % of English figure
11/80ths	80	11	13.75
Standard Year (1913–14)	£13,470,966	£2,306,835	17.1
Population (1911 census)	36,070,492	4,760,904	13.2
Scholars average enrolment (1914)	6,288,103	857,000 approximately	13.63
Scholars as % of population	17.4	18.0	–
Teachers (1914)	174,502	20,800 approximately	11.92
Scholars mainly average attendance (1914)	5,569,805	765,621	13.75
Scholars per teacher (1914)	31.9	36.8	–

Source: NAS, SOE, 6/1/26.

The Goschen myth

General expenditure was not based on the 11/80s formula. Sir Henry Craik MP who had first-hand experience having been Secretary of the Scotch Education Department from 1885 to 1904 failed to stem the tendency amongst Scottish MPs of using Goschen as a measurement of the fairness of changes in Scotland's share of public expenditure. According to Craik in July 1909, Goschen had told him:

> I am not going to lay down rules which can be made the foundation of serious encroachments on the Treasury. It is your business to find out where the shoe pinches in regard to the Education Grant, what are the difficulties, and how much is wanted in each case, and then you can come to me and ask for money, and we will see whether it can be granted.[95]

Every case for increasing an element in educational expenditure was 'separately examined' Craik maintained. Three years later he was more explicit:

> Many Hon. Members are apt to speak as though the proper proportion were that proportion which arose on one occasion, and was

invented only for a special emergency, namely, eleven eightieths. The sooner Hon. Members disabuse their minds of any lingering belief in that proportion the better it will be for the financial stability of education. It was accidently taken up in the year 1890, when Mr Goschen's Local Government Taxation Bill was first brought forward. It was taken up because for the moment there was no other course to be pursued. It has been repudiated over and over again by the Treasury; it has been, and ought to be, repudiated by the Scottish authorities as well.[96]

In 1913 Major John Hope, Unionist MP for Midlothian, asked whether there was 'any agreement with the Treasury that, in respect of Grants in aid of local expenditure, Scotland should be entitled to £11 for every £80 which England and Wales receive?' Scottish Secretary McKinnon Wood replied that 'no universal rule relating to Grants for local expenditure' existed and that the 11/80 fraction was 'an approximate figure, which is sometimes used as a criterion'.[97] Nevertheless, many Scottish Liberal MPs were grateful that Goschen had been used in whatever way it had, as it could be used as a benchmark of financial fairness. This formula became the measure used and helped, by its nature as a proportion of the English and Welsh figure, to rigidify the demarcation of Scotland and England. On the other hand, however, it meant that Scottish educational progress would be tied to England's. This did not please Craik who criticised those MPs whose,

> endless and tiresome comparisons of the exact proportions between England and Scotland are absolutely wide off the mark. We ask to be paid for what we have done educationally, not by any comparison with England. If we have earned twice as much as England, we still put forward the claim which I trust the right hon. Gentlemen will advance on our behalf.[98]

By 1918, Goschen, which had initially been introduced as a means of allocating probate duty between Scotland, Ireland and England and Wales in the vain hope of separating imperial and local finance, had become a benchmark of financial justice for many Scots. It did not and could not reflect Scotland's changing needs and resources. Neither did Goschen represent a method of allocation clearly linked to anything other than a fairly crude account of contributions to the Exchequer in the late 1880s. Goschen was an arbitrary fraction which linked Scottish educational developments with those in England and Wales. By the outbreak of the First World War any Scottish distinctiveness and advance over the southern neighbour which had once justifiably given Scotland an enviable and independent education tradition was drastically diminished by Scottish education being linked to Whitehall considerations. Innovations were now less likely in Scotland. England and Wales, as a consequence of size, became the base and the engine of educational change. Scotland would react to English developments. Occasionally, the SED might win victories but these were bound to be concerned with the calculation of Scotland's 'equivalent'. The SED could not hope to lead the way if, as was always expected by the Treasury, it would provoke similar demands south of the border.

Defending Goschen's advantage

The inter-war period was marked by severe economic crises. The immediate post-war boom soon gave way to financial difficulties resulting in an austerity programme. The Geddes cuts were imposed on Government Departments in the early 1920s. Public expenditure and state intervention was reined back after a long period of growth. Ten years on, following the international crisis after the Wall Street Crash, the May Committee performed a function similar to Geddes by inquiring into possible public expenditure cuts. Coping with retrenchment and determining how these changes should be distributed territorially raised as many thorny issues as had the determination of Scotland's equivalent in increases in expenditure.

A note written by a Treasury official in 1939 expressed surprise that the Geddes and May Committees, which had investigated ways of cutting public expenditure, had both failed to consider whether some alteration in the Goschen formula would effect a 'justifiable economy in the vote for Scottish Education'.[99] But the failure to challenge Goschen was not so surprising. Its main use, to determine changes in the education budget, had been settled in the Education (Scotland) Act of 1918 only a short period before Geddes was set his task of finding means of cutting expenditure. It had been used in some form or other from 1888 and reaching agreement on an alternative would probably have proved too much trouble. The major issue of contention had not been the Goschen formula but the base year. The backlash from Scotland would have been considerable. Some minor changes in the formula which might have been agreed would have had a fairly marginal impact overall on public expenditure. Targeting English public expenditure and anticipating equivalent savings in Scotland was a simpler approach.

There were fears in the SED that the arrangement would be challenged. In October 1921, John Struthers, SED Secretary, urged officials to prepare a defence of the Goschen principle in case it should be challenged by the Geddes Committee.[100] In a memorandum in December, Struthers presented a defence of the formula to the Scottish Secretary and warned that experience proved that the 'maintenance of this principle is essential if justice is to be done to Scotland'.[101] In this case, Goschen was not challenged. Struthers may have been responding to suggestions in the Scottish press that Scotland's claim should not be based on the expenditure of another country but in Government he defended the practice. Further trouble emerged sixteen months later when Hawkins, an SED official, reported that the Educational Institute of Scotland was raising the 'familiar cry of being "dragged at the heels of England" in connection with Grants'.[102]

In private meetings and through its contacts with local government, the SED attempted to convince its Scottish detractors that it was dangerous to raise the issue of the Goschen formula. Hawkins reports a meeting he had with a group of MP, Messrs Pringle, Cowan and Dickson, in April 1923 at which he impressed upon them the 'obvious dangers of bringing the arrangements too closely under review at the present time'.[103] Matters were not always so simply resolved. Col. Patrick Blair, the Scottish Unionist Party's political secretary, wrote to the SED Secretary in 1927 requesting information which Unionist MPs could confront home rulers with.[104] In reply, MacDonald reiterated a point he had made earlier that day to F.C. Thomson, Scottish Unionist MP. It was,

> not too wise to emphasise unduly the advantages of our present financial arrangement. What may be merely a salutary reminder for home rule extremists in Scotland might easily produce awkward reactions in Whitehall.[105]

Having written this, MacDonald still supplied Blair with over two pages of figures and arguments to make the case that Scotland was being treated favourably. Significantly, the statement concluded by quoting a letter which appeared in the *Scotsman* in March 1924 written by Henry Keith, a leading local authority official.[106] What he did not state was how Keith had arrived at his conclusions. Not for the first time, Keith had gained information privately from central government. As noted earlier, he had used SED supplied statistics in 1912 to argue for increased Government grants. Nor was this the last occasion when Keith acted as the public voice for the SED. Eight years later, in 1932, he brought an issue of the *Scottish Educational Journal* (SEJ) to the attention of Hawkins at the SED.[107] In an editorial on Scottish education grants, the SEJ argued against the 'financial nexus that binds us' and asked for an enquiry into the 11/80 formula.[108]

A likely consequence might well have been closer alignment with English education rather than greater autonomy. In a private letter to Keith from MacDonald in March 1923, the SED Secretary was certain that a departure from the existing arrangements would not mean the abandonment of Goschen but that Scotland would be cut down to a 'total of 11/80ths of the English Grant – in other words, to deprive us of the advantage of the standard year.'[109] Further correspondence between Keith and the SED in 1923, which at one point was almost on a daily basis, gives an indication of the SED's position. The SED strongly opposed measures which might involve it adopting certain practices of the English Board of Education. MacDonald's concern was that the Board's methods of forcing economy from the centre would damage Scottish education. As far as he was concerned, the fault lay not with the English local authorities but pressure exerted by the Treasury and Board of Education.[110] In May 1927, Ronald McNeill, Financial Secretary to the Treasury informed a Scottish MP that the Goschen formula was,

> now very favourable to Scotland as it gives her 11 to England's 80, whereas on recent population figures the true ratio would be 10.08 to England's 80. Moreover, in the case of many very important grants, for example, the General Aid Grant to Education the system in force is more favourable to Scotland than even the plain Goschen proportion would be.[111]

There was a view that Scotland did not benefit as much as it might under a different financial dispensation, at least as far as certain items of expenditure was concerned. George Pottinger has suggested that in 1932 Sir Archibald Sinclair, when Scottish Secretary, considered that Scotland might do better by getting a grant based on need rather than Goschen.[112] However, the context and strange wording of a letter to an SED official written by Sinclair suggests that he was probably only considering abandoning Goschen in one particular case.

> I should not think I am right in saying that the Department would think it undesirable to prefer any such claim for the reason that the preservation of the eleven-eightieths grant is the paramount consideration in Scottish educational finance and that we ought not on

our own initiative to suggest any weakening on or exception to that principle.[113]

The actual use of Goshen was fairly limited. Education was the most important item of expenditure determined by the formula. Neil MacLean had asked a Parliamentary Question in May 1935 seeking information on the application of Goschen in each year from 1930. The information which was presented to the Commons demonstrated how limited the application of Goschen actually was (Table 8.11).

In a letter responding to Nationalist criticisms, a Treasury official summed up the situation regarding the application of Goschen:

> In general, Scotland's share of the expenditure on social and other services is, wherever possible, determined not by that formula but either by her ability to qualify for grants which are not specifically limited in amount (for example, housing subsidies) or in the light of all concrete and relevant data (for example, the block grants under the Local Government Act, 1929, and the Local Government (General Exchequer Contributions) Act, 1933). The Goschen formula is now only adopted in exceptional cases where there is an absence of accurate data and where a rough and ready division between the two countries is required to be made.[114]

The former Chancellor of the Exchequer and Scottish Unionist MP, Sir Robert Horne expressed his outrage at the use of Goschen for allocating distressed areas grant to local authorities. At second reading of the Unemployment Assistance (Temporary Provisions) (No. 2) Bill, Horne accused the Treasury of segregating Scotland from England and treating them as different countries in the case of what was, he maintained, a universal question. He argued that Goschen had 'no relation to the question of unemployment or the need of one country against the other':

> Suppose that half the unemployment was in Scotland and half in England, it would be ridiculous to say that Scotland was to get 11/80ths. When it came to the distribution of this £500,000 there were four distressed areas in this country. Suppose that an arrangement had been made, a rough division equally among those distressed areas, Scotland would have got £125,000. If a calculation had been made as to what it had been costing Scotland at that time to support its able-bodied unemployed the figure would have been between £160,000

Table 8.11 Statement of services in Scotland to which the Goschen formula applies with expenditure on those services in the financial years 1930–34

Vote	1930	1931	1932	1933	1934
Public education					
i. Part of General Aid Grant[a]	4,163,145	4,122,233	3,645,320	3,431,912	3,623,206
ii. Grant for teachers' superannuation[b]	718,886	777,312	829,232	930,772	975,235
Department of Health, Scotland					
i. Housing (Rural Authorities) Act, 1931[c]					3,055
ii. Rural Water Supplies Act, 1934[d]				232	662
Department of Agriculture, Scotland					
Grants for scholarships for sons and daughters of agricultural workers etc.	2,223	2,174	1,692	1,958	1,918
Grants in respect of Employment Schemes (Necessitous Areas) (Scotland)[e]	39,341	16,196	4,463		
Grants to Local Authorities in Distressed Areas (Scotland)				60,000	55,000

a The Exchequer Grant for Education in Scotland calculated in accordance with section 21 (1) of the Education (Scotland) Act, 1918 consists of two parts (i) a sum equal to the total grant for Scottish Education (with certain exceptions) in 1913 and (ii) 11/80 of the amount by which the grant for Education in England and Wales in any year exceeds the grant in 1913 (with exceptions as in the case of Scottish basic grant). The figures given in the statement above relate only to (ii) the figure of expenditure under (i) for each of the financial years 1930–1934 was £2,306,835.

b The Goschen formula applies not only to Exchequer payments in respect of teachers' superannuation in Scotland but also to Exchequer receipts. The Exchequer receives from Scotland 11/80ths of the superannuation contributions paid by teachers and their employers in England and Wales. The payments made to the Exchequer under this head were:

1930	1931	1932	1933	1934
£728,745	£705,926	£664,255	£675,219	£717,035

c The Housing (Rural Authorities) Act, 1931, limited the contributions to be made by the Ministry of Health and Department of Health for Scotland to 80/91 and 11/91 respectively of a total sum of £2,000,000. Actual expenditure is shown in columns 5 and 6.

d The Rural Water Supplies Act, 1934 made available for Scotland £137,000, being 11/80 of the sum off £1,000,000 made available for England and Wales. Actual expenditure up to 31 March 1935, is shown in column 6.

e The sum of £60,000 was provided in 1930 for Grants in respect of employment schemes (Necessitous Areas) Scotland and revoted in 1931. Actual expenditure shown in columns 3, 4 and 5. The amount shown in columns 3, 4 and 5 were borne by Civil Contingencies Fund and included in the 1933 and 1934 Votes for Repayments to that Fund, this procedure being required by the fact that expenditure was delayed until a date when the Necessitous Areas vote had ceased to exist.

Source: Hansard, Commons, vol. 302, 27 May 1935, cols. 778–80; PRO, T160/796, part 3.

and £170,000. Upon this 11/80ths basis Scotland got £60,000, and, as I have said, this miserable, unjust grant perpetuates itself in legislation which we had in 1934 and the legislation of today.[115]

Horne made his argument in terms of justice for Scotland. He found allies in Davie Kirkwood and Neil Maclean, the latter invoking the emotive argument that Goschen had not been applied 'when men from the shipyards and the fields were wanted to go into the Army during the War'.[116] Sir Godfrey Collins, the Scottish Secretary had a difficult task in trying to convince the Scottish backbenchers that Scotland was not being unjustly treated and resorted to referring to other items of expenditure:

> I say nothing here to my Scottish colleagues of the fact that the Post Office might say that because of the heavy cost of delivering letters to the Outer Hebrides the rates should be raised, but let me remind them of the extra sums that Scotland gets under the Housing Acts and suggest that if a strict analysis is made between what Scotland is entitled to get and what she does get, it will not be an advantage to the people of Scotland.[117]

Horne had described the application of the distressed areas grants as resulting in an 'extraordinary mosaic of irregularities'.[118] This could equally be said of the application of Goschen and the pattern of methods of determining Scottish public expenditure generally.

Conclusion

In March 1939 a note written by a Treasury official explained the situation regarding the Goschen formula,

> The Treasury view on the Goschen formula has been that there is certainly no justification for increasing Scotland's share, and that wherever possible, the formula should be disregarded and Scotland should receive grants in particular cases appropriate to her actual needs, rather than a grant calculated in accordance with a formula which was introduced as early as 1888. It is clear, however, that any change in the formula which meant that Scotland received less money for the services which are at present provided for on this basis would call forth loud protest from certain elements in Scotland.[119]

It was more trouble to try to dismantle the system than to keep it. By the outbreak of the Second World War, through a process of messy incrementalism, Scotland's share of public expenditure had come to be determined by a number of different methods. The Goschen formula could not be described as rational either in its constitution or its application. Few people seemed to be able to recall the original application of Goschen. Fewer still could explain why it should have come to be used as it was. But it had come to represent a powerful precedent.

9

Scottish Office Ministers

One of the claims made for having a Scottish Secretary in the 1880s was that it would give Scotland a direct say in decision-making. Anything short of a Cabinet post was thought to be inadequate. But the office of Secretary for Scotland that was established, as distinct from a Secretary of State, did not carry with it automatic membership of the Cabinet. The Duke of Richmond and Gordon accepted the office in 1885 in exchange for his previous office as President of the Board of Trade with no alteration in his status as a member of Salisbury's Cabinet. In the immediate years that followed, despite this precedent, Scottish Secretaries were not assured of a place in the Cabinet. The Earl of Dalhousie, the Marquess of Lothian and, for a period, A.J. Balfour were excluded from the Cabinet. Balfour's accession to the Cabinet was facilitated by his undoubted abilities rather than by virtue of the office. From 1892, War Cabinets apart, Scottish Secretaries were always appointed to the Cabinet.

There was some controversy surrounding the position of the Scottish Office during the First World War. In 1915 reports in the *Times* and *Morning Post* that the Scottish Secretary should be dropped from the Cabinet for the duration of the war incited Thomas McKinnon Wood to write to the Prime Minister protesting that such a proposition would be a 'degradation of the national position' and would make the efficient discharge of his duties difficult because of this 'inferior position' allotted to the office.[1] Agreement that the Scottish Secretary should remain in the Cabinet, though not the War Cabinet, was confirmed in a letter sent to McKinnon Wood from John Gulland, Parliamentary Secretary to the Treasury, following a conversation with Asquith.[2] Despite his comments on the importance of the Scottish Office, McKinnon Wood in July 1916 accepted the Financial Secretaryship to the Treasury and Chancellorship of the Duchy of Lancaster and told Asquith that he felt that the Treasury was the most important department and required two Cabinet Ministers. While he did not 'undervalue' the Scottish Office, Asquith had informed McKinnon Wood that it had 'little to do with the conduct of war'.[3]

The Scottish Secretary was invariably a junior member in the Cabinet. This was not only because most Scottish Secretaries were fairly unimpressive individuals but because of the nature of the office. In Salisbury's Cabinets, the Scottish Secretary was there on sufferance and the post was regarded by successive Prime Ministers and other Ministers as a backwater. If some talented individual happened to be appointed then he (and it always was a 'he') might manage to impress his colleagues and lead on to a more senior post, as occurred in the case of A.J. Balfour.

There was no formal ranking within the Cabinet until 1929, though some idea of rank was clear and the Scottish Secretary was always seen as a very junior member. In 1929, after Labour had been in office for a few months, a list of Ministers was published which was intended to rank them in terms of political importance. The Scottish Secretary was listed second from the bottom of nineteen Cabinet Ministers.[4] There might be shuffling around from time to time depending on which party was in power, which issues were at the forefront of politics or what the Prime Minister perceived as important. But there is no reason to believe that the Scottish Office was ever anything other than a very lowly Cabinet position under any party, Prime Minister or circumstance.

Raising the status of the Office

There were constant murmurings of discontent that the office remained only a Secretaryship prior to the First World War and demands for the office to be upgraded to a Secretaryship of State became more intense following the war. Successive Governments from the end of the war favoured a measure to increase the status of the office and, initially anyway, also to increase the remuneration of the Scottish Secretary. In December 1918, Robert Munro, Scottish Secretary, wrote to the Prime Minister and Bonar Law on a 'matter which I regard as of the first importance to Scotland'.[5] He appealed to the Prime Minister to support legislation to 'elevate the office of the Secretary for Scotland into that of a Secretary of State', and maintained that the growth in importance and multiplicity of duties made the 'restricting provisions in the Act of 1885 an anachronism'.[6] Later, as Lord Justice Clerk for Scotland, Munro expressed his dissatisfaction with the status of the Scottish Secretaryship. In a speech he stressed the national dimension of the

Table 9.1 Background, incumbencies and future offices of Scottish Secretaries, 1885–1939

Date of appointment	Scottish Secretary	Education School Uni.	Duration of office (months)	Higher office attained
17/8/1885	Duke of Richmond and Gordon	Winchester, Oxford	6	
8/2/1886	George Trevelyan	Harrow, Cambridge	2	
5/4/1886	Duke of Dalhousie	Private	4	
5/8/1886	A.J. Balfour	Eton, Cambridge	7	Chief Secretary for Ireland; First Lord of the Treasury; Prime Minister
11/3/1887	Marquis of Lothian	Eton, Oxford	65	
18/8/1892	George Trevelyan	Harrow, Cambridge	34	
29/6/1895	Lord Balfour of Burleigh	Eton, Oxford	100	
9/1/1903	A.G. Murray	Harrow, Cambridge	16	
2/2/1905	Marquis of Linlithgow	Eton	10	
10/10/1905	J. Sinclair (Lord Pentland)	Edinburgh Academy, Sandhurst	74	
13/2/1912	T. McKinnon Wood	Mill Hill, London	53	Duchy of Lancaster/Financial Secretary to Treasury
9/6/1916	H. Tennant	Eton, Cambridge	5	
10/12/1916	Robert Munro	Aberdeen Grammer, Edinburgh	70	
24/10/1922	Viscount Novar	Private, Sandhurst	15	
22/1/1924	Willie Adamson	Elementary	10	
6/11/1924	Sir John Gilmour	Glenalmond, Edinburgh and Cambridge	55	Minister for Agriculture; Home Secretary
7/6/1929	Willie Adamson	Elementary	26	
25/8/1931	Sir A. Sinclair	Eton, Sandhurst	13	Secretary of State of Air
28/9/1932	Sir Godgrey Collins	H.M.S. Britannia	49	
29/10/1936	Walter Elliot	Glasgow Academy, Glasgow	19	Minister of Health
16/5/1938	John Colville	Charterhouse, Cambridge	24	

Source: Chris Cook and Brendan Keith, British Historical Facts, 1830–1900, pp. 36–47 plus private papers etc.

office: 'The Secretary for Scotland, moreover, represents a nation. And yet he is not a Secretary of State, and his emoluments remain those of a minor Minister.'[7] Giving his support to those who were campaigning for the elevation in the status of the Scottish Secretary to that of a Secretary of State, Munro felt it would be wrong to press the matter on the Government 'as an urgent reform' but wanted to record his opinion that the 'present arrangement is not fair to the holder of the office of Secretary; it is not fair to the staff: above all, it is not fair to Scotland'.[8] Inertia, opposition from those who saw themselves as upholders of the historic English constitution and the assumed need to increase the salary of the office commensurate with an increase in status appear to have been reasons for the delay in passing the necessary legislation to upgrade the office to one of His Majesty's principal Secretaries of State.

By the outbreak of the First World War, the office had evolved from being what was an attempt to placate Scottish sensibilities into a department of state with a panoply of administrative responsibilities. It had gained new responsibilities while its status in government remained the same. To a large extent this was the consequence of the individuals who held the office more than anything else. That the Scottish Secretary was not a member of the War Cabinet undoubtedly lessened his potential influence but this was only part of the picture. Even over those matters which were his responsibility, particularly respecting the unrest on Clydeside, the Scottish Secretary 'played an extraordinarily limited part', as one account of Red Clydeside noted.[9] McKinnon Wood, Tennant and Munro, who successively held the office during the war, were 'unimportant figures who had little to say for themselves'[10] on important matters, Ian McLean has remarked, the Scottish Office 'was simply by-passed'.[11] Probably the most notable and lasting contribution to the politics of this period by these Scottish Secretaries was their belief, in particular Munro's, in the revolutionary nature of the Clydeside unrest. Munro's Cabinet memorandum of January 1919 in which he maintained that it was 'a misnomer to call the situation in Glasgow a strike – it was a Bolshevist rising'[12] encouraged exaggerated fears within the Government and fostered a myth which has had significance for Scottish politics which linger yet.

In August 1919 the Government did introduce a bill which would have increased the number of Secretaries of State, and transferred the powers and duties of the Scottish Secretary to a principal Secretary of State and removed the 'statutory limitation on the salaries of certain Ministers'[13] but it was not proceeded with beyond second reading. The following year a Select Committee on the Remuneration of Ministers reported in favour of a classification of offices which would have raised the Scottish Secretary, as well as the President of the Board of Education, to first class rank with a pay of £5000 per annum. The Committee, which included six Scottish Members – Charles Barrie, Sir Godfrey Collins, Sir Henry Dalziel, Sir Harry Hope, James Hogge and John Robertson – amongst its fifteen members, noted that a former Lord Advocate 'on being appointed Secretary for Scotland, has had to sacrifice £3000 of his salary, the superior position being paid less than the lower'.[14] This encouraged agitation for the enhancement in the status of the office.

However, by no means was there the same degree of support for an increase in the salary of the office as there was for the establishment of the office of a Secretaryship of State for Scotland. After the war, representations were made in Parliament and a memorial signed by forty-seven MPs in April 1919 was sent to the Prime Minister. However, Scottish Members who raised the issue were divided as to whether the salary of the Scottish Secretary should be increased.[15] Finally, in December 1925, after a series of Parliamentary Questions over nearly six years, Prime Minister Baldwin announced that the office would be upgraded but that there would be no alteration in the salary attached to the office.[16] During this period, resolutions had been passed by various bodies in Scotland in support of the movement to raise the Secretary for Scotland's status. From Kirkwall Town Council to the South of Scotland Chamber of Commerce and from Edinburgh Conservative Working Men's Association to the Scottish Liberal Federation's Executive, Scotland appeared to be united on this matter as it had been in 1884 in favour of the establishment of the office. Once more, the Convention of Royal Burghs played a prominent part in the campaign, passing a resolution addressed to the Prime Minister favouring a Secretaryship of State in April 1919.[17] In March 1924, a deputation from the Convention met with the Secretary for Scotland, William Adamson and argued for an increase in the office's status – somewhat perversely the Treasury reporter who took notes of the meeting included the 'Secretary of State for Scotland' amongst those present.[18] Adamson expressed his agreement with the deputation and suggested that they should approach the Prime Minister and Scottish Members.

A further deputation met Baldwin in February 1925 in the House of Commons when the Prime Minister stated that he would examine the question 'without delay'.[19] Support for the Secretaryship of State also came from Lord Rosebery, the 'official progenitor of the Department',[20] in June 1922.[21] Reginald MacLeod of MacLeod, Permanent Under Secretary at the Scottish Office from 1902–09, wrote to Sir John Gilmour in 1924, on the latter's appointment as Scottish Secretary, urging the new Scottish Secretary to 'get the S. for S. made one of the Secretaries of State. It is preposterous that this should be denied'.[22] Files of the Nationalist organisation, the Scots Secretariat, include cuttings showing that even the *Times of India* and the *Shanghai Times* sided with Scotland in its claim for a Secretaryship of State.[23]

In April 1926, the Government introduced the Secretaries of State Bill which received the Royal Assent in July that year. Opposition to the bill was formal and was not pressed to a division, probably because it did not propose to increase the salary of the office and because the Government had negotiated with its opponents before the bill was introduced. Five years before, in April 1921, it had been agreed in Cabinet that the Government should undertake to pass a bill on condition that it was unopposed and that 'negotiations with possible opponents should be entered into . . . with a view to the Bill being treated as unopposed'.[24] The financial stringency imposed after Geddes and the divisions amongst those who wanted to upgrade the office regarding remuneration meant that the legislation was not passed until 1926 and was really more concerned with styles and appearances than substance. The opposition of two traditional Conservatives, Commander Bellairs and Sir John Marriot, the latter being an historian at Worcester College, Oxford was not pressed to a vote. The essence of their opposition lay in their fear that increasing the numbers of those holding the office of Secretaryship of State might effect 'some little dissipation of its ancient dignity'.[25]

The support for upgrading the office was considerable in Scotland. A campaign was waged over the seven years up to 1926. The Scottish Secretaries had been openly in favour of the proposal and made their positions clear to other members of the Government, deputations and the public. The wartime activities of the Scottish Secretaries had not augured well for an early increase in the office's status. The reaction to the upgrading of the office suggested that something worthwhile had been won. Walter Elliot remarked during the Bothwell by-election in March 1926 that the Government had given the 'country a status unknown since the '45' while 'Home Rule and other associations had been talking'.[26] Following the Prime Minister's announcement, Sir Henry Keith, chairman of the Convention of Royal Burghs, welcomed the proposed change at the Convention's annual general meeting in April 1926 as one of historic importance:

It is the restoration of the Scottish peoples' Chief Secretary to that equality of privilege and dignity in the Councils of State of which he ... has been arbitrarily and unconstitutionally deprived since the Rebellion of 1745.[27]

Elliot's speech during the Bothwell bye-election and Keith's statement read now as exaggerated praise for a fairly inconsequential change. Both appear to have tapped a strain of Scottish sentiment suggesting that their much aggrieved country was at last to be restored to its rightful position – by adding 'of State' to the title of the office of Secretary for Scotland. Even the salary of the office did not rise in 1926. What is most significant were the political symbolism and historical allusions which were attached to the upgrading of the office.

Salary and status

There were hardly any changes in the salaries of Government Ministers over the period from 1885 to the First World War. When the Duke of Richmond and Gordon accepted the post of Scottish Secretary in 1885 with a salary of £2000 per annum this had meant no change in remuneration from his previous position as President of the Board of Trade. By 1914, the Scottish Secretary still received £2000 but the President of the Board of Trade and the President of the Local Government Board had been awarded salaries of £5000 from 1910–11, in line with most other Cabinet Ministers. When it had been decided to raise the salary of the President of the Board of Trade, Asquith stated his personal opinion that 'it would be an invidious thing that the President of the Local Government Board should not be in the same position'.[28] Notably, the Prime Minister did not expect to provoke the envy of other members of the Cabinet who still received £2000 per annum, including the Scottish Secretary and the Lord President of the Council.

A dilemma which critics of the office faced in attempting to make their case for improvements in the Scottish administration was that they found that the traditional method of censuring Government, by moving a reduction in the salary of the office, would run contrary to one of the demands they were making. John Stirling Ainsworth MP expressed this dilemma in June 1911 when he explained that though he wanted to criticise the Scottish Secretary he had not ventured to move a reduction in the salary simply because he felt that it was already too low.[29] This had not prevented earlier moves to reduce the remuneration of the office by the more radical Members who felt that if uniformity was desirable then the higher salaries should be cut to the lower rate. A.C. Morton MP expressed this opinion in 1910 when the salary of the President of the

Local Government Board was raised from £3000 to £5000. Another Liberal Member, Lees Smith stated in the same debate that the salary of £5000 was suitable 'at a time when Ministers of the Crown were expected to be what is called Society' and asked 'why should we, the Liberal Party, expect our Parliamentary leaders to take their standard of life from the wealthy and ostentatious classes?'[30]

The salaries of Scotland's law officers rose over the period up to the First World War. The Lord Advocate's salary rose from £3238 to £5000 per annum and the Scottish Solicitor-General received £2000 compared with £995 in 1880.[31] Though the Scottish Secretary was the senior Minister, the remuneration for the post was less than half the salary of the Lord Advocate and by 1914 the junior law officer for Scotland, the Solicitor General was on the same rate as the Scottish Secretary. When the salaries of the Lord Advocate and Solicitor General had been raised in 1885, James Weir MP asked the Chancellor of the Exchequer whether an increase in the salary of the Scottish Secretary could be expected, comparing the Scottish Secretary's less favourable position with the Chief Secretary for Ireland, who received £2225 more and also had an official residence. Harcourt's answer was simple. He had not received an application on the subject from the Scottish Secretary and suggested that it would 'depend upon who, in the future, may be the Secretary for Scotland',[32] referring perhaps to the prospects of a General Election, which was to occur only four months later.

In addition to his salary, the Lord Advocate was able to earn much from legal work so that the promotion of Scotland's senior law officer to the Secretaryship for Scotland could mean a very substantial decrease in salary. This was pointed out to the Prime Minister by Graham Murray in October 1903 when the latter was offered the Scottish Office. Murray's problems with the offer were not limited to the fact that he would lose his salary of £5000 and the possibility of continuing to earn an additional £2000 from legal fees in exchange for a salary of £2000 as Scottish Secretary, but also that he had already fought five elections and could not 'dip into capital forever' for this purpose.[33] His problem was compounded by his fear that by leaving law he might lose his legal practice which he saw as his security in the event of the Conservatives losing the General Election. Accepting that his age would make the prospect of senior Cabinet office unlikely, Murray proposed that a number of peers might be considered for the post but was not enthusiastic about any of them and concluded that he could only accept the Secretaryship on condition that he should be considered available for judicial appointment. The appointment of Murray the following day as Scottish

Secretary would appear to confirm that his condition was the 'admissible stipulation', of which he had been uncertain in his letter. This was confirmed by Murray's remark, in a letter to Henry Craik in November 1903, that he viewed his Secretaryship as 'only temporary' and that he intended to return to the law.[34] The judicial vacancy in early 1905 which provided the realisation of Murray's ambition with his appointment as Lord President of the Court of Session re-opened the problem for Prime Minister Balfour which Murray's Scottish Secretaryship had solved.

Baldwin informed a deputation from the Royal Burghs, published by the Convention in 1925:

> So long as human nature is what it is, a higher paid office would receive higher consideration, and an underpaid office would be apt to be regarded as an inferior one: so, from the point of view of salary, and, indeed, on the main point, he was very much in agreement with the deputation.[35]

However, from the second reading of the Ministries and Secretaries Bill in the Commons in August 1919 when Scottish Liberals Wedgewood Benn and James Hogge argued against an increase in the remuneration of the Scottish Secretary,[36] it was clear that any increase in salary would be met with stronger opposition than any move to raise the office's constitutional status.

In 1929–30, the Select Committee on the Remuneration of Ministers had considered the position of the Scottish Secretary, amongst others, though it was mainly concerned with the Prime Minister's salary. In light of the financial problems facing the Government, it concluded that only the Prime Minister should receive an increased salary, despite the evidence of both Stanley Baldwin and Ramsay MacDonald who recognised the inadequacy of the Scottish Secretary's pay.[37] In March 1936, Sir John Gilmour received a letter from Robert Bruce, editor of the *Glasgow Herald*, in which the question of the salary of the Scottish Secretary was raised:

> my recollection may be faulty, but am I not right in thinking that when your office was raised to that of a Secretaryship of State it was understood that the salary would also be raised – not during your term of office but during that of your successor?[38]

Gilmour's response is not recorded but over a decade after the office became a Secretaryship of State the salary was finally raised. Without the campaign and without the fanfare of success which had accompanied the upgrading of the office in 1926, the remittance paid to the Scottish Secretary was increased under the Ministers of the Crown Act, 1937.

The multifunctional Scottish Minister

H.J. Hanham made reference to the 'passivity' of the pre-1914 Scottish Office. This passivity, he maintained was 'intentional, and arose from the concept of the Secretary for Scotland as a grandee. It was not that the Secretary for Scotland had no work to do, as the Duke of Richmond feared would be the case when he took the office in 1885. But the work he had to do was essentially that of co-ordinator.'[39] There is much truth in this comment. Having to cope with the statutory and non-statutory duties, ensured that managerialism would be the Office's most obvious feature. Ranging from initiating and leading the Small Landholders Act through Parliament creating the Board of Agriculture to acting as a mediator in the inter-Church discussions,[40] the Scottish Secretary may not have had much time to devote to particular matters. However, much legislation was passed in the field of education, major reforms of local government took place and during the most interesting incumbency, that of John Sinclair's, there was a long struggle to pass the Small Landholders (Scotland) Act which created the Board of Agriculture for Scotland and a system of small landholding in Scotland. The Liberal Governments in which Sinclair served were remarkable for the passage of fairly radical measures, though in the Scottish Office most of the enthusiasm for change seemed to be devoted to land legislation, though progressive measures were passed in education. The Education (Scotland) Act, 1908 was to a large extent a consolidating piece of legislation, establishing an Education (Scotland) Fund in place of various other funds, though it did give a broader and fuller interpretation to the scope of education.

The lack of innovation in the legislative enactments of successive Scottish Secretaries up to 1914 may be accounted for by the essentially 'co-ordinating' role of the Scottish Office, as suggested by Hanham. Additionally, and a common criticism of the office, the Secretary headed many boards. James MacPherson's speech at the second reading of the Government of Scotland Bill in 1914 expressed dissatisfaction with this aspect of the administration:

> Except my right Hon. Friend the Prime Minister, there is no one in modern politics who is so comparable to Atlas as my right Hon.

Friend the Secretary for Scotland. The whole of Scotland is upon his broad shoulders alone. He is a sort of political Pooh-bah. Land, law, lunacy, local government, agriculture, prisons, housing, roads, the Board of Agriculture, and a host of other things he has to administer, not in Scotland, not with the aid of a Scottish Board, but 400 miles away.[41]

Other home rulers had been equally critical of the Secretary's wide-ranging powers: John Gulland argued that sufficient attention had not been paid to administrative work because there was no Under Secretary in the office;[42] and in 1902 James Weir had accused Lord Balfour of Burleigh of fogetting his responsiblities for the many boards which he headed.[43] However, the most perceptive appraisal of the office's extensive scope came from Robert Munro who served as Scottish Secretary between 1916 and 1922. He described the difficulties of holding such an office:

> A Secretary for Scotland must put a severe curb upon his personal predilections, and endeavour to deal with those branches of his activities, whatever they may be, that call for immediate attention. He cannot, being merely human, expand habitually to the width such a catalogue would demand. He has to live from day to day, to attend Cabinets, to think of Upper Silesia as well as, let us say, Auchtermuchty.[44]

Membership of the Cabinet had its advantages, most obviously that it brought access to the centre of power, but it also required the Secretary's consideration of extra-departmental matters and added to his burdens. The multifunctional character of the office could be seen to limit the nature of the Scottish Secretary's role, leaving initiatives to his officials or following English initiatives. However, much depended on the predilections and personal influence of the individual holding the office.

The New Despotism and the Scottish Secretary

In one of the very few books on Scottish central government published prior to 1939, John Percival Day's study of public administration in the Highlands and Islands, published in 1918, observed that:

> a comparatively independent Executive is called upon to do its work with tools largely of its own fashioning, and the efficiency of the

result is due, not so much to any legal control exercisable by the people, as to the traditions and calibre of the Civil Service and the sensitiveness of the administrators to the manifestations of popular feeling.[45]

For Day, the control of the Scottish Office by Parliament was British not Scottish. Such criticism of the Scottish Office assumed a constitutional requirement for the Scottish Secretary to be answerable to Scotland, whether by this was meant Scottish MPs, Scottish MPs of the governing party or some other indefinite Scottish body. Though a case for home rule could be made, many critics of the Scottish Office went beyond making such a case and seemed to believe that the Scottish Secretary was constitutionally bound to be answerable to a Scottish rather than Westminster body. But there was never any suggestion in the legislation that the Scottish Office required a 'Scottish mandate'.

It may have been the idea that the Secretary should be answerable to a Scottish constituency which had provoked the resolution being laid before the Scottish Liberal Association in 1909 concerning the 'Tory' appointments being made to official bodies by Liberal Scottish Secretary John Sinclair.[46] The resolution was withdrawn. Furthermore, the thinking that the views of the Scottish Members should be taken into account was evident in the letter to McKinnon Wood from John Gulland during the First World War when the position of the Scottish Secretary was being considered. Gulland informed Wood that he had told Asquith that the Scottish Secretary 'must be a Liberal'.[47] With fifty-five Scottish Liberals and fifteen Unionists, Gulland felt that a Tory Secretary would be 'impossible and intolerable', a view with which Asquith was in agreement. Accepting this view was not the same as arguing that the Scottish Secretary should always be chosen from the majority party but it was a notable consideration in the wartime coalition.

But the concern that civil servants and Ministers had too much power was not peculiar to Scotland. In a series of lectures on delegated legislation in Cambridge in April 1921, C.T. Carr spoke on a subject which during the inter-war period became controversial both amongst students of public administration and government and those more directly involved in government and politics in Britain. Carr maintained that the 'statute book is not only incomplete but even misleading unless it be read with the delegated legislation which amplifies and amends it',[48] and noted three ways in which delegated legislation was allowed to affect the statute book – by direct amendment of an Act, through the creation of additional machinery affecting the commencement, duration or application of an Act, and in the elaboration of detail to facilitate the objects or working of an Act. That such delegated legislation was necessary so long as Parliament lacked the time and expertise to deal with the minutia of the increasing complexities of government was obvious, but the implications did give rise to fears that Ministers or their officials were becoming over-powerful, fears which had been heard in the 1830s but seemed to decline in the Victorian era, perhaps in consequence of the formal 'professionalisation' of the central civil service. However, as Carr again noted, looking back on the matter twenty years after his Cambridge lectures, the situation had changed after the First World War:

> Dicey had told the islanders that so far as administrative law was concerned they could sleep peacefully in their beds, and now all the alarm bells were ringing.[49]

This arose because of the failure to deregulate the wartime regulations completely and abandon wartime administrative machinery. In addition, the implications of Lloyd George's election slogans. 'A land fit for heroes' meant better houses and health care but also meant new or extended machinery of government, increased delegated legislation and, arguably, the 'new despotism', as Lord Hewart was to characterise the lack of accountability with respect to central government's executive functions. An important distinction which seems to have been blurred in discussions during the period concerning the increased powers and duties of the executive was that of the respective positions of Ministers and of their officials. Indeed, when the Lord Chancellor appointed the Committee on Ministers' Powers in 1929, the remit given was for the consideration,

> by or under the direction of (or by persons or bodies appointed specially by) Ministers of the Crown by way of (a) delegated legislation and (b) judicial and quasi-judicial decision.[50]

In the case of the Scottish Office at least, the distinction would seem valid. The scope of responsibilities over which the Scottish Secretary was charged, the location in Edinburgh of a growing population of officials while the Minister's work remained concentrated in London, and the diverse, disparate and unco-ordinated administrative boards and departments were causes for concern.

In November 1929, the Scottish Departments received a request from the Select Committee on Ministers' Powers for information concerning the powers they possessed, as did all government departments.[51] Even the Librarian at the National Library of Scotland was in receipt of such a letter though as he replied, 'I think you may safely assure the Committee that the sovereignty of Parliament is not menaced by the encroachments of our Trustees !'[52] However, the committee failed to consider the peculiarities inherent in the Scottish Office, perhaps because both Scottish Members, the Duchess of Atholl and the Rev. James Barr, resigned before it reported. The committee noted that the Local Government (Scotland) Act, 1929 was among eight Acts of Parliament passed between 1888 and 1929 in which power was conferred on a Minister to modify the provisions of the legislation so far as was necessary for the purpose of bringing the Act into operation – a so-called 'Henry VIII' clause. However, the committee could only conclude that Henry VIII clauses should be exceptional and its other recommendations could hardly be expected to have satisfied the critics. The 'new despotism' of Whitehall, having thus been put upon trial, was, in Lord Eustace Percy's phrase, dismissed with a farthing fine.[53]

To some extent the questions considered by the Committee on Ministers' Powers were set in a Scottish context by the Gilmour Committee though the central issue concerning the powers of the Scottish Secretary was not considered by Gilmour. In July 1939, James Henderson Stewart, Liberal National Member for East Fife, unsuccessfully urged the Prime Minister to allow a discussion on a motion which stated that the Gilmour Committee had 'dealt only with the form and inter-relations of the various Departments under the control of the Secretary of State' and stated that the time had come for an examination of the duties, powers and authority vested in the Secretary of State and urged,

> the immediate appointment of a Joint Committee to inquire into these and related matters and to recommend what changes, legislative or otherwise, should be made with a view to equipping the Secretary of State adequately for the task confronting him.[54]

Notably, the stress was on how to improve the functioning of the Scottish Secretary rather than how to limit his functioning. This seems to have been the concern of Scottish Members opposed to home rule. They feared that the civil servants might be too powerful, with echoes, however diminished, of the pre-war the SED officials' 'bureaucratic despotism'.

On the other hand, home rulers in the inter-war period were obviously inclined to criticise what they regarded as the concentration of power in the hands of the Scottish Secretary and the extensive powers permitted to permanent officials. The *Times*, in a report on a debate on Scottish Estimates in April 1925, referred to that 'Pooh-Bah, the Secretary for Scotland, who combines in his person, in respect of half the kingdom, all those offices for which a more complex England requires half a dozen separate Ministers.'[55] The condescending tone of the *Times* compares with the affronted dignity of Scottish home rulers including Tom Johnston who declared,

> The Secretary of State controls 16 departments. He cannot do it. There is no human being capable of controlling 16 departments. This Pooh-bah business, this conglomeration of 16 offices in the person of one individual is an insult to a proud nation.[56]

At the second reading of the Reorganisation of Offices Bill in 1928, the Rev. James Barr had drawn an historical parallel with King James VI, who had once stated, as could the Scottish Secretary according to Barr, 'here I sit and govern Scotland with my pen. I write, and it is done, and by the clerk of the Department I govern Scotland now, which others could not do by sword.'[57] It was hardly surprising that the Scottish Secretary should be compared with the character in the Mikado who held many offices simultaneously or with a Stuart King and became known as the 'Little King' by home rulers[58] or 'Scotland's Minister' by the Gilmour Committee.[59]

The Parliamentary Under Secretary for Scotland

The Parliamentary Under Secretary for Scotland, appointed in 1919 with responsibility for Health and from the Act of 1926 with general responsibilities, was thought to have improved the situation of the Scottish Secretary. However, while holding the junior office, both Walter Elliot and Tom Johnston, were at times given responsibilities not associated with the Scottish Office. Elliot became involved with the work of the Empire Marketing Board in October 1927 when he was appointed a Vice President of the Imperial Research Conference meeting at Westminister Hall. In both posts he argued the case for increased scientific research.[60] In May the following year it was reported that Elliot together with A.M. Samuel, Financial Secretary to the Treasury, was to assist Winston Churchill, Chancellor of the Exchequer in the debates on the budget while still a Parliamentary Under Secretary at the Scottish Office.[61] Tom Johnston, as Parliamentary Under Secretary, along with Mosley and Lansbury, according to Ramsay MacDonald's biographer, 'was also supposed to assist Thomas [Lord Privy Seal] and became parliamentary secretary [sic] at the Scottish Office'.[62] These additional responsibilities may have been temporary and not very onerous but it is striking that the dissatisfaction with the Scottish Office Ministerial team was beginning to be voiced just when Elliot and Johnston were being given responsibilities outwith the Scottish Office.

The issue of a second Parliamentary Under Secretary was raised by the Gilmour Committee at the end of its report. The committee remarked on the heavy burden falling upon the Secretary of State and the arduous nature of his responsibilities:

> Though it is hardly within our province to make suggestions regarding the Parliamentary assistance available to the Secretary of State, we think it right to refer to a suggestion frequently put before us, namely, that there should be a second Parliamentary Under Secretary of State for Scotland, possibly with a seat in the House of Lords. We make no specific recommendation on this matter, and content ourselves with bringing the suggestion forward for consideration.[63]

An internal Scottish Office memorandum on the subject in 1938 stated that Sir Godfrey Collins had raised the question with the Prime Minister in 1935 but noted that the 'matter was deferred on the ground that a new Ministerial office could not be introduced at that time'.[64] However, with the matter being raised once more, the memorandum noted:

> The question has since been the subject of consultation by the Secretary of State with the Chancellor of the Exchequer, and afterwards with the Prime Minister. On the 19 July, 1938, the Prime Minister asked the Secretary of State not to raise the matter in the Cabinet, partly because serious criticism would arise if the already large number of Members holding Government office were increased, and partly because repercussions would ensue in relation to Wales. The Prime Minister undertook, however, to consider the position afresh after experience had been gained of the working of the new arrangements contemplated in the Report of the Committee on Scottish Administration.[65]

However, as the memorandum made clear, the official response to the idea was that it was not justified in the circumstances. In 1940 with the extra responsibilities involved with the war, a second Parliamentary Under Secretary of State was appointed.

The Scottish Secretaries and the conception of the office

When he was offered the Scottish Secretaryship in October 1903, Andrew Murray suggested instead the appointment of certain members of the House of Lords. Included among these was the Marquess of Linlithgow, who had recently returned from Australia where he had served as the first Governor General. Despite his ill-health, Linlithgow was appointed on 2 February, 1905 but he offered his resignation in a rather sad letter just over a month later in which the ailing Scottish Secretary felt that he was neither mentally nor physically fit enough to serve in the Cabinet and to administer the Scottish Office.[66] His letter of resignation, in parts quite illegible, stated that his memory had gone. However his resignation was refused and Linlithgow remained in office until Balfour's resignation as Prime Minister in December that year. The imminence of a General Election, the prospect of a massive defeat and the need to project a confident image rather than that of confusion and haste, which Linlithgow's resignation would have signalled a month after his appointment, probably encouraged Linlithgow to hang onto office against his own wishes. Lord Salisbury's comment on the light workload combined with its symbolic importance was still relevant. Had it been otherwise, someone more capable of carrying the increasing administrative load but a less notable figure in Scottish society might have been appointed.

In the debates on the establishment of the Scottish Office the conclusion had been reached that the Secretary should be Vice President of the SED and education became the principal function in the gamut of responsibilities, largely on the grounds that Scottish educational distinctiveness was undisputed. Yet, ironically, the holders of the office to 1918 rarely had much experience of the peculiarities of Scottish education themselves. If any school could claim to have educated Scottish Secretaries then it was Eton: five of the Secretaries to 1918 attended England's most prestigious fee-paying school; there were two Harrovians; and one former pupil of Westminster amongst their number. Of the twelve individuals who held the office to the end of the First World War only two had attended school in Scotland; John Sinclair at Edinburgh Academy and Robert Munro at Aberdeen Grammar School.

Only Robert Munro was educated at a Scottish University, Edinburgh while there were four former Cambridge students and three Oxford-educated Secretaries, including the Earl of Dalhousie who left Balliol College only a few months after matriculating. Though Scottish education had been deemed to be distinctive enough to merit separate administrative treatment and the Scottish Secretary was Vice President of the SED, effectively the Education Minister for Scotland, there appears to have been no intention of making appointments on the basis of educational experience in Scotland. This exemplifies the dichotomous nature of the Scottish Office. Scots may have expected the Vice President of the SED to have had practical experience of Scottish education whereas Prime Ministers regarded the more important qualification to be administrative competence or loyalty in the Cabinet.

Iain McLean has described the Scottish Office under McKinnon Wood during the First World War as a 'broken reed', in reference to the Clydeside agitation and consequent rent control which, McLean maintains, resulted largely due to Lloyd George's advocacy.[67] At the Scottish Office from February 1912 to July 1916, McKinnon Wood appears to have had neither the determination of his predecessor, John Sinclair, nor the ambition of Balfour of Burleigh but perhaps typified other Scottish Secretaries in the period up to 1914. No major initiative is associated with his term, though the newspaper of the Temperance Reform Organisation paid tribute to Wood after he had died, claiming him to be the 'only British statesman who has carried through the Imperial Parliament a Local Option measure and secured it a place on the Statute Book.'[68]

The transition from war to peace may have been marked by continuity in the Scottish Office in the person of Robert Munro but such continuity was, in Christopher Harvie's opinion, 'Scotland's tragedy'.[69] As a Coalition Liberal, Munro's tenure ended in 1922 and he was succeeded by Viscount Novar who had been, as Robert Crauford Munro Ferguson, Liberal Member for Leith from 1886–1914. As a Liberal, Munro Ferguson had espoused the cause of Scottish home rule and had been a critic of the Scottish Office. In 1922, two years after returning from Australia where he had served as Governor-General, Novar accepted the office of Scottish Secretary. In a letter to Baldwin in November 1924, after the Prime Minister informed him that his services would no longer be required at the Scottish Office, Novar wrote that he recognised that his original nomination was 'due to the friendship of Mr Bonar Law and not to party claims'.[70]

The first Labour Scottish Secretary, Willie Adamson had spent twenty-seven years as a miner before becoming a union official and then entering Parliament in December 1910. Both in 1924 and in 1929–31, Adamson made little impact as Labour's first Scottish Secretary. In 1924, it had been John Wheatley, Minister of Health, who had led the housing legislation affecting Scotland and the rest of Britain, through a House of

Commons without a Labour majority. Without intending any slight, Patrick Dollan wrote of Adamson in March 1938: 'His major gift to Glasgow and the rest of Scotland was his support of the late John Wheatley's Housing Act.'[71] His local paper the *Dunfermline Press* summed up Adamson's Secretaryship in an obituary notice in February 1936: '... caution, allied to shrewdness was clearly discernible in practically everything he said and did while a member of the Cabinet.'[72]

Succeeding the ebullient Walter Elliot at Dover House in May 1938 was Sir John Colville. Colville was the grandson of the founder of Colvilles, the steel manufacturers. It was during Colville's time that the Reorganisation of Offices (Scotland) Act, 1939 was passed through Parliament. Gilmour's committee had reported in September 1937 and the St Andrews House building on Calton Hill was already in the process of being built when Colville obtained Cabinet approval to introduce legislation to reorganise the Scottish central administration in July 1938. Colville was not a Conservative in the mould of his predecessor at Dover House. His interests were not those of social reform and, though he led the Reorganisation legislation through Parliament, it is doubtful whether Colville had much interest in the machinery of government. For the most part Scottish Secretaries were unimaginative individuals who played a comparatively limited role in Government. On demitting office many Scottish Secretaries returned to the obscurity from which they should probably never have emerged.

Disputes with the Prime Minister

Balfour of Burleigh was an ambitious Scottish Secretary but his ambition was not confined to the passage of Scottish legislation but rather to his career, his desire to hold higher office in Government. In a 'strictly private' letter to A.J. Balfour in November 1900, while Secretary for Scotland, Balfour of Burleigh bemoaned the fact that he had not been promoted in changes in the Cabinet which had just taken place and suggested that his full potential was not being realised as Scottish Secretary. His grievance, however, did not come to anything as he was disinclined to allow his grievances to be made known to Salisbury, as A.J. Balfour suggested would have been the proper course to take.[73]

Burleigh's ambitions to influence matters outwith his direct remit eventually led to his political demise. His advocacy of free trade and his secretive Cabinet manoueverings, part of the 'Cabinet within a Cabinet' as Prime Minister Balfour saw it, allied with rumours of intrigue against the Prime Minister, led to Burleigh's dismissal from office at the Cabinet meeting on 14 September, 1903. Officially, Balfour of Burleigh resigned four days later but, in reality was removed from office by his Prime Minister on a policy difference, and one which had no direct relation to his office. Lady Francis Balfour's memoir of Balfour of Burleigh records her impression that 'there was a good deal of the benevolent Despot about his character' in reference to his term as Secretary for Scotland[74] and evidence of this style is suggested in a letter from A.J. Balfour in June 1901 in which the latter suggests that the Scottish Secretary ought to think about permitting the Cabinet to see the Local Taxation Return before it was published.[75]

Apart from the ten weeks from May to August 1945 during the Caretaker Government at the end of the Second World War when the sixth Earl of Rosebery served as Scottish Secretary, Viscount Novar was the last Scottish Secretary in the House of Lords. In his letter to Novar, Baldwin explained that he had 'always felt it a weakness not to have the Scottish Secretary in the Commons and after the popular verdict in Scotland I regard it as more than ever essential'.[76] The 'popular verdict' referred, of course, to the support shown in Scotland for the Labour Party. Novar obviously doubted the sincerity of the Prime Minister; at the foot of Baldwin's letter Novar noted: 'This is weak but his best line of argument. The reasons were quite different & originated possibly in Scotland – though I don't trust Mr B!'[77] In his formal reply to Baldwin, Novar was more subtle but gave the reasons why he was not appointed:

> Your reference to 'loyalty' is welcome as showing that you under-
> stand that my opposition to Protection and to the Dissolution of
> 1923 was actuated solely by my fear of its ill consequences to the
> country and party.[78]

Baldwin's biographers have recorded the differences in Cabinet over the British Debt to the United States and Novar's siding with Bonar Law against Baldwin's settlement of January 1923. As Middlemas and Barnes noted, only Novar gave 'any real support to the Prime Minister' when Law advocated the repudiation of the Chancellor's proposed settlement if not the debt itself.[79] Further to this were the issues of tariff reform and the election of 1923. Novar was one of three or perhaps four Cabinet Ministers not consulted on the issue of tariff reform prior to the Cabinet meeting in October 1923, just two days before the Plymouth Conservative Conference when Baldwin announced the dramatic change of policy from free trade to protection.[80] Novar's residual liberalism was evident in his support of free trade and explains the widening of an existing breach with Baldwin.

Sir Archibald Sinclair's period at the Scottish Office lasted just over one year and ended with his resignation with other Free Trade Liberals who formed part of the Coalition Government under Ramsay MacDonald. During the course of the year, Sinclair had considered abandoning the Goschen formula basis of educational finance in favour of a grant based on need. However, his tenure at the Scottish Office was not long enough to permit the realisation of this aim. Pottinger records the high opinion of Sinclair held by Sir David Milne, who was Sinclair's private secretary. However, a letter which seems to have been privately written by Sir John Jeffrey, head of the Department of Health for Scotland, to Gilmour in September 1932, noted that Sinclair's departure was 'very welcome'.[81] Whatever the relations with his staff, Sinclair hardly had the time to be an innovative Secretary nor were economic conditions propitious for innovation. His dispute was again unusual as it focussed on something not directly under the Scottish Secretary's responsibility.

Administrative competence and business-like styles

Sir John Gilmour was the Scottish Secretary in 1926 when the office was raised to a Secretaryship of State but his name is more often associated with the committee which he chaired and the Reorganisation of Offices (Scotland) Act, 1939 which resulted from its report. Without doubt, he was the Scottish Secretary who most influenced the development of the machinery of government in Scotland during the twentieth century. A major reform of local government was enacted in 1929 during Gilmour's Secretaryship which remained the basis of the Scottish local government system for over fifty years. With respect to the Scottish central administration, it was under Gilmour that the Departments of Health, Agriculture and Prisons replaced boards in legislation passed in 1928 and the Act of 1939 owed much to the report of the Gilmour Committee. Yet, despite such considerable importance in shaping the structure of Scottish administration, Sir John Gilmour is not considered to have been a great innovator or reformer. This is probably because he was not a noted social reformer.

Neville Chamberlain, who was in a sense Gilmour's English counterpart as Minister of Health, had a low opinion of the Scottish Secretary. Chamberlain wrote privately of Gilmour:

> I wish I had the conduct of Scottish affairs instead of Gilmour. He is thoroughly honest, courageous and well meaning but he strikes me as lacking in knowledge of how to deal with his people.[82]

Gilmour was 'hardly a Demosthenes',[83] as Colin Coote put it, and may not have impressed Chamberlain but his quiet style probably belied considerable administrative competence. Scottish Unionist MPs had been amongst the most ardent supporters of the Coalition Govenment headed by Lloyd George and Sir John Gilmour had been one of thirteen Unionists who had issued a manifesto justifying their decision to support the coalition after the Carlton Club meeting and made clear their determination not to help Bonar Law form a Government.[84] Gilmour refused to accept office in the Baldwin Government because he took 'gravest exception to shutting out the possibility of working usefully with the Coalition Liberals'.[85] As a consequence, Viscount Novar, a member of the Lords and only a recent convert to the Conservative Party, became Scottish Secretary. However, the rift within the Conservative Party did not last long and Gilmour accepted the office of Scottish Secretary in November 1924: as Middlemas and Barnes stated, the Scottish Office then was 'destined for Gilmour'.[86]

Gilmour attained office following an election when the Labour Party in Scotland won more votes than the Conservatives for the first time. The Scottish Unionist political secretary, P.J. Blair remarked on being a 'little apprehensive in some ways about the political future' in a congratulatory letter to Gilmour on his appointment.[87] The Conservatives had problems in 1922 appointing Scottish Ministers when the Lord Advocate, William Watson and the Parliamentary Under Secretary for Health, James Kidd had been defeated and the Solicitor-General David Fleming did not stand again. In 1923, Watson had failed to be re-elected and Walter Elliot, who had succeeded Kidd, lost his seat. Difficulties in the appointment of the Scottish Ministerial complement from amongst Scottish Members of the Commons filled Conservatives with genuine concern in the 1920s.

Disputes over the Ottawa Agreements had resulted in the former Scottish Secretary, Sir John Gilmour replacing Sir Herbert Samuel at the Home Office and Walter Elliot in turn replaced Gilmour at the Agriculture Ministry and Sir Godfrey Collins being appointed Scottish Secretary in Sinclair's place. Elliot had been expected to be given the Scottish Office. In a letter to Gilmour, Donald Fergusson, Permanent Secretary at the Ministry of Agriculture described how he had 'indulged in Cabinet making' with Tony Muirhead, Gilmour's Parliamentary Private Secretary. While correctly predicting that Gilmour would be made Home Secretary, Fergusson and Muirhead made what was probably a fairly common mistake: 'We appointed Walter Elliot for Scotland. ... We did not spot Godfrey Collins for a place.'[88]

However surprising the appointment of the Liberal publisher, it proved to be of importance in the develpoment of Scottish central administration. Collins served for four years until his death in September 1936 during which time he played an active part in the Cabinet advocating special measures for Scotland during years of economic depression and he instigated a major reorganisation of the Scottish administration. Sir William Murrie served as private secretary to Collins and described the Secretary of State as having been the driving force behind the concentration of offices in Edinburgh.[89] Sinclair had not been an active proponent of concentrating the offices in Edinburgh but Collins, perhaps reflecting his business experience, felt that a more administratively efficient structure could emerge from a reorganisation of the Scottish departments. In July 1936, Collins wrote to Sir John Gilmour and others inviting their participation in the review of the structure of Scottish government. The announcement of the establishment of the Gilmour Committee was postponed when Collins died and it was Elliot, who succeeded Collins, who made the formal announcement in the Commons and took the credit for the initiative.

Pressure from within Scotland were at their height during Collins' term. On taking office, he was faced with what was then viewed as the serious phenomena of home rule agitation. The National Party of Scotland had been established in 1928 and the more moderate Scottish Party, with respectable senior members such as Sir Alexander McEwen and the Duke of Montrose, was formed in 1932. Scottish public records and the private papers of individuals such as Elliot and Gilmour demonstrate that though treated publicly as a fringe issue, the Scottish home rule question attracted much more attention within the Scottish Office and Conservative Party than would be expected of something irrelevant. Though home rule agitation may have partly sprung from the economic conditions, allied with the feeling that Scotland was being neglected, the manifestation of discontent in this new form in Scotland was seen as more challenging than were previous demonstrations of Scottish dissatisfaction. Part of the response was the reorganisation of the central administration.

Collins was unwell towards the end of his period as Scottish Secretary and this impaired his performance. In November 1935, Sir John Stirling Maxwell, former Unionist MP, in a letter to Gilmour, hoped that Gilmour could influence the Prime Minister and ensure the appointment of a 'live wire for the Scottish Office':

Collins did his best I am sure, but he has no health and can bring no energy to an office which lacks it. Now that the Housing Act is on the

Statute Book it is a good opportunity to tackle new questions which
want tackling.
One would want to see one much younger given a chance – Clydesdale
for instance, or Colville or Dunglass, all of whom seem to have some
life in them. Or Arthur Rose [Special Areas Commissioner] if he cd. be
released from his present hopeless job and a seat found for him ?[90]

Maxwell's evident dismay at the lack of vitality in Dover House – where 'no
one seems capable of more than messing about with a Deer Forest Bill
which is ten years out of date' – did not take account of Collins' Cabinet
advocacy of special Scottish measures but shows that amongst
Conservatives there were worries about the appearance of Scottish Office
inactivity. Maxwell's comments highlight the public role which 'Scotland's
Minister' was presumed to adopt. It was not enough to be an effective
advocate of Scottish interests in Cabinet. The Scottish Secretary was
expected to be seen to act publicly as the advocate of Scottish interests.

Collins' successor as Secretary of State for Scotland was Walter Elliot.
Throughout his Parliamentary career to the outbreak of the Second
World War, Elliot was regarded by commentators in the press as a politician with a bright future. In 1921, Herbert Sidebotham of the *Times*
singled out Elliot as a young politician with much potential.[91] Other
journalists over the years would appear to have agreed.[92] It has been suggested that Neville Chamberlain had pressed for Elliot being moved to
the Scottish Office from an English one.[93] Evidence of this is suggested in
a letter Chamberlain wrote to his sister in October 1936, but it is difficult
to know for certain the extent of Chamberlain's influence respecting
Cabinet appointments. What is notable is that Chamberlain perceived
the Scottish Office as a backwater from which it would be difficult for an
ambitious politician, such as Elliot, to make much of an impact and be
noticed. Gilmour and Elliot did succeed in moving on from the Scottish
Office. Part of the problem for Scottish Secretaries, particularly
Conservatives, was that there was a more limited field of potential
Ministers for a Prime Minister to choose from, thus able and competent
Scottish MPs found that there were few colleagues able to replace them at
Dover House.

Conclusion

The office of Scottish Secretary was seen in Scotland as a post open only
to a Scottish MP and by 1939 even a Scottish peer was regarded as unacceptable, whatever the constitutional situation may have permitted.

In this respect, the office had become a parochial backwater. Demands for such special treatment had brought the benefit of a representative in Cabinet but meant that Scottish politicians could find themselves in the Cabinet but with only a remote prospect of promotion. The Scottish Office was not even a middle-ranking Cabinet post so that Scottish Secretaries could rarely expect to move directly on to such offices as Chancellor of the Exchequer, Foreign Secretary or to the Premiership. As a consequence, the Scottish Secretaryship allowed a number of politicians to enter the Cabinet who would otherwise have had little chance of doing so. At the same time, though Gilmour and Elliot were clearly exceptions, able and ambitious Scottish MPs might find the Secretaryship of State more of a burden than a stepping stone in their political careers.

In his book on the Secretaries of State for Scotland, one of the main themes developed by George Pottinger was that the 'very personal contributions of Scottish Ministers is often underrated'.[94] If this is so, or when this has been the case, partly it has been because the Scottish Secretary's most important work is done in Cabinet and Cabinet committees which, because of secrecy and collective ministerial responsibility, means that 'Scotland's Minister' would be unable, openly at least, to publicise this work. Partly, it was because personal contributions were so limited.

10
Conclusion

The establishment of the Scottish Parliament in 1999 owed much more to the evolution of the Scottish Office than has generally been imagined. Scholars of nationalism have long understood that history or, at least, collective memory is important. Scholars of public administration and political institutions are increasingly aware of the importance of the past in understanding how institutions and policies are shaped. Two principal factors explain the establishment of the Scottish Parliament: a Scottish base and a political dynamic. The dynamic that combined with the Scottish base to create the Scottish Parliament was the perceived threat to Scottish distinctiveness that was posed by Thatcherism.[1] The Scottish base had existed since 1707 when the new British state allowed for the continued existence of distinct Scottish institutions but this thinking also allowed for the institutional expression of distinctiveness to change over time. The United Kingdom had no entrenched written constitution nor a body of constitutional cases to guide the development of its structures of government that existed elsewhere but there was (and remains) what amounted to a set of constitutional norms. The continued existence of these norms owed much to pressures from Scotland.

The historic institutionalist school offers an explanatory framework for understanding developments discussed in this book. The 'basic, deceptively simple' idea of historic institutionalism is that 'policy choices made when an institution is being formed, or when a policy is initiated, will have a continuing and largely determinate influence over the policy far into the future'.[2] This draws on the seminal work of Skocpol, King and Krasner.[3] Krasner's notion of 'path dependency' suggests that when a policy is initiated it sets out on a path that will remain set short of major pressure for change.[4] The work on historic institutionalism that rings most true with this study is that of Margaret Levi. Levi's metaphor is particularly appropriate:

> Perhaps the better metaphor is a tree, rather than a path. From the same trunk, there are many different branches and smaller branches. Although it is possible to turn around or to clamber from one to the other – and essential if the chosen branch dies – the branch on which a climber begins is the one she tends to follow.[5]

In the context of this study, the establishment of the Scottish Office ensured that separate administrative arrangements would not only persist but would apply to new or expanding areas of public policy. Famously seen by Prime Minister Lord Salisbury as a fairly insignificant event, the establishment of the Scottish Office proved in time to have great significance. The roots lay in the separate administrative bodies that preceded the Scottish Office but the Scottish Office became the trunk. This path dependency has also been evident in the case of territorial public finance and in particular the Goschen formula. Decisions on public finance taken long before continued to influence policy and institutional development throughout the twentieth century.

Historic institutionalism has been criticised for its lack of a predictive quality.[6] It would not have been possible to predict the precise course central administration would have taken but what was clear was that from even before the establishment of the Scottish Office, a pattern of distinct central administrative apparatus had been established which provided the basis for continued distinct treatment of Scotland at the heart of British government. The UK was a union state, not a unitary state. Integration in the union state is 'less than perfect' and while 'administrative standardisation prevails over most of the territory' some 'pre-union rights and institutional infrastructures which preserves some degree of regional autonomy and serve as agencies of indigenous elite recruitment' remain[7] and this would continue to be the basis of Scotland's position within the union short of some dramatic pressure for change or through the gradual erosion of Scottish distinctiveness. Its form changed but its essentials remained the same. More than this, the union state had dynamic properties. It was not just that these pre-union rights and institutional infrastructures were preserved as some kind of static heritage but had implications for later developments in policy and administration. As this book has shown, the existence of distinct Scottish institutions, most notably the Scottish Office after 1885, created interests and demands for further concessions. These would make any effort to alter the institutional balance and create a more integrated, uniform unitary state more difficult. The status quo was on the side of Scottish distinctiveness and, indeed, there appears to have been a ratchet-like effect, the kind of path dependency identified by historical institutionalists.[8] It may not have been predictable at the outset but it is explicable from an historic institutionalist perspective.

The importance of ideas in shaping policy has been noted in historical institutionalist writings.[9] Throughout the history of Scottish central administration and, indeed, a key feature of the union state, have been the twin ideas of allowing, encouraging, even celebrating Scottish distinctiveness alongside centralised authority. These twin themes took the form of a Scottish and Whitehall view in the context of the development of Scottish central administration. Vying with each other, this tension formed the basis of the Scottish Office's foundation and development. This idea of a union state – though, of course, the term itself was never used – captures the developments which had the Scottish Office at their centre.

The union state tradition did not prescribe the manner in which Scotland should be governed but set parameters within which authoritative decisions could be made. It was a versatile tradition able to take account of changing circumstances. The greatest challenge came in the form of the expansion of the state's activities. So much that had made Scotland distinct in the early post-Union period focussed on civil society. The state was very limited in its reach. But the union state tradition successfully accommodated the remarkable transformation of state activity in the late nineteenth and early twentieth centuries. As institutions such as the Church of Scotland declined, most notably in educational matters, the state assumed a larger role not only in replacing the Church but also in response to social, political and economic pressures. This increased state intervention and allied institutional structures could conceivably have led to a more uniform, unitary state but this did not occur. The Scottish Office became the chief manifestation of the union state.

The media's role in the establishment of the Scottish Office and its development was notable. Not only did newspapers campaign actively for a Scottish Office, celebrate major reforms but they ensured that the Scottish view was heard. Political parties in Scotland too ensured that the Scottish view was loudly, if sometimes incoherently, articulated. All of this served to deepen the Scottish dimension of UK politics.

Path dependency is not path determinism. In the case of Scottish central administration, there was a tendency to continue to treat matters which already had a Scottish dimension as distinct and to provide separate Scottish administrative arrangements for related matters. This did not mean that a Scottish dimension would always emerge even in matters that had already developed Scottish apparatus. As the reforms of the late 1920s and late 1930s confirm, it was possible to change course and absorb the patronage-based but distinctly Scottish boards though, crucially, this was done within the union state tradition. Within this broad pattern of organising government, significant changes were brought about but these had to be articulated in Scottish terms and concede much to the Scottish view.

Reverses in 'administrative devolution' were less likely as time went by and as institutions and policies became deeply rooted. In some cases, notably public finance, the practice of treating Scotland as a distinct entity made it very difficult to change course. This was also true of the broader picture of public administration. Even with pressure for a more professional system of administration, this was completed within parameters that had evolved over time. The tension between the Scottish and Whitehall views was one that could be creative and one that was unlikely to result in either being completely victorious over the other. By 1939, the prospect of having a system of central government in which the territorial dimension had disappeared and functional organisation dominated was almost inconceivable. The union state nature of central administration had been affirmed in each development of the Scottish Office up to 1939. We may speculate on what might have happened had the Scottish Office not been set up in 1885, though it should be noted that there already existed a distinct pattern of Scottish central administration and that this would not have disappeared immediately even if the Scottish Office had not come into being. What is clear is that the addition of new responsibilities and development of existing ones created a pattern that was re-established again and again making an alternative course – at least one based on unitary principles with UK-wide Ministries or Boards for public policy – less likely. Indeed, even the modernisation that occurred could be presented as a victory for the Whitehall view and a victory for the Scottish view. The consolidation of central administration under the Scottish Office rather than British-wide functional departments protected the Scottish base. By the time of the First World War, the Scottish Office was in little danger of being abolished and integrated into other parts of Whitehall. By the opening days of the Second World War, the Scottish Office's position was secure. The only threat to its existence was a 'more Scottish' alternative.

Potential path inefficiency as a consequence of early decisions 'locking an institution into a set pattern' from the outset has been much debated amongst historical institutionalists.[10] To relate path inefficiency to Scottish central administration it might be contended that the Scottish Office was a sub-optimal institution with which Scotland was stuck. The best evidence of sub-optimal institutionalisation from this study is to be found in the chapter on finance. The Goschen formula was repeatedly criticised – by all sides – as sub-optimal but difficult to alter. The formula had few staunch and consistent friends. It had its supporters in given situations who might in other situations be its detractors. But it served a purpose and it was difficult to find an alternative without major disruption to the existing arrangements. The Goschen formula, like the Barnett formula that has been used in a similar way since the late 1970s, was one that was defended not because it was the best tool for the job of determining how much public expenditure Scotland should receive over a range of public policies but because finding an acceptable alternative proved too difficult.

However, as this book shows, change is possible. The case of administrative development was not set in stone as the significant changes in the inter-war period demonstrate. Additionally, much government activity was conducted through British-wide functional departments. It would be easy to lose sight of this in focussing on Scottish central administration. Two aspects to the changes from a Board system to a Whitehall system are notable. First, it was gradual and second, as already discussed, it was achieved by working within, not against, the union state tradition.

From a unitary state perspective, that is given the assumption that such a state is the best form of government, it would certainly make sense to argue that the establishment of the Scottish Office created something inefficient that proved increasingly difficult to get rid off. From a union state perspective in which the value of plurality and difference is accepted, the creation of the Scottish Office might be welcomed, even celebrated. In other words, it is difficult to find means of measuring efficiency free of value judgements. Similarly, it is easy to criticise Goschen for its apparent inefficiency but as was noted again and again it proved difficult to agree to an alternative.

Of course, the Scottish Office was itself part of Whitehall. This was one of the limits of administrative devolution and the union state. The union state was not a form of federalism. Integration may have been 'less than perfect',[11] as Rokkan and Urwin's definition suggested, but there was still a strong centre. The union state was marked by centralisation and diversity and only limited autonomy for its component parts. It is not a decentralised or regionalised state. Scotland did not have meaningful autonomy. Paterson has rightly criticised those who have been overenthusiastic in pointing to Parliamentary sovereignty as evidence of an all-powerful centre.[12] However, in arguing that Scotland had autonomy through the involvement of the Scottish Office as well as its attendant agencies in implementation, he exaggerates its extent in three respects. First, this ignores the ability of bureaucracy in general to alter policies at implementation stage. A well established literature on implementation[13] demonstrates the ability of those implementing public policy to alter policy as intended by legislators. To cite this as evidence of autonomy reduces the value of the term and makes it fairly meaningless in the Scottish context. Scotland's 'autonomy' becomes nothing more than would be found anywhere that involves the implementation of public policy. Second, it ignores the tight financial control exerted by the Treasury within the UK system of government. Time and again, the Scottish Office found itself constrained by what Lloyd George amongst others noted: 'the sum which might be a comparatively small figure if it were confined to Scotland, when multiplied by 10 becomes a very considerable sum.'[14] Third, Parliamentary sovereignty cannot be dismissed quite so lightly especially in contexts when the governing party had minority support in Scotland – again raising doubts about any notions of autonomy. What Scotland possessed was not autonomy in any meaningful sense but rather it was assured a distinct status as part of a union state. In criticising the notion that the UK is a unitary state it is wrong to leap to the conclusion that Scotland had autonomy. As John Macintosh pointed out thirty years ago in reviewing James Kellas's *Scottish Political System*, it is 'wrong' to suggest that there is 'considerable autonomy in certain aspects of policy-making. This is impossible where the Secretary of State is a member of a UK Cabinet and where English and Welsh Ministers of Education, Health and Housing have to take collective responsibility for actions in these fields of the Secretary of State.'[15] Mackintosh noted that Kellas had himself conceded that differences in policy could only occur when Scottish Ministers convinced anxious English Ministers that a Scottish experiment would not create a precedent for England and Wales.[16]

In inventing the term 'administrative devolution' and then fleshing it out, the civil servant Patrick Laird was attempting to find a reconciliation of the Scottish and Whitehall views on how Scotland should be governed. Imposing Whitehall solutions would not be politically acceptable unless they had a Scottish dimension. The term administrative devolution encapsulated this perfectly. At the time this was seen as a way of placating fears that assimilation or at least more integration was being proposed. It had little cost. There never was an intention behind those arguing along these lines for the abolition of the Scottish Office. The increasing use of the term devolution, even reference to 'self-government' to refer to the Scottish Office,[17] was a 'cheap' response. It had no immediate financial consequences but its use proved symbolically important. However, as noted in another context, 'cheap talk' can prove expensive in time.[18] The connotations of devolution that came to be associated with the Scottish Office built up expectations that proved unrealistic. Related to this was the notion of a Scottish political system, that decisions affecting Scotland should be taken in Scotland. 'Administrative devolution' created a belief and expectation that Scotland was somehow autonomous. This was not a short jump from self-government as normally understood. From this perspective, it is impossible to disentangle the existence of a Scottish Office from notions of a Scottish political system and in turn that Scotland should have its own Parliament.[19] Home rulers developed an argument for a Scottish Parliament that was based on democratising this autonomy, this 'administrative devolution'.[20]

The rhetoric of devolution went beyond the reality of the union state as it existed by 1939. It served the purpose of emphasising the Scottishness of the structure of government. It also created a problem of expectations that this system could not meet, at least at times when the party in government in London and consequently providing the political leadership of the Scottish Office, was out of sympathy in Scotland. A feature of twentieth-century UK politics was its increasing democratisation. The Scottish Office symbolised plurality within the union state and difference in policy outputs to a greater extent than was ever likely. Pluralistic and democratic pressures combined to create pressures which the language of administrative *devolution* encouraged. Even in the decades before 1939 the evidence of this kind of pressure was evident. In the early arguments on how Scottish education should be governed and the criticisms of bureaucratic despotism there was more than a hint of the need for devolution of a more robust kind. This would be a theme that grew louder and louder after 1939.

Conclusion: the 1939 Scottish Office model

By 1939, the Scottish Office was firmly established and had more than survived a succession of unimaginative Scottish Secretaries. C.L. Mowat characterised Britain in the years 1922–39 as having been subject to the 'rule of the pygmies',[21] an apt description, for the most part, of holders of the Scottish Secretaryship. Individuals such as Sir Godfrey Collins and Sir John Gilmour left their mark on the Scottish Office and on Scotland. Both Gilmour and Elliot left the Scottish Office to assume more senior posts in the Cabinet, a development which was not to occur again until 1985 when George Younger moved to Defence. But the pattern was set of a lowly placed cabinet office filled by people who would often, without its existence, have failed to make it to cabinet rank. It should, however, be noted that, at least for many, holding the office of Scottish Secretary was a great national honour.

The Scottish Office had come to have three main functions:

(i) it was the institutional expression of the union state demonstrating that Scotland would be treated distinctly within a centralised state;
(ii) articulating Scottish interests at the heart of government, especially in the cabinet and Whitehall;
(iii) administering a growing range of responsibilities.

These combined to give it an unusual position in government. In the period after 1939, the pattern already established continued. Scottish Secretaries were men (and always men) who would generally otherwise not have made it to the cabinet. Further administrative devolution developed in an *ad hoc* manner. As was commonly noted, the Scottish Secretary was both Scotland's man in the cabinet and the cabinet's man in Scotland. The Scottish Office could on occasion develop different policies from those operating south of the border but for the most part the differences were in degree rather than substance. Its role as lobbyist for Scotland meant it was expected that the Scottish Office would ask for more resources. Less acceptable was the notion that the Scottish Office should be allowed to pursue wholly different policies. Difference, then, was more acceptable in degree than direction. Ultimately, that proved its undoing. By the end of the twentieth century the expectations that had built up around the office, most notably associated the Scottish view, could not be fulfilled. Lord Salisbury's remark at the time the Scottish Office was being established proved accurate: the expectations of the Scottish people were 'approaching the Arch-angelic'.[22] But these expectations had been encouraged by notions of administrative devolution operating in a democratic age. Moreover, the expectations the public had of the state grew over time. The functions of the Scottish Office were summed up in 1936 in a memorandum prepared by the Scottish Office for an address by John Colville, then a junior Minister at the

Scottish Office and echoed many times over the years:

> ... unfortunately the Secretary of State for Scotland is expected on all hands to watch over all Scottish affairs including those outside the scope of his own office or his Departments or indeed sometimes of any Department. Every piece of proposed legislation which is applicable to Scotland, whether promoted by another Minister or by a private member, requires to be scrutinised to see whether its application to Scotland is made in the right terms, does not conflict with existing law, and is generally equitable.[23]

However much Scotland gained financially from having the Scottish Office, Michael Fry has argued that it had a damaging effect on Scottish politics:

> Debates are predictable and lifeless. Policies are geared to institutions and interests either themselves adjuncts of the bureaucracy or else unconcerned with any but their own fixed demands.[24]

The Scottish office was the institutional embodiment of treating Scotland favourably. It proved to be extremely successful in getting more resources for Scotland, winning extensions to policies decided for other parts of Britain but less successful in innovation. In one sense, this was as it should be. The Scottish Office was administrative devolution and as such lacked a specifically Scottish democratic legitimacy. It is no irony that it was the poll tax, that most innovative and radical policy that proved its undoing.

Notes

Preface

1. C.H. Allen, 'The Study of Scottish Politics: A Bibliographical Sermon', *Scottish Government Yearbook, 1980*, p. 12.
2. David Milne, *The Scottish Office*, 1957.
3. John Gibson, *The Crown and the Thistle*, 1985.

1 Introduction

1. In a letter from Prime Minister Lord Salisbury to the Duke of Richmond and Gordon inviting him to accept the newly constituted post of Secretary for Scotland August 7, 1885. Quoted in H.J. Hanham 'The Creation of the Scottish Office, 1881–87', *Juridical Review*, 1965.
2. Ibid.
3. Richard Rose, *Understanding the United Kingdom*, 1982.
4. James Kellas, *The Scottish Political System*, 3rd edition, 1984.
5. For a discussion of the evolution of the Welsh Office see E.L. Gibson, *A Study of the Council for Wales and Monmouthshire, 1948–1966*; Ivor Gowan, *Government in Wales*; K.O. Morgan, *A Study of the Attitudes and Policies of the British Political Parties Towards Welsh Affairs, Disestablishment of the Church, Education and Governmental Devolution in the Period 1870–1920*; P.J. Randall, *The Development of Administrative Devolution in Wales from the establishment of the Welsh Department of Education in 1907 to the creation of the post of Secretary of State for Wales in October 1964*; P.J. Randall, 'Wales in the Structure of Central Government', *Public Administration*, Autumn 1972, vol. 50; Ian Thomas, *The Creation of the Welsh Office: Conflicting Purposes in Institutional Change*; Sir Percy Watkins, *A Welshman Remembers*.
6. James Molyneaux in speech to Unionist party conference, November 19, 1983: 'It is time we started moving to a pattern resembling the Scottish Office which in 1929 [sic] was transplanted from Whitehall to Edinburgh for the purpose of making the Department more responsive to Scottish needs and more closely in touch with Scottish thinking.' Molyneaux believed that this had led to continuity in both Ministerial and civil service appointments, an increased number of Scots in senior positions and a movement of Scots 'outwards to Whitehall Departments'. As this book makes clear that was not quite what happened though Molyneaux shared his misunderstanding with many Scots.
7. B.C. Smith, *Field Administration*, 1967.
8. John Mackintosh, *The Devolution of Power*, p. 163.
9. Jack Brand, *The National Movement in Scotland*, p. 29.
10. B.C. Smith, *Decentralisation*, London, George Allen and Unwin.
11. Preston King, *Federalism and Federation*, London, Croom Helm, 1982, p. 133.
12. Ibid., ch. 11.

13. S. Rokkan and D. Urwin 'Introduction: centres and peripheries in western Europe' in S. Rokkan and D. Urwin (eds) *The Politics of Territorial Identity: Studies in European Regionalism* London: Sage, 1982, p. 11.
14. Ibid.
15. James Mitchell, *Strategies for Self-Government*, Edinburgh, Polygon, 1996.
16. Walker Connor, 'The Politics of Ethnonationalism', *Journal of International Affairs*, vol. 27, 1973, p. 21.
17. James Kellas, *The Scottish Political System*, 1984.
18. For an alternative view see Arthur Midwinter, Michael Keating, James Mitchell, *Politics and Public Policy on Scotland*, 1991, especially, pp. 195–202.
19. W. Bagehot, The English Constitution, London, Fontana, 1981 [1867], p. 61.
20. See J. Mitchell, *Conservatives and the Union*, Edinburgh: Edinburgh University Press, 1990, p. 34.
21. S. Rokkan and D. Urwin 'Introduction: centres and peripheries in western Europe' in S. Rokkan and D. Urwin (eds) *The Politics of Territorial Identity: Studies in European Regionalism* London: Sage, 1982, p. 11.
22. Ibid.

2 The Origins of the Scottish Central Administration

1. H.J. Hanham, 'The Creation of the Scottish Office, 1881–1887' *Juridical Review* 1965, p. 205.
2. George S. Pryde, *Central and Local Government in Scotland since 1707*, pp. 18–19.
3. The one board which originated in the previous century was the Board of Manufactures in 1726 which was initially funded by Parliament for the 'improvement and encouragement of fishery and manufactures in that part of Great Britain called Scotland'. However during the following century the board became increasingly concerned with industrial design, decorative arts and education in the fine arts. Sir David Milne, *The Scottish Office*, p. 212.
4. Sir Andrew Grierson, 'One Hundred Years of Scottish Local Government' *Public Administration* vol. 13, 1935, p. 230.
5. Ironically the principle advocate of the voluntary system, Dr Thomas Chalmers also led the disruption which made any scheme operated by the church impracticable and made a statutorily based compulsory scheme necessary.
6. Ian Levitt, *Welfare and the Scottish Poor Law, 1890–1948*, Edinburgh, Edinburgh University Press, 1983, p. 13.
7. Ibid., p. 18.
8. Mabel Atkinson, *Local Government in Scotland*, p. 369.
9. Ibid., p. 375.
10. Ian Levitt, *op. cit.*, p. 19.
11. *Report of the Commissioners appointed by the Lord Commissioners of Her Majesty's Treasury to inquire into certain Civil Departments in Scotland*, March

1870. The report states that the Board of Supervision gave written legal advice on their application on matters of law on 140 occasions in 1868, p. 3.

12. William C. Smith, *The Secretary for Scotland*, p. 2.
13. Ibid., p. 10.
14. Under the Fisheries Regulation (Scotland) Act, 1895, 58 and 59 Vict., c. 42 the constitution was amended to include a chairman and six Crown appointees, four of who were to be representatives of sea-fishing interests, one a sheriff and the other a scientist.
15. Henry Craik, *The State and Education*, p. 125.
16. Ibid., pp. 130–1.
17. Quoted in Sir Lewis Amherst Selby-Bigge, *The Board of Education*, p. 2.
18. Ibid., p. 361.
19. *Second Report of the Argyll Commission inquiring into the schools of Scotland, Elementary Schools* c. 3845, 1867, p. xliv.
20. It was proposed that the Board should have fourteen Members with a chairman and secretary nominated and paid by the Crown. Each of the four Scottish Universities were to have a representative and another four were to be chosen by the chief magistrates by Glasgow, Edinburgh, Dundee and Aberdeen who would all serve for three year terms. Each year the Commissioners of Supply of Inverness, Perth and Ayr would appoint one representative each. Three permanent members, named in the Act, would make up the board. Report of the Argyll Commission p. clxxvii.
21. James Scotland, *A History of Scottish Education,* vol. 1, p. 362.
22. Education Act, 1870, section 2 states that the Act 'shall not extend to Scotland or Ireland'.
23. James Scotland, *op. cit.,* vol. 1, p. 367.
24. The term 'Scotch' Education Department applied statutorily until the passage of the Education (Scotland) Act, 1918 from which time the Department became known as the 'Scottish' Education Department.
25. Quoted in James Scotland, *op. cit,*. vol. 1, p. 364.
26. Henry Craik, *op. cit.*, p. 153.
27. For example see Hansard, Series 3, Commons, vol. 232, 15 February 1877, col. 374; vol. 241, 4 July 1878, col. 800.
28. Hansard, Series 3, Commons, vol. 232, 13 March 1877, col. 1852.
29. Ibid., vol. 241, 4 July 1874, col. 804.
30. William Watson, the Lord Advocate, became a Privy Councillor that year and became a member of the Committee on Education in Scotland on 2, April 1878. Lord Gordon of Drumearn, a Conservative, had been a Solicitor-General for Scotland from 1866–67 then became Lord Advocate from 1867–December 1868 and again from 1874–76. He became a Privy Councillor in 1874 and died on 21 August 1879.
31. Hansard, Commons, vol. 241, 4 July 1878, cols. 809–10.
32. Ibid., vol. 265, 6 August 1881, col. 34.
33. NAS, SOE 1/35. Thomas Cooper in note to Millar Craig, 29/10/1937.
34. A Secretary of State responsible for Scotland existed for much of the time from the Union until 1746:

1707 Earl of Loudon and Earl of Mar
1708–9 Duke of Queensberry

1713 Earl of Mar
1714 Duke of Montrose
1716 Duke of Roxburghe
1741–2 Marquess of Tweeddale.
1717 The post was abolished finally in 1746 during the '45 Rising. 'The function of the third secretary [i.e. the Secretary of State for Scotland] had not been so much to justify such an appointment – as the control of parliamentary elections and the dispensing of government patronage in line with English practice.' Robert Rait and George S. Pryde, *Scotland* p. 163.

35. Henry Dundas, first Viscount Melville and Baron Dunira: Solicitor-General for Scotland 1766–75; Lord Advocate 1775–83; Home Secretary 1791–94; Secretary of State for War 1794–1801. Dundas was Scottish political manager from 1775–1805. In 1785, Boswell described him as 'Henry the Ninth, Uncrowned King of Scotland' and at the election of 1802 Dundas nominated forty-three of the forty-five Scottish MPs.

36. 'The Powers and Duties of the Lord Advocate of Scotland', *Edinburgh Review,* vol. 39, 1824, p. 370. The piece, unattributed at the time, was written by Lord Cockburn: Henry, Lord Cockburn, *Memorials of His Times,* p. 386.

37. Ibid., pp. 363–92. George W.T. Omond, *The Lord Advocates of Scotland,* vol. II, pp. 283–4.

38. Ibid., p. 285.

39. William Smith, *The Secretary for Scotland,* p. xii.

40. Hansard, Commons, vol. 150, 15 June, 1858, col. 2119.

41. The Scottish Rights Society, as it came to be known, included members such as the poet and Tory, W.E. Aytoun; Duncan McLaren, Lord Provost of Edinburgh and a leading Liberal; and P.E. Dove, a radical journalist.

42. Hansard, Lords, 6 April 1854, vol. 132, cols. 496–514.

43. *Journal of Jurisprudence,* vol. 1, 1857, p. 3.

44. Sir Reginald Coupland, *Welsh and Scottish Nationalism,* pp. 281–96.

45. Hansard, Series 3, Commons, vol. 139, 22 June 1855, cols. 19–21; vol. 150, 15 June, 1858, cols. 2118–50.

46. Ibid., vol. 150, 15 June 1858, cols. 2118, 2120.

47. Ibid., col. 2150.

48. One novel proposal put forward by Mr W. Williams to get round the problem of finding work for a territorial Minister for Scotland was that this post should be combined with that of the Chief Secretary for Ireland. Hansard, Series 3, Commons, vol. 150, 1858, col. 2134.

49. Ibid., Lords, vol. 175, 3 June 1864, col. 1168.

50. Ibid., col. 1191.

51. Ibid., Commons, vol. 185, 12 February 1867, col. 283; 21 February 1867, col. 721; vol. 186, 22 March 1867, cols. 398–410; vol. 188, 20 June 1867, cols. 166–7. The Lord Advocate had changed on 28 February 1867 but neither George Patton nor his successor, Edward Gordon were MPs.

52. Hansard, Series 3, Commons, vol. 186, 22 March 1867, col. 408.

53. Copy of letter from Anstruther and Craufurd sent to Gladstone. 22 March 1869 contained in appendix to *Report of Inquiry into Civil Departments in Scotland,* Parliamentary Papers, 1870, vol. 18, p. 64.

54. Hansard, Series 3, Commons, vol. 198, 5 August 1869, cols. 1296–7.
55. *Report of Inquiry into Civil Departments in Scotland*, Parliamentary Papers, 1870, p. 64.
56. Remit of Camperdown Commission:

   1. To ascertain how far it might be possible to effect economy in the management of the Public Boards in Edinburgh, it having been represented to Her Majesty's Government, that if the Boards were concentrated under one Parliamentary head, considerable financial reductions might be made.
   2. To consider what, if any, administrative changes in this direction might be desirable.
   3. To enquire into Boards, their constitution, establishments, and the duties which they perform.
   4. To ascertain whether it might be practicable to consolidate any of the Boards, and in that case to consider what staff, and salaries for that staff, would be sufficient for the new establishment.

57. *Report of Inquiry into Civil Departments in Scotland*, Parliamentary Papers 1870, p. 7.
58. Ibid., p. 8.
59. In his evidence to the Commission, the chairman of the Lunacy Board agreed that the Secretary of the Board was unnecessary but opposed amalgamation, as did William Walker, chairman of the Board of Supervision.
60. Duke of Argyll, Secretary of State for India, in debate. Hansard, Series 3, Lords, vol. 201, 20 May 1870, col. 1040.
61. Hansard, Series 3, Commons, vol. 150, 15 June 1858, col. 2130.
62. F.M.G. Willson, 'Ministries and Boards: Some Aspects of Administrative Development Since 1832' *Public Administration,* vol. 33, 1955, p. 44.
63. Henry Parris, *op. cit.,* p. 83.
64. William Smith, *op. cit.,* p. xiv.
65. Hansard, Series 3, Commons, vol. 239, 10 May 1878, col. 1691; vol. 248, 21 July, 1879, col. 857; vol. 262, 13 June, 1881, cols. 309–25; vol. 285, 6 March, 1884, cols. 648–9; vol. 287, 1 May, 1884, cols. 1050–1.
66. Hansard, Series 3, Lords, vol. 262, 1881, col. 318–19.
67. Camperdown in 1881 complained that the share of time being devoted to Ireland was resulting in the rest of the United Kingdom being forgotten. Hansard, Series 3, Commons, vol. 261, 31 May 1881, col. 1767.
68. Ibid., vol. 209, 12 March 1872, col. 1858.
69. Hansard, Series 3, Lords, vol. 261, 31 May 1881, col. 1768.
70. ' Hansard, Series 3, Commons, vol. 282, 3 August 1883, col. 1490.
71. William Smith, *The Secretary for Scotland.*
72. George W.T. Omond, *op. cit.,* p. 334.
73. Hansard, Series 3, Commons, vol. 248, 21 July 1879, col. 857.
74. Ibid., vol. 265, 6 August 1881, cols. 32–3. The differences over the matter which Gladstone had with Rosebery are recounted in Robert Rhodes James, *Rosebery: A Biography of Archibald Philip, Fifth Earl of Rosebery* ch. 4.
75. Hansard, Series 3, Lords, vol. 262, 13 June 1881, cols. 308–25.
76. Robert Rhodes James, *op. cit.,* p. 121.
77. Hansard, Series 3, Lords, vol. 262, 13 June 1881, col. 320.

78. Earl of Camperdown, Hansard, Series 3, Lords, vol. 262, 13 June 1881, cols. 321–2.
79. Hansard, Series 3, Lords, vol. 262, 13 June 1881, cols. 324–5.
80. Robert Rhodes James, *op. cit.*, p. 138.
81. Ibid., p. 147.
82. 'Scotland in 1882', *The Times*, 1 January, 1883.
83. Robert Rhodes James, *op. cit.*, p. 148.
84. H.J. Hanham, 'The Creation of the Scottish Office, 1881–87' *Juridical Review*, 1965, p. 209.
85. The bill had been obstructed by the 'Fourth Party' and when it reached the Lords the Parliamentary session had only four days to go, so the Lords had rejected it by a majority of fifteen. Hansard, Series 3, Lords, vol. 283, 21 August 1883, cols. 1460–77.
86. William Smith, *op. cit.*, p. xv.
87. Ibid., p. xvi.
88. *The Times*, 17 January, 1884, p. 10.
89. Ibid. Including the Marquess of Lothian, chairing the meeting, on the platform were the Marquis of Bute, Marquis of Huntly, Earl of Aberdeen, Earl of Stair, Earl of Breadalbane, Earl of Elgin, Earl of Dalhousie, Earl of Mar and Kellie, Lord Balfour of Burleigh, Lord Saltoun, Lord Napier and Ettrick. Sir John D. Hay MP, Sir George Balfour MP, Sir George Campbell MP, Sir A.H. Gordon MP, Sir J. Don Wauchope MP, Hon. E. Majoribanks MP, Mr J.W. Barclay MP, Mr A.J. Balfour MP, Dr C. Cameron MP, Mr Cochran-Patrick MP, Mr Craig Sellar MP, Mr Fraser-Mackintosh MP, Mr R. Farquharson MP, Mr W. Holms MP, Mr J. Dick Peddie MP, Mr J. Ramsay MP, Mr R.F.F. Campbell MP, Mr Maclagan MP, Mr Anderson MP, Mr Duncan McLaren, and Mr J.J. Grieve.
90. Ibid., p. 10.
91. Hansard, Series 3, Lords, vol. 287, 8 May 1884, cols. 1664–5.
92. Ibid., vol. 289, 26 June 1884, cols. 1334–70.
93. Ibid., Commons, vol. 293, 17 November 1884, col. 1853; vol. 294, 19 February, 1885, col. 859.
94. Ibid, Lords, vol. 299, 9 July 1885, col. 87.

3   Settling Down to Business

1. A. MacCallum Scott, 'The Government of Scotland' in the *Scots Magazine*, October 1925, p. 11.
2. H.J. Hanham, 'The Creation of the Scottish Office, 1881–87', *Juridical Review* p. 213.
3. Hansard, Commons, vol. 300, 3 August 1885, col. 932.
4. Ibid., cols. 936–7.
5. Sir Thomas Wemyss Reid, *Memoirs and Correspondence of Lyon Playfair*, Letter to Gladstone, 8 December 1888, pp. 335–7.
6. Ibid., Letter to S.H. Russell, 20 May 1885, p. 337.
7. Report from the Select Committee on Education, Science, and Art (Administration) c. 312 July 1884, p. iii, paras. 2–3.
8. Ibid., p. 14, para. 266.
9. Ibid., para. 267.

10. Ibid., paras. 268–9.
11. Ibid., p. 75, paras. 1241–2.
12. Ibid., p. 80, para. 1331.
13. Ibid., p. 21, paras. 389–91.
14. Hansard, vol. 300, 4 August 1885, col. 1137.
15. Ibid., vol. 293, 6 November 1884, col. 1116.
16. Ibid., vol. 299, 9 July 1885, cols. 92–93.
17. 48 & 49 Vict., c. 1, section 6.
18. Hansard, Lords, Series 3, vol. 299, 14 July 1885, col. 587.
19. Ibid., 16 July 1885, cols. 899–900.
20. Ibid., 21 July 1885, col. 1375.
21. Ibid., col. 1373.
22. Quoted in H.J. Hanham, 'The Creation of the Scottish Office, 1881–87', *Juridical Review*, p. 229.
23. CAB 37/20 no. 36, 12 July 1887.
24. Ibid., Lothian quotes this 'narrow interpretation' of the Act of 1885 in the memorandum but does not give its source other than that it was that of the 'then Secretary of State'.
25. Max Egremont, *Balfour: A Life of Arthur James Balfour*, p. 77.
26. Sydney H. Zebel, *Balfour: A Political Biography*, p. 57.
27. D.W. Crowley, 'The "Crofters Party", 1885–1892', *Scottish Historical Review*. Though not a formally constituted political party the group of MPs in 1885 included the two Highland Land League Members – Dr G.B. Clark (Caithness-shire), Dr R. MacDonald (Ross-shire) – and three 'Independent Crofters' – D.H. Macfarlane (Argyllshire), J. MacDonald Cameron (Wick Burghs), C. Fraser-Mackintosh (Inverness-shire).
28. H.J. Hanham, 'The Creation of the Scottish Office, 1881–87', *Juridical Review*, p. 221–5.
29. CAB 37/19, no. 19, 18 March 1887, p. 3. MacDonald included this answer to Cross as an appendix to his memorandum on the memorandum by the Secretary for Scotland.
30. CAB 37/18, no. 42, 21 August 1886.
31. Ibid., p. 3.
32. Ibid., p. 2.
33. Ibid., p. 3.
34. Max Egremont, *Balfour: A Life of Arthur James Balfour*, p. 79.
35. CAB 37/19, no. 29, 10 May 1887.
36. CAB 37/18, no. 42, 21 August 1886, p. 1.
37. Quoted in memorandum by Lord Lothian to Cabinet on Scottish Business. CAB 37/20, no. 36, 12 July 1887, p. 3.
38. CAB 37/19, no. 19, 18 March 1887.
39. Ibid., p. 2.
40. 48 & 49 Vict., ch. 61, section 9.
41. CAB 37/19, no. 19, 18 March 1887, p. 2.
42. Hansard, Commons, Series 3, vol. 319, 24 August 1887, col. 1767.
43. CAB 37/20, no. 36, 12 July 1887, p. 1.
44. Ibid., p. 2.
45. Hansard, Lords, Series 3, vol. 318, 1 August 1887, col. 691.
46. CAB 37/20, no. 36, 12 July 1887, p. 6.
47. Hansard, Commons, Series 3, vol. 318, 10 August 1887, col. 1928.

48. Ibid.
49. Hansard, Commons, Series 3, vol. 319, 24 August 1887, col. 1760.
50. Ibid., col. 1761.
51. *Journal of Jurisprudence,* September 1887, vol. 31, p. 453.
52. Hansard, Lords, Series 3, vol. 318, 1 August 1887, col. 692.
53. Ibid., Commons, vol. 318, 10 August 1887, cols. 1927–8; vol. 321, 9 September, 1887, col. 150.
54. CAB 37/20, no. 36, 12 July 1887, p. 7.
55. Hansard, Lords, Series 3, vol. 318, 1 August 1887, cols. 688–9.
56. Ibid., 5 August 1887, col. 1341.
57. Ibid., col. 1342.
58. Ibid., col. 1954.
59. Ibid., vol. 331, 11 December, 1888, col. 1782.
60. Ibid., col. 1788.
61. Ibid., vol. 313, 31 March 1887, col. 84; vol. 313, 22 April 1887, col. 1631; vol. 318, 5 August 1887, col. 1378; vol. 321, 13 September 1887, cols. 496–502.
62. Ibid., Commons, vol. 331, 11 December 1888, col. 1802.
63. Ibid., col. 1807.
64. Ibid., Commons, vol. 331, 11 December 1888, col. 1802.
65. Ibid., vol. 300, 3 August 1885, col. 924.
66. Ibid., Lords, vol. 299, 9 July 1885, col. 96.
67. Ibid., vol. 324, 19 April 1888, col. 1743.
68. Ibid., col. 1744.
69. Ibid., c. 1.
70. CAB 37/24, no. 19, 6 April 1889.
71. 50 & 51 Vict., ch. 52, section 2 (1).
72. Sir Reginald Coupland, *Welsh and Scottish Nationalism* p. 290.
73. Salisbury to Richmond, 7 August 1885. Quoted in 'The Creation of the Scottish Office', *Juridical Review* 1965, p. 229.
74. *Journal of Jurisprudence*, vol. 31, September 1887, p. 449.
75. Hansard, Commons, Series 3, vol. 275, 27 November 1882, col. 142.
76. Ibid., col. 316.
77. Ibid., col. 318.
78. Ibid., col. 318. This suggestion was adopted on an experimental basis in 1981 and the Scottish Grand Committee met in Edinburgh on 15 February, 1982. During the Second World War an attempt to hold meetings in Edinburgh of Scottish MPs were regarded as a failure because of the lack of attendance.
79. Ibid., vol. 323, 6 March 1888, col. 401.
80. Ibid., col. 458.
81. Ibid., col. 452.
82. Ibid., col. 454.
83. PRO, CAB 41/22/22. 17 December 1892.
84. Ibid.
85. Hansard, House of Commons, vol. 21, 26 February 1894, col. 1044.
86. Ibid., vol. 22, 2 April 1894, col. 116.
87. Ibid., vol. 33, 9 May 1895, col. 822.
88. Ibid., vol. 34, 23 May 1895, col. 173.
89. Ibid., vol. 23, 17 April 1894, col. 669.

90. Ibid., col. 658.
91. Ibid., vol. 33, 9 May 1895, cols. 26–7. Bright's speech of 1 July 1886 was extensively quoted by Trevelyan in 1895 when, as Scottish Secretary, he moved once more the establishment of a Scottish Standing Committee.
92. Ibid., vol. 23, 17 April 1894, cols. 655–6.
93. In 1900–01 the vote on the Congested Districts Board, which had been established in 1897, was transferred from clause 7 (miscellaneous category) to the vote on the office of the Scottish Secretary in class 2 (civil departments) and was later transferred to the Board of Agriculture, still under class 2. The Scottish Land Court was placed under Class 3 (law and justice) after the enactment of the Small Landholders legislation in 1911.
94. Hansard, Commons, vol. 46, 15 February 1897, col. 414.
95. Ibid., Series 4, vol. 171, 26 March 1907, col. 1672.
96. Ibid., vol. 175, 11 June 1907, cols. 1207–8.
97. Ibid., vol. 175, 30 May 1907, col. 143.
98. Ibid., vol. 191, 25 June 1908, col. 123.
99. Ibid., 29 June 1908, col. 380.
100. Ibid., 8 July 1908, cols. 1663–4.
101. Ibid., Series 5, vol. 7, 8 July 1909, cols. 1423–4, 1515.
102. Ibid., col. 1484.
103. Ibid., vol. 19, 18 July 1910, cols. 936–89.
104. Ibid., Series 5, vol. 26, 15 June 1911, cols. 1676–7.
105. H.J. Hanham, *Scottish Nationalism,* p. 95.
106. CAB 37/105, no. 16, February 1911; CAB 37/105, no. 18, March 1911.
107. Pirie and Gulland attempted to strengthen the Scottish Grand Committee in the debate on the Standing Orders when the Committee was established in 1907. Hansard, Series 4, vol. 171, 25 March 1907, cols. 1561–2; vol. 172, 15 April 1907, cols. 642–3; vol. 174, 15 May 1907, cols. 1026–7. In a contribution to the debate on the second reading of the Government of Ireland Bill in 1912, Pirie raised the difficulties he had had regarding his attempts to amend Standing Orders in 1907 and related this to the question of home rule all round; Hansard, Commons, vol. 38, 7 May 1912, col. 336.
108. Sir Reginald Coupland, *Welsh and Scottish Nationalism* p. 307.
109. Hansard, Commons, vol. 62, 20 May 1914, col. 1935.
110. Ibid., vol. 41, 22 July 1912, cols. 814–15.
111. Ibid., 23 July 1912, col. 1012.
112. Ibid., 25 July 1912, cols. 1501–2.
113. Ibid., col. 1505.
114. Ibid., cols. 1503–4.
115. Ibid., 1 August 1912, col. 2288; 6 August 1912, col. 2928; vol. 42, 22 October 1912, col. 1930; vol. 44, 20 November 1912, col. 294.
116. Ibid., vol. 36, 11 April 1912, cols. 1403.

4　Educational Administration

1. George Elder Davie, *The Democratic Intellect*, p. xi.
2. Walter Bagehot, *The English Constitution*, London, Fontana, 1981 [1867], p. 61.

3. Coal Mines Regulations Act, 1887, 50 & 51 Vict., c. 58. Clause 6 included a part on the employment of boys, girls and women which dealt with the payment of school fees out of the wages of boys working in the mines.
4. NAS, SOE 2/12; ED 7/3/21, SED Minute Book no. 1, 1872–1946.
5. 1915 Session Cases p. 236, from the pursuers submission.
6. Martin Gilbert, *Winston S. Churchill* Companion vol. 5, pp. 689–90. Churchill to Warren Fisher, 30 April 1926. Also, E.O'Halpin, *Sir Warren Fisher, Head of the Civil Service, 1919–1939*, p. 108.
7. 35 & 36 Vict., c. 62, clause 1 and 52 & 53 Vict., c. 63, clause 12 (7). *Graham's Handbook* 1911 edition, much used by officials, did not include the amendment introduced in the Act of 1889, neither was it included in Roxburgh's *The Law of Education in Scotland*.
8. NAS, ED 7/3/21, SED Minute Book no. 1, 1872–1946.
9. Hansard, Series 5, vol. 41, 23 July, 1912, col. 1055.
10. Henry Craik, 'A Minister for Education', *Fortnightly Review,* vol. 37, April 1885, p. 479.
11. Hansard, Series 5, vol. 42, 22 October 1912, col. 1918.
12. NAS, ED 7/3/2. Correspondence between Craik and Grant-Ogilivie, 19/1/95; 21/1/95; 23/1/95; 19/2/95.
13. NAS, ED 7/3/2.
14. Ibid., Note to Vice President from Henry Craik, 20/11/94.
15. Ibid.
16. Ibid., Note to Trevelyan from Craik, 4 February 1895.
17. Ibid., J. Struthers reply, 30 January 1895.
18. *Glasgow Herald* 13 December 1921, quoted in Ian Russell Findlay, *Sir John Struthers KCB – Secretary of the Scotch/Scottish Education Department (1904–1922) – a study of his influence upon Scottish educational development* p. 47.
19. James Donaldson, 'The Scottish Education Department'. Address to western branch of Association of Secondary Teachers in Scotland, 29 October 1892 printed in *Scottish Review* p. 188.
20. Alexander Morgan, *The Rise and Progress of Scottish Education*; James Scotland, *A History of Scottish Education* vol. 2, p. 25; Andrew L. Stevenson, *The Development of Physical Education in the State Schools of Scotland, 1900–1960*.
21. Ian Russell Findlay, *Sir John Struthers KCB – Secretary of the Scotch/Scottish Education Department (1904–1922) – a study of his influence upon Scottish educational development* p. 54.
22. Alexander Morgan, *Makers of Scottish Education* p. 208.
23. *Glasgow Herald*, 8 June 1903.
24. *Scotsman*, 8 June 1903.
25. Ian Russell Findlay, *Sir John Struthers KCB – Secretary of the Scotch/Scottish Education Department (1904–1922) – a study of his influence upon Scottish educational development* p. 70.
26. *Educational News*, 14 November 1903.
27. J.H. Walker, *The Ad Hoc Administration of Education in Scotland, 1872–1929*, pp. 67–8.
28. Andrew L. Stevenson, *The Development of Physical Education in the State Schools of Scotland, 1900–1960* p. 27.

29. T.R. Bone, *School Inspection in Scotland, 1840–1966* p. 148.
30. Ibid., p. 149.
31. James Donaldson, 'The Scottish Education Department'. Address to western branch of Association of Secondary Teachers in Scotland, 29 October 1892 printed in Scottish Review p. 204.
32. Ibid.
33. 8 & 9 Geo.5, cap. 48, section 20.
34. CAB 37/51, 1899, no. 97, 13 December 1899. Memorandum on Education (Scotland), 1900, Balfour of Burleigh.
35. CAB 37/51, 1899, no. 97, 13 December 1899.
36. Duncan MacGillivray, 'Fifty Years of Scottish Education: Retrospect and Outlook' in John Clarke (ed.) *Problems of National Education*, London, Macmillan & Co. 1919. p. 10.
37. *Scotsman* 8 June, 1903.
38. R.B. Haldane, 'Preface' in Charles M. Douglas and Henry Jones, *Scottish Education Reform* p. 7. Also see chapter 5.
39. Rev. John Smith, *Broken Links in Scottish Education* p. 159.
40. Sir James Donaldson's address on the Scotch Education Department to the Education section of the British Association at Dundee, September 1912, reprinted in booklet form, *St Andrews Citizen* 14 September 1912. Copy in NAS, ED 7/3/8.
41. Ibid., pp. 11–12.
42. NAS, ED 7/3/8. Letter to Struthers from James Leishman, 6 May 1908.
43. Ibid., Letter to Leishman from Struthers, 8 May, 1908, marked private. At top of the letter are penned the question and answer, 'Was this ever sent ? Apparently not. AB 17.8.11'.
44. Ibid.
45. NAS, ED 7/3/8. Letter to Dr Kerr from Struthers, 4 November 1912.
46. Ibid., Note on Advisory Council on Education in Scotland.
47. Hansard, Series 5, Commons, vol. 42, 22 October 1912, cols. 1919–20.
48. Ibid., vol. 97, 8 August 1917, col. 423.
49. Ibid., cols. 428–9.
50. EIS Papers, GD 342/79/2. Reform in Scottish Education, report of Scottish Education Committee, pp. 24–5.
51. Struthers to Balfour of Burleigh, 24 October 1918, SRO, ED 14/30. Quoted in Ian Russell Findlay, *Sir John Struthers KCB – Secretary of the Scotch/Scottish Education Department (1904–1922) – a study of his influence upon Scottish educational development* pp. 301–2.
52. Hansard, Series 3, Lords, vol. 288, 20 May 1884, col. 804. This is misquoted in James Scotland, *A History of Scottish Education* vol. 2, p. 24.
53. Charles M. Douglas and Henry Jones, *Scottish Education Reform* p. 6.
54. Ibid., pp. 68–9.
55. EIS Papers, GD 342/1/11. Report of 57th Annual General Meeting in Edinburgh on Saturday, 19 September 1903, p. 16.
56. Papers of Sir Henry Craik, MS 7174. Letter from J.A. Chamberlain to Sir Henry Craik, 1/3/4, fols. 68–9.
57. Hansard, Series 4, Commons, vol. 162, 2 August 1906, col. 1455.
58. NAS, ED 7/3/6. Note to MacDonald from Struthers, 9/1/07.
59. Ibid., Note to Treasury and Office of Works from Struthers, 2/13/07.

60. Ibid., Note from the Treasury, signed by J.H. Murray to the Secretary of SED, 6 December, 1907.
61. Ian Russell Findlay, *Sir John Struthers KCB – Secretary of the Scotch/Scottish Education Department (1904–1922) – a study of his influence upon Scottish educational development* p. 40.
62. NAS, ED 7/3/6. Note to Vice President from Struthers, 28/7/09 giving Sinclair Struthers' views on the transfer of the SED to Edinburgh.
63. Ibid.
64. Ibid.
65. Ibid., Letter to Lord Pentland from Pirie, 24 June 1909.
66. NAS, ED 7/3/6. Letter to Pentland from Pirie, 24 June 1909.
67. Hansard, Series 4, Commons, vol. 196, 20 November 1908, cols. 1574–5; Series 5, Commons, vol. 31, 15 November 1908, col. 49; 22 November 1911, col. 1348, 1366–8.
68. EIS Papers. GD 342/13/1. Parliamentary and Tenure Committee Minute Book, 1901–02; GD 342/13/2, Parliamentary and Emergency Committee Minute Book, 1905–10; GD 342/13/3, Parliamentary and Emergency Committee Minute Book, 1910–14.
69. NAS, ED 7/3/6. Note to Vice President from Struthers, 28/7/09.
70. Ibid.
71. Ibid., Letter to Lord Pentland from Pirie, 24 June 1909.
72. Ibid., Note to MacDonald from A.D.K., 3/5/12.
73. Ibid., Letter to A.D.K. from Office of Works, 18 September 1912, signed by W.J. Downer.
74. NAS, ED 7/3/6. Note to MacDonald from A.D.K., 3/5/12.
75. NAS, ED 7/3/6, 12/3/12. Press reports gave the figure as forty-two MPs but as Struthers pointed out in a note to Mr Rose, the signatures given amounted to only forty-one.
76. *Scotsman* 30 July, 1909.
77. *Glasgow Herald* 11 July 1912.
78. J.A. Bryce, G.B. Esslemont, James Falconer, J.H. Henderson, P. A. Molteno, J.E. Sutherland and J.D. White.
79. *Glasgow Herald* 13 July 1912.
80. Letter in *Aberdeen Free Press* 22 July 1912.
81. Hansard, Series 5, Commons, vol. 41, 23 July 1912, cols. 1015–16.
82. Ibid., col. 1027.
83. Hansard, Series 5, Commons, vol. 19, 18 July 1910, col. 989.
84. *Aberdeen Free Press* 13 July 1912.
85. Hansard, Series 5, Commons, vol. 197, 24 November 1908, col. 215.
86. Ibid., Series 5, Commons, vol. 19, 18 July 1910, col. 976.
87. Hansard, Series 5, Commons, vol. 10, 30 August 1909, col. 50.
88. Ibid., Series 4, vol. 33, 29 April 1895, col. 20.
89. Royal Commission on the Civil Service, 1912–15, report 3, minutes of evidence, 21 November 1912, p. 169, para. 19,468.
90. Ibid., Graham Wallas, p. 185, para. 19,830.
91. Ibid., Struthers, p. 185, para. 19,831.
92. Ibid., p. 172, para. 19,537.
93. Ibid., p. 174, para. 19,607.
94. Walker Connor, 'The Politics of Ethnonationalism', *Journal of International Affairs*, vol. 27, 1973, p. 21.

5 Administering Agriculture, Health and the Highlands and Islands

1. Sir Austen Chamberlain, Politics From Inside – An Epistolary Chronicle 1906–1914, Letter to Balfour, 29 January 1910, p. 198.
2. D.W. Crowley, 'The Crofters Party, 1885–1892', *Scottish Historical Review,* vol. 35, 1956; James Hunter, *The Making of the Crofting Community* chs. 9 and 10.
3. Sir John Winnifrith, *The Ministry of Agriculture, Fisheries and Food* 1962, pp. 23–4.
4. Hansard, Series 4, vol. 2, Commons, 18 March 1892, col. 1275.
5. Ibid., col. 1276.
6. NAS, AF 43/6, Item 1. Memorandum to Sinclair from Sheriff Brand, 25 August 1903.
7. MS Asquith, 23 (238–9). Memorandum to Asquith from R.M. Ferguson, 12/1/1910.
8. NAS, AF 43/6, Item 18, Centralisation in Scotland.
9. John Brown, 'Scottish and English Land Legislation, 1905–11', *Scottish Historical Review,* vol. 47, p. 77. From British Museum Ripon Papers Add. MS 43544, liv, fos. 117–18. Ripon to Carrington, 19 January 1907.
10. Ibid.
11. Asquith Papers, Bodleian, Oxford, MS Asquith 84 (53); 1 February 1907.
12. Ibid., 11 (178–189). To Asquith from Sinclair, 7 September 1908.
13. Ibid.
14. NAS, AF 43/6, Item 9A.
15. *Scotsman* 7 October 1911.
16. NAS, GD 325/1/12, Scottish Landowners Federation Papers.
17. Ibid., cols. 1389–92. By 150 votes to 90.
18. Ibid., cols. 1431–2. By 89 votes to 39.
19. Ibid., cols. 1298, 1299.
20. James Hunter, *op. cit.* p. 193.
21. Scots Secretariat Papers, National Library of Scotland, Acc. 3721, Box 128, no. 56. Letter from Jim Dunlop to Roland Muirhead, 11 June, 1920.
22. Ibid., no. 65. Note attached to a letter from Dunlop to Muirhead, 25/5/20.
23. NAS, AF 68/18. Cutting from the North British Agriculturalist 7 March, 1912. Wright was a former professor of agriculture and principal of the West of Scotland Agricultural College (1901–11), author of a revision of Blackie's Agriculture and editor of the Standard Encyclopaedia of Modern Agriculture. R.B. Greig was an agriculture lecturer in Aberdeen University and the North of Scotland Agricultural College and had been appointed an inspector of agriculture under the Board of Education following his return from Australia where he had served on a Commission for two years which reported on agriculture. John D. Sutherland was an original member of the Crofters Commission and a member of Hosack & Sutherland, bank and law agency with a special interest in forestry and had been a member of the Royal Commission on state forestry appointed two years before.
24. Royal Commission on the Civil Service, minutes of evidence, report 3, 14 November 1912 (44th day), p. 154, para. 19,032.

25. Ibid., report 4, April 1914, ch. 9 (xii), p. 77, para. 69.
26. NAS, AF 75/1, no. 130.
27. NAS, AF 75/1.
28. Royal Commission on Poor Laws and Relief of Distress (Scotland), 1909, p. 152, para. 30.
29. Highlands and Islands Medical Service Committee. Report to the Lords Commissioners of His Majesty's Treasury, December 1912, Cd. 6559.
30. Ibid., Part II, p. 9, para. 19.
31. Ibid., p. 13, para. 31.
32. Ibid., Part IX, p. 41, para. 164.
33. PRO, CAB 37/115, June 1913, no. 34.
34. Ibid., p. 2.
35. Ibid., pp. 2–3.
36. PRO, CAB 37/115, 10 June 1913, no. 38.
37. Ibid., p. 3.
38. PRO, CAB 41/34/20, 11 June 1913.
39. NAS, AF 43/40.
40. Report of the Royal Commission on the Housing of the Industrial Population of Scotland, 1917, Cd. 8731.
41. Report of Her Majesty's Commissioners for Inquiry into the Housing of the Working Classes (Scotland), 1885, c. 4409.
42. Report of the Royal Commission on the Housing of the Industrial Population of Scotland, 1917, Cd. 8731, p. 9, para. 51.
43. Ibid., p. 4, para. 23.
44. NAS, HH/6/1170. Note to Sinclair from H.M.C. [Conacher], 16/1/09.
45. Royal Commission on Mines, second reading, 1909, Cd. 4820, part 18, p. 189.
46. Report of the Royal Commission on the Housing of the Industrial Population of Scotland, 1917, Cd. 8731, p. 293, para. 1938.
47. Ibid., p. 293, para. 1940.
48. A. Campbell Munro, 'Public Health Administration in England and Scotland: Points of Contrast and Contact', *Public Health Administration*, October 1898, vol. 11, p. 14.
49. Royal Commission on the Poor Laws and Relief of Distress, Report on Scotland 1909, Cd. 4922, part 3, ch. 2, paras. 35–6.
50. Ian Levitt, *Welfare and Scottish Poor Law, 1890–1914* pp. 88–89.
51. Sir Henry Bunbury (ed.), *Lloyd George's Ambulance Wagon: Being The Memoirs Of William J. Braithwaite, 1911–1912,* 20 April 1911, p. 148.
52. Ibid., 'Introduction', p. 31.
53. NAS, DD/1/1/1. Letter to W.J. Braithwaite from John Jeffrey, 12 February 1912.
54. Ibid., Letter to the Secretary, H.M. Treasury from the Secretary of the Scottish Insurance Commission, 24 May 1916.
55. Report of the Machinery of Government Committee, 1918, Cd. 9320, part 2, ch. 9 p. 58, para. 3.
56. Ibid., part 1, p. 11, para. 31.
57. Ibid.
58. Ibid., p. 165, para. 19,362.
59. Ibid., reprt 4, ch. 9, (xii), para. 70.

60. Christopher Addison, *Four and a Half Years,* vol. 2, p. 543, 12 June 1918.
61. Ibid., p. 546, 21 June 1918.
62. Hansard, Commons, Series 5, vol. 114, 27 March 1919, col. 606.
63. Ibid., 1 April 1919, col. 1136.
64. Ibid., cols. 1136, 1143.
65. Ibid., cols. 1146, 1153.
66. Ibid., col. 1157.
67. Ibid., 10 April 1919, col. 2394.
68. *British Medical Journal*, 17 August 1918; 5 April 1919.
69. Hansard, Commons, Series , vol. 114, 1 April 1919, col. 1160.
70. Hansard, Series 5, vol. 114, 1 April 1919, col. 1150.
71. *British Medical Journal,* 5 April, 1919; 17 May 1919; 26 July 1919.
72. NAS, HH/1/468. Note to Secretary for Scotland from J.L., 24/2/22.
73. Ibid., Memoranda, 6, 8, 9 March 1922.
74. Ibid., Letter from P.J. Grigg, Treasury to C.C. Foster, Scottish Office, 25 April 1922.
75. Ibid., Letter from C.C. Foster to P.J. Grigg, 1 May 1922.
76. Royal Commission on the Civil Service, Cmd.7338, 1914, Fourth Report, ch. 9, p. 779, para. 70.
77. Christopher Addison, *Four and a Half Years,* vol. 2, pp. 428–9, 12 September, 1917.
78. Hansard, Commons, Series 5, vol. 112, 26 February 1919, cols. 1829–30.

6   MacDonnell, the Boards and the 1928 Act

1. Royal Commission on the Civil Service (MacDonnell) Report, 1914, Cd.7338, report 4, ch. 1.
2. Ibid., ch. 2, p. 27, para. 20.
3. Ibid., para. 21.
4. Ibid., ch. 9, p. 77, para. 67.
5. Ibid., ch. 4, p. 45, para. 5.
6. Hansard, Commons, Series 5, vol. 204, 23 March 1927, col. 474.
7. MacDonnell Commission, report 3, p. 152, para. 18,993.
8. Ibid., p. 152, para. 18,992.
9. Ibid., p. 155, para. 19,065.
10. Ibid., report 4, ch. 9, p. 79, para. 70.
11. Ibid., report 3, p. 156, para. 19,093.
12. Ibid., report 4, ch. 4, p. 44, para. 4.
13. Ibid., ch. 9, p. 77, para. 69.
14. This method was fully explained in ch. 2, p. 26 of the report.
15. MacDonnell Commission, report 3, p. 153, para. 19,009.
16. Civil Service Commissioners, 47th report, 1903, Cd. 1695; 51st report, 1907, Cd. 3602; 54th report, 1910, Cd. 5277; 56th report, 1912, Cd. 6332.
17. MacDonnell Commission, report 4, ch. 3, p. 42, para. 48.
18. Ibid., p. 160, para. 19,223.
19. Appendix to third report of MacDonnell Commission, 1913, Cd. 6740, p. 159, paras. 19,181–2.
20. Ibid., p. 156, para. 19,104.

21. Ibid., p. 158, paras. 19,160–2.
22. Ibid., pp. 164–6, para. 19,357.
23. Ibid., p. 165, para. 19,361.
24. Ibid., p. 166, paras. 19,409, 19,411; p. 163, para. 19,309.
25. Ibid., p. 163, para. 19,312.
26. Ibid., p. 156, para. 19,130.
27. Asquith Papers, MS Asquith 89 (3–12). Deputation from Scottish Liberal MPs to the Rt Hon. H.H. Asquith. Transcript of meeting, 6 May 1912.
28. Hansard, Commons, Series 5, vol. 38, 9 May 1912, col. 581.
29. PRO, CAB37/105, no. 23, 9 March, 1911.
30. Ibid., vol. 26, 1 June 1911, col. 1290.
31. Ibid., vol. 34, 28 February 1912, col. 1454.
32. Ibid., cols. 1457–8.
33. Ibid., vol. 62, 15 May 1914, col. 1547.
34. Ibid., Series 4, vol. 153, 12 March 1906, col. 932.
35. NAS, HH/1/887. Memorial sent to Prime Minister, April 1919.
36. *Scotsman*, 16 January 1923.
37. Sir Colin Coote, *A Companion of Honour – The Story of Walter Elliot,* p. 81.
38. Hansard, Lords, Series 5, vol. 54, 30 July 1923, col. 1457.
39. NAS, HH/1/518. Note to Mr Laird mentions consultations of 1922, 2/8/23.
40. NAS, HH/1/520. Note of meeting in Lord Chancellor's room, 29 April 1924.
41. *British Medical Journal,* 18 August 1923, p. 29.
42. NAS, HH/1/521. Letter from Miss Margaret W. Hamilton, Hon. Secy. of Standing Committee of Scottish Insured Women to James Stewart MP, Parliamentary Under Secretary for Health, 29 July 1924.
43. Ibid., Commons, Series 5, vol. 214, 5 March 1928, col. 914.
44. NAS, HH/1/525. Letter to P.R. Laird, Scottish Office from James Rae, Assistant Secretary, Treasury, 18 January 1927.
45. Hansard, Commons, Series 5, vol. 139, 8 March 1921, cols. 229–30; vol. 144, 21 July, 1921, cols. 2409–10; vol. 147, October 20, 1921, cols. 273–274.
46. NAS, HH/1/531. Memorandum by Robert Greig, 9 January 1925.
47. Ibid.
48. NAS,HH/1/525. Note for resumption of second reading debate, 26/10/27.
49. NAS, HH/1/527. Telegram to Scottish Office from A.W, Hunter, 30 March 1928.
50. NAS, HH/1/531. Memorandum by Ewan MacPherson, 6 January 1925.
51. Ibid.
52. NAS, HH/1/521. Letter from Miss Margaret W. Hamilton to James Stewart MP, 29 July, 1924.
53. NAS, HH/1/525. Note for resumption of second reading debate, 26/10/27.
54. Civil Service Opinion, November 1923, p. 36.
55. NAS, HH/1/521. Report of deputation from Executive Officers' Association received by James Stewart MP, 3 April 1924.
56. Ibid., Letter to James Stewart MP from Walter G. Boys, 8 April 1924.
57. Ibid., Report of deputation from Executive Officers and Other Civil Servants received by the Secretary for Scotland, 16 February, 1925.
58. Hansard, Commons, Series 5, vol. 185, 25 June 1925, col. 1738.
59. NAS, HH/1/520. Supplementary note on any suggestion to effect immediately the reduction in the Board of Health from four to three.

60. Hansard, Commons, Series 5, vol. 204, 23 March 1927, col. 473.
61. Report of the Scottish Departmental Committee on the North Sea Fishing Industry, Report 1, 8 January 1914, Cd.7221.
62. Ibid., p. 168.
63. NAS, HH/1/527. Letter from Boys enclosing Memorandum on the position of the Fishery Board, 4 April, 1927.
64. Ibid.
65. NAS, HH/1/525. Home affairs Committee Memorandum, 4 March 1927.
66. The Prisons Chairman, Lord Polwarth would have been 65 in February 1929 and Dr Devon would have been 65 in October 1931 and Mr Crombie (Secretary and Inspector of the Commission) was 65 in February 1928.
67. NAS,LAD/A5/5. Prison Commission for Scotland, undated, unsigned memorandum.
68. NAS, LAD/A5/5. Report by the Committee on Bills of the Society of Writers to His Majesty's Signet on the Reorganisation of Offices (Scotland) Bill, June 1924.
69. Ibid.
70. Ibid., Report of the Committee of the Faculty of Advocates on the Reorganisation of Offices (Scotland) Bill, June 1924.
71. Ibid.
72. Ibid., Report by the Council of the Society of Solicitors in the Supreme Courts of Scotland on the Reorganisation of Offices (Scotland) Bill, July 1924.
73. Ibid.
74. NAS, HH/1/520. Note of meeting in Lord Chancellor's room, 29 April 1924.
75. Ibid.
76. Ibid.
77. Hansard, Commons, Series 5, vol. 204, 23 March 1927, cols. 467–70.
78. Ibid., Lords, Series 5, vol. 58, 2 July 1924, col. 104.
79. Hansard, Commons, Series 5, vol. 204, 23 March 1927, col. 465.
80. Ibid, col. 467.
81. NAS,HH/1/527, letter to Under Secretary, Scottish Office from Convention of Royal Burghs, 16 June, 1927, reporting resolution passed at previous day's meetings of the Parliamentary Bills Sub-Committee of the Convention.
82. Hansard, Commons, Series 5, vol. 204, 23 March 1927, col. 474.
83. NAS, HH/1/520. Note of meeting in Lord Chancellor's room, 29 April 1924.
84. NAS, HH/1/525. Note for resumption of second reading debate, 26/10/27.
85. Hansard, Commons, Series 5, vol. 204, 23 March 1927, col. 482.
86. Thurso Papers, Churchill College Archives' Centre, Cambridge, Thrs I 8/5, 14 October 1924.
87. Hansard, Commons, Series 5, vol. 214, 28 February 1928, cols. 265–6.
88. Ibid., col. 266.
89. Ibid., Lords, Series 5, vol. 58, 2 July 1924, col. 106.
90. Ibid., Commons, vol. 214, 28 February 1928, col. 267.
91. NAS, HH/1/526, Position of Fishery Board for Scotland, undated, unsigned.
92. Ibid.
93. Reorganisation of Offices (Scotland) Act, 1928, 18 & 19 Geo.5, ch. 34, section 1(5)(a) and (b).

94. W.I.R. Fraser, *An Outline of Constitutional Law,* p. 138.
95. NAS, LAD/A5/5. Note for amendments in Committee.
96. Hansard, Commons, Series 5, vol. 214, 28 February 1928, col. 296.
97. Ibid., Lords, Series 5, vol. 71, 10 July 1928, col. 1053.
98. Interview with Sir William Murrie, 6 January 1983.
99. NAS, HH/1/526. Copy of letter from John Gilmour sent to forty Scottish Conservative MPs, 23 April 1928.
100. NAS, HH/1/527. Letter from F.C. Thomson MP to Sir John Gilmour, 10 February 1928.
101. Hansard, Commons, Series 5, vol. 214, 28 February 1928, col. 865.
102. Ibid., col. 870.
103. Ibid., col. 870–1.
104. Ibid., col. 286.
105. Ibid., col. 873.
106. Ibid., cols. 881–2.
107. NAS, Gilmour Papers, GD 383/29/32x. Impressions of the General Election, 12 July 1929.

7 The Reorganisation Debate and Gilmour

1. Arthur Turner, *Scottish Home Rule*, ch. 3.
2. Andrew Dewar Gibb, *Scotland in Eclipse*, p. 96.
3. Scottish Grand Committee debates 1932/33, volume of Committees C and Scottish, cols. 717–3.
4. *Glasgow Herald*, 13 October 1937.
5. Ibid.
6. J. Henderson Stewart MP, 'A Plan for "Cinderella Scotland" ', *The People's Journal*, 24 December 1938.
7. NAS, HH/1/1228.
8. *Scotsman*, 5 October 1937.
9. NAS, HH/36/120. Draft of Confidential Memorandum, 29 November 1937.
10. Ibid.
11. Ibid.
12. Ibid., Letter to Elliot from Simon, 10 February 1938.
13. Ibid., Letter to Simon from Elliot, 18 February 1938.
14. Ibid., Letter to Elliot from Simon, 31 March 1938.
15. White Paper on Revenue and Expenditure (Scotland's Relations), December 1932.
16. Richard Finlay, *Independent and Free*, Edinburgh: John Donald, 1994.
17. W.E. Whyte, *The Case for the Reform of Local Government in Scotland*, address delivered at Glasgow University, 11 February 1926, p. 4.
18. NAS, HH/1/471. Letter from John Lamb, 24 November 1928.
19. NAS, HH/45/56. Speech prepared for Scottish Division of Society of Labour Candidates at Glasgow, 4 January 1930.
20. NAS, HH/45/55. Speech in Greenock by Sir Godfrey Collins, 18 October 1935.
21. Ibid.
22. NAS, HH/45/51. Note to Registry, 9/10/23.

23. Ibid., Letter to Gilmour from Messrs. Hillier, Parker, May and Rowden, 11 December, 1924.
24. NAS, HH/45/44. Case for Edinburgh building.
25. NAS, HH/1/799. 'A note as to the possibility of extending devolution', P.R. Laird, 12 September 1928.
26. Ibid.
27. Ibid.
28. Ibid.
29. Ibid.
30. Ibid.
31. Ibid., Note attached to memorandum by P.R. Laird for Under Secretary of State, 17/11/32.
32. Ibid., P.R. Laird, 'Administrative Devolution', 17 November 1932.
33. Ibid.
34. Ibid.
35. Ibid., Note by Mr Stewart, undated.
36. NAS, HH/45/44. Letter to Collins from McKechnie, 30 September 1933.
37. Hansard, Commons, Series 5, vol. 287, 13 March 1934, col. 184.
38. *Glasgow Herald*, 16 February 1935.
39. Hansard, Commons, Series 5, vol. 272, 24 November 1932, cols. 260–4.
40. NAS, HH/45/61l. Committee on Scottish Administration, 21 November 1935.
41. Ibid., Letter to Jeffrey from Rae, 26 June 1936 and 30 June 1936.
42. Sir John Gilmour Papers (GP), GD/383/68/7. Copy of letter to Collins from Tom Johnston MP, 27 July 1936.
43. Ibid., GD/383/61/1. Letter to Gilmour from Collins, 9 June 1936.
44. Interview with Sir William Murie, January 6 1983.
45. NAS, HH/45/61. Letter to Elliot from Alexander Gray, 5 November 1936. Jeffrey, Peck, Highton and Laird were, respectively, Permanent Under Secretary of State at the Scottish Office, Secretary of the Scottish Education Department, Secretary of the Department of Health for Scotland, and Secretary of the Department of Agriculture for Scotland.
46. Report of Committee on Scottish Administration, October 1937 Cmd.5563, p. 4.
47. NAS, AD/62/111/1. Memorandum by Permanent Under Secretary of State, November 1936, p. 38, para. 40.
48. Ibid.
49. Ibid., p. 39, para. 41.
50. Ibid., p. 39, para. 42.
51. NAS, HH/45/62. Third meeting, 9 December 1936.
52. NAS, HH/45/66. Memorandum by George MacDonald, February 1937, p. 19, para. 20; p. 20, para. 20.
53. Ibid., p. 20, para. 20.
54. NAS, HH/45/62. Seventh meeting, 18 February 1937.
55. Ibid.
56. Ibid., Fifth meeting, 10 February 1937.
57. Ibid., Tenth meeting, 12 April 1937.
58. Ibid.
59. Ibid., Fourth meeting, 16 December 1936.

60. NAS, HH/45/65. Society of Civil Servants Evidence, April 1937.
61. Gilmour Report, part 1, pp. 26–7, paras. 50,52,53.
62. NAS, AD/62/111/1. Memorandum by Permanent Under Secretary, part I, para. 22.
63. Gilmour Report, part V, p. 42, para. 83.
64. NAS, HH/45/62. Tenth meeting, 12 April 1937.
65. NAS, HH/45/64. Memorandum by General Board of Control.
66. NAS, HH/45/62. Tenth meeting, 12 April 1937.
67. Committee on Scottish Health Services (Cathcart) Report, 1936, Cmd.5204.
68. Ibid., p. 300, para. 830.
69. Ibid., p. 301, para. 830.
70. Gilmour Report, part I, p. 34, para. 68.
71. NAS, HH/45/62. Fourth meeting, 16 December 1936.
72. NAS, AD/62/111/1, p. 40, para. 43(2).
73. NAS, HH/45/62. Second meeting, 2 December 1936.
74. NAS, HH/45/73. Letter to Elliot from Gilmour, 19 September 1937.
75. NAS, AD/62/111/2, SAC7. Note by Sir Horace Hamilton, 12 November 1937.
76. Ibid.
77. Gilmour Report, part I, p. 26, para. 50.
78. NAS, AD/62/111/2, SAC 7. Note by Sir Horace Hamilton, 12 November 1937.
79. NAS, HH/45/73. Letter to Hamilton from Rae, 19 January 1938.
80. NAS, AD/62/111/2, SAC 10. Note by Sir Horace Hamilton, 15 November 1937.
81. NAS, AD/62/111/2, SAC 4. Note by J.W. Peck, 3 November 1937.
82. Ibid., Letter from Fishery Board for Scotland to Under Secretary of State, 20 November, 1937; HH/54/75. Letter to Hamilton from George Hogarth, 12 November, 1937; Note to Hamilton from Duke, 25 November 1937.
83. NAS, AD/62/111/2, SAC 17. Letter to Hamilton from General Board of Control, 30 November 1937; HH/45/76.
84. NAS, HH/45/74, SAC 13. Memorandum by McNicoll, 21 October 1937.
85. Ibid., Letter to Duke from R.J.P. Harvey, 31 January 1938; Letter to Harvey from Duke, 3 February 1938.
86. Ibid., Letter to D.J. Colville from Glasgow branch of NUJ, 5 September 1938; Letter to Colville from General Secretary of NUJ, 2 December 1938.
87. PRO, T 162/476. Note from Sir James Rae to Warren Fisher, Treasury 24/6/36 with hand-written reponse, 25/6/36.
88. NAS, AD/62/111/1. Letter from Depute Clerk to Privy Council to the Lord Advocate, 28 October 1937; Note to Millar Craig from Lord Advocate Cooper, 29 November 1937.
89. NAS, HH/45/44. Copy of letter to Ormsby-Gore from MacDonald, 30 June, 1933.
90. *Scotsman*, 28 July 1933.
91. NAS, HH/45/44. Proposed Government Buildings, Edinburgh. October 1934.
92. Ibid. Letter to Duke from R.E.W. Baird, Secretary, Prisons Department for Scotland, 26 September 1934.

93. NAS, HH/45/44. Letter from Wing-Commander E.J. Hodsoll, Home Office to Office of Works, 24 January 1938.
94. *Glasgow Herald*, 15 October 1937.
95. Ibid., 16 October 1937.

8   The Origins and Development of the Goschen Formula

1. Robert Christie, *Injustice to Scotland Exposed, in a Letter to the Scottish Representatives in Parliament* Edinburgh: Thomas Constable & Co., 1853.
2. William Ferguson, *Scotland: 1689 to the Present* Edinburgh: Mercat Press, 1987, p. 322.
3. David Heald, *Territorial Equity and Public Finances: Concepts and Confusion*, p. 11.
4. David Heald, *Public Expenditure*, p. 246. For example, Lawrence Boyle, *Equalisation and the Future of Local Government Finance*, pp. 70–1; Michael Keating and Arthur Midwinter, *The Government of Scotland*, p. 183; James G. Kellas, *The Scottish Political System*, p. 195.
5. Sir Robert Rait and George S. Pryde, *Scotland* second edition London: Ernest Benn, 1954, p. 169; William Ferguson, *Scotland: 1689 to the Present op. cit.*, p. 328.
6. Sir David Milne, *The Scottish Office* London: Allen and Unwin, 1957, p. 94.
7. Sydney and Olive Checkland, *Industry and Ethos*, p. 170.
8. Thomas J. Spinner George Joachim *Goschen: The Tranformation of a Victorian Liberal* London: Cambridge University Press, 1973, p. 164.
9. Sir Edward Bridges, *Treasury Control* London: Athlone Press, 1950, p. 8.
10. Fisher to Baldwin, February 16, 1926. Quoted in E. O'Halpin, *Sir Warren Fisher*, p. 113.
11. Expenditure and Revenue of Local Authorities, 1848, 1867, 1881, 1893.

In 1848, the expenditure of local authorities, excluding loan expenditure, was	£1,684,000
and the total receipts, excluding loans, were of which there was obtained from	1,623,000
Rates that is direct taxation	903,000
Tolls, dues and other indirect taxation	475,000
Imperial subventions	15,000
All other sources	230,000
In 1867, the expenditure of local authorities, excluding loan expenditure, was	£2,854,000
and the total receipts, excluding loans, were of which there was obtained from	2,841,000
Rates that is direct taxation	1,793,000
Tolls, dues and other indirect taxation	600,000
Imperial subventions	151,000
All other sources	297,000
In 1881, the expenditure of local authorities, excluding loan expenditure, was	£4,664,000

and the total receipts, excluding loans, were of which there was obtained from	4,933,000
Rates that is direct taxation	2,956,000
Tolls, dues and other indirect taxation	928,000
Imperial subventions	546,000
All other sources	503,000
In 1893, the expenditure of local authorities, excluding loan expenditure, was	£7,593,000
and the total receipts, excluding loans, were of which there was obtained from	7,743,000
Rates that is direct taxation	3,780,000
Tolls, dues and other indirect taxation	868,000
Imperial Subventions	1,357,000
All other sources	1,738,000

Source: Report on Local Taxation in Scotland C.7575, 1895, p. xlvi.

The figures were imprecise, as Skelton noted in his report, but some idea of the changes over the latter half of the nineteenth century is clear (Report on Local Taxation in Scotland C.7575, 1895, p.viii.). Not only had the amount paid in subventions from the state increased dramatically but as a proportion of the expenditure of local authorities imperial subventions had increased from only 0.89% in 1848 to 17.87% in 1893.

12. Local Government Act 1888, 51 & 52 Vict., ch. 41, section 20, first schedule.
13. Finance Act, 1894, 57 & 58 Vict. c.30, s.19.
14. Hansard, Series 3, Commons, vol. 324, 26 March, 1888, col. 301.
15. Ibid.
16. K.B. Smellie, *A History of Local Government*, p. 80.
17. Hansard, Series 3, Commons, vol. 324, 26 March, 1888, col. 302.
18. Ibid., vol. 332, 18 December, 1888, col. 790.
19. Correspondence between Chancellor of the Exchequer and the Secretary for Scotland in regard to the Allocation of the Grant in aid of Local Taxation for the year, 1888–89. Parliamentary Paper, June 1888, c.5418.
20. Local Government (Scotland) Act, 1889, 52 & 53 Vict., ch. 50, section 22.
21. Alexander Morgan, *The Rise and Progress of Scottish Education*, p. 179.
22. K.B. Smellie, *A History of Local Government*, p. 80.
23. Sheriff W.C. Smith 'Imperial Grants as Adjustments of Taxation' *Proceedings of the Philosophical Society of Glasgow*, vol. 30, 1898–99, Glasgow: John Smith and Son, 1899.
24. Local Taxation (Customs and Excise) Act, 1890, 53 & 54 Vict., ch. 60, section 2.
25. Customs and Inland Revenue Act, 1890, 53 & 54 Vict., ch. 8.
26. Ibid., section 7.
27. SRO, ED 7/5/18, SED Memorandum, Grants for Technical Education in England and Scotland, 9/xi/97.
28. Alexander Morgan, *The Rise and Progress of Scottish Education*, p. 180.
29. SRO, ED 7/5/18, SED Memorandum, Grants for Technical Education in England and Scotland, 9/xi/97.

30. 1894–95 amounts falling to England and Wales and Scotland by Customs and Excise Duties:

England and Wales	£1,055,278
Scotland	145,100
that is in proportion of 80:11	
Deductions which fell to be made:	
England and Wales	300,000
Scotland	105,800
(£95,000 plus £10,800 variable)	
Resulting Residue Grants available for distribution amongst the Counties and Burghs:	
England and Wales	755,278
Scotland	39,300
that is in proportion of 80:4.2	

Source: NAS, ED 7/5/18.

31. £40,000 under section 2 (2) of Local Taxation (Customs and Excise) Act, 1890; section 2 (6) of Education and Local Taxation Act, 1892; section 22 of Local Government (Scotland) Act, 1889.
32. NAS, ED 7/5/17. Draft of note to Treasury sent to Vice President of SED for approval by Craik, 2/3/95.
33. NAS, ED 7/5/17. Referred to in draft of note to Treasury sent to Vice President of SED for approval by Craik, 2/3/95.
34. NAS, ED 7/5/17. Draft of note to Treasury sent to Vice President of SED for approval by Craik, 2/3/95.
35. NAS, ED 7/6/2. Copy of letter to Treasury from Craik, 26 March 1896.
36. NAS, ED 7/5/17. Letter to SED from Sir Francis Mowatt, Permanent Secretary to the Treasury, 1 February 1896.
37. Ibid., Draft of note to Treasury sent to Vice President of SED for approval by Craik, 2/3/95.
38. Ibid., Draft of note to Treasury for Vice President's approval, 17/3/96.
39. Hansard, Series 4, Commons, vol. 39, 30 March, 1896, col. 371; 31 March 1896, cols. 516–17; vol. 43, 27 July 1986, col. 697; 28 July 1896, cols. 822–3; 30 July 1896, col. 1045.
40. Ibid., vol. 43, 27 July 1896, col. 697.
41. NAS, ED 7/5/17. Letter to SED from R.W. Hanbury, 23 April 1896.
42. Ibid., Letter to SED from R.W. Hanbury, 12 March 1897.
43. Ibid., Note to Vice President from Craik, 19/3/97.
44. Ibid.
45. Hansard, Series 3, Commons, vol. 351, 24 March 1891, col. 1801.
46. Ibid., col. 1809.
47. NAS, ED 7/5/18. 'Confidential' memorandum on Claim for Additional Grant to Scotland, Balfour of Burleigh, 2 April 1897.
48. Ibid.
49. Agricultural Rates Act, 1896, 59 & 60 Vict., ch. 16, section 2.
50. Agricultural Rates, Congested Districts and Burgh Land Tax Relief (Scotland) Act, 1896, 59 & 60 Vict., ch. 37, section 3 (1).
51. NAS, ED 7/5/7. Note to Lord Balfour of Burleigh from Craik, 22/11/02.

52. Ibid., Memorandum from Balfour of Burleigh to Ritchie, 2 December 1902.
53. Ibid., Memorandum from Ritchie to Balfour of Burleigh [Dec. 1902 ?].
54. Ibid.
55. Royal Commission on Local Taxation, Final Report on Local Taxation (Scotland) 1902, cd.1067, p. 15.
56. Ibid.
57. Cd.616, 1902. Population proportions of UK given as 78.4% in England and Wales, 10.8% in Scotland, and 10.8% in Ireland.
58. NAS, ED 7/5/7. Note to Craik, 28/1/03.
59. Ibid., Ritchie to Balfour of Burleigh, 21 February 1903.
60. Ibid., Letter to Craik from W. Blair, Treasury, 26 February 1903.
61. Ibid., Memorandum of arrangement between Secretary for Scotland and Chancellor of the Exchequer as to General Aid Grant to be given to Scotland in respect of grant to England under 1902 Education Act. Also, reply to Parliamentary Questions from Mr O'Mara MP, Kilkenny South, Hansard, Series 4, Commons, vol. 120, 2 April 1903, cols. 898–9.
62. Ibid., Memorandum of arrangement between Secretary for Scotland and Chancellor of the Exchequer as to General Aid Grant to be given to Scotland in respect of grant to England under 1902 Education Act.
63. Revenue and Expenditure (England, Scotland and Ireland), Return, 1 July 1914, cd.387.
64. Sir Lewis
Selby-Bigge, *The Board of Education*, p. 80.
65. NAS, ED7/5/9. SED Note to Treasury, 15/10/06.
66. Ibid.
67. Education (Scotland) Act, 1901, ch. 9, section 1.
68. NAS, ED 7/5/9. SED Note to Treasury.
69. NAS, ED 7/5/7. Paper giving comparison of grants paid to SED, 7/7/02.
70. Education (Scotland) Act, 1908, 8 Edw.7, ch. 63, section 15.
71. Ibid., subsection 6.
72. Hansard, Series 4, Lords, vol. 198, 7 December 1908, col. 14.
73. NAS, ED 7/5/9. Memorandum to Treasury from SED, December 18, 1907; Letter to SED from Sir G.H. Murray, 6 January 1908.
74. NAS, ED 7/5/22. Note from Struthers to Vice president, 26/2/09.
75. Ibid., Memorandum, 12 December 1909.
76. *Glasgow Herald*, 19 April 1911.
77. NAS, ED 7/5/22. Comparison of figures used by Mr D.M. Wilson at Oban EIS Congress on 18 April 1911 with those of Accountant's Report for 1908–09.
78. S.M. Murray, *A Short Manual of the Education (Scotland) Act, 1908*, p. 3.
79. NAS, ED 7/5/22, LLoyd George. Transcript of proceedings of meeting between LLoyd George and deputation from Scottish MPs, 18 June 1912.
80. Ibid.
81. Ibid., Paper by Henry Keith, Scottish Educational Finance copy sent to SED with a letter on 4 May 1912.
82. Letter to Scotsman, 19 July 1912.
83. NAS, ED 7/5/22. Letter to Keith from Struthers, 24 July 1912.
84. *Scotsman* and *Glasgow Herald*, 19 July 1912; 27 July 1912; 29 July 1912; 1 August 1912.
85. 8 & 9 Geo. 5, ch. 48, section 21.

86. NAS, ED 14/149. Correspondence with Treasury, unsigned and undated memorandum, Vote Grants paid into the Education (Scotland) Fund, Section 14 (6).
87. Ibid., Letter to Struthers from Sydney Armitrage-Smith [Assistant Secretary to the Treasury], 17 December 1917.
88. Ibid., Letter to Sydney Armitrage-Smith from Struthers, 17 December 1917.
89. Ibid., Letter to Munro from Stanley Baldwin, 18 December 1917.
90. Ibid., Letter to SED Secretary from Stanley Baldwin, December 1917.
91. Ibid., Draft letter to Baldwin from Secretary for Scotland, 22 December 1917.
92. Hansard, Series 5, Commons, vol. 100, 17 December, 1917, cols. 1653–7.
93. NAS, SOE 6/1/26. Note to Mr Alexander from R.T.H. [Hawkins], 11/4/23. Hawkins was private secretary to Dr George MacDonald, SED Secretary.
94. NAS, SOE 6/1/26. Note to Mr Alexander from R.T.H. [Hawkins].
95. Hansard, Series 5, Commons, vol. 7, 8 July 1909, col. 1437.
96. Ibid., vol. 41, 23 July 1912, col. 1015.
97. Ibid., vol. 55, 24 July 1913, col. 2220.
98. Ibid., vol. 41, 23 July 1912, col. 1015.
99. PRO, T/160/796 pt.3. Note to Mr Brittain from M.T. Flett, 9/3/39.
100. NAS, SOE 6/1/31. Note to Mr Aitkin from JWP [Peck], 21/10/21.
101. Ibid., Note to Vice President from J.S. [Struthers] 1/12/21.
102. NAS, SOE 6/1/26. Note from R.T.H. to Mr Alexander, 5/4/23.
103. Ibid.
104. Ibid., Letter from Col. P.J. Blair, political secretary of Scottish Unionist Party, to Sir George MacDonald, 11 October 1927.
105. Ibid., Reply to Blair from MacDonald, 14 October 1927.
106. *Scotsman* 19 March 1924.
107. NAS, SOE 6/1/26. Letter to Reginald T. Hawkins, SED from Sir Henry Keith, 12 November 1932.
108. Scottish Educational Journal Friday, 11 November 1932.
109. NAS, SOE 6/1/26. Letter to Henry Keith from George MacDonald, 29 March 1923.
110. Ibid. Letters from Keith to MacDonald, 9 and 29 March 1923.
111. PRO, T160/796 part 2. Letter to Sir Aylmer Hunter-Weston MP from Ronald McNeill, Financial Secretary to the Treasury, 5 May, 1927.
112. George Pottinger, *The Secretaries of State for Scotland, 1926–76*, p. 50.
113. Thurso Papers, Letter from Sir Archibald Sinclair MP to Peck, 10 August 1932.
114. PRO, T160/796 Part 3. Note to Mr Waterfield from A. Wilson Smith 25/5/35.
115. Hansard, Commons, 5 Series, vol. 301, 9 May 1935, cols. 1171–2.
116. Ibid., col. 1247.
117. Ibid., col. 1186.
118. Ibid., col. 1173.
119. PRO, T160/796 part 3. Note to Mr Brittan from M.T. Flett, 9/3/39.

9   Scottish Office Ministers

1. McKinnon Wood Papers, letter to Asquith, 20/5/15.
2. Ibid., Letter from Gulland to McKinnon Wood, 22 May 1915.

3. Ibid., Letter from McKinnon Wood to Aunt Anne, 16/7/16.
4. D.J. Heasman, 'The Ministerial Hierarchy' Parliamentary Affairs vol. 15, 1961–62, p. 319.
5. NAS, HH/1/887, draft of letter to Prime Minister prepared 23 December 1918.
6. Ibid.
7. Robert Munro, *Looking Back: Fugitive Writings and Sayings*, p. 346.
8. Ibid., p. 348.
9. Iain MacLean, *The Labour Movement in Clydeside Politics, 1914–22*, p. 20.
10. Ibid.
11. Ibid.
12. PRO, CAB 23/9, War Cabinet no.523, 31 January 1919.
13. Ministries and Secretaries Bill, 1919, Bill 162. Hansard, Commons, Series 5, vol. 118, First Reading, 1 August 1919, col. 2429; vol. 119, second reading, 5 August 1919, cols. 280–324.
14. Report from the Select Committee on the Remuneration of Ministers, House of Commons, 15 December 1920, cd.241.
15. Hansard, Commons, Series 5, vol. 112, 27 February 1919, col. 1947; vol. 117, 1 July 1919, col. 780; vol. 120, 5 November 1919, cols. 1494–95; vol. 128, 22 April 1920, cols. 650–1; vol. 130, 17 June, 1920, col. 1443; vol. 132, 22 July 1920, col. 620; vol. 134, 1 November 1920, col. 46; vol. 141, 12 May 1921, col. 2119; vol. 145, 2 August 1921, col. 1166; vol. 162, 16 April 1923, col. 1669; vol. 180, 24 February 1925, cols. 1729–30; vol. 182, 25 March 1925, cols. 427–8; vol. 185, 17 June 1925, col. 501.
16. Ibid., vol. 189, 17 December 1925, cols. 1612–13.
17. *Glasgow Herald* editorial, 21 April 1919.
18. NAS, HH/1/887. Notes of deputation from the Convention of Royal Burghs to the Secretary of State for Scotland, 13 March 1924.
19. Ibid., Report of deputation to Prime Minister on 23 February 1924. Published by the Convention of Royal Burghs, March 1925.
20. *Scotsman*, editorial, 12 June 1920.
21. *Scotsman*, 12 June 1920.
22. NAS, Sir John Gilmour papers, GD 383/20/9, MacLeod of MacLeod to Gilmour, 9 November, 1924.
23. NAS, Scots Secretariat Papers, Acc.3721, box 127, no. 55, *Times of India*, 19/12/25; *Shanghai Times*, 15/3/26.
24. PRO, CAB 23/38, 6 April 1921.
25. Hansard, Commons, Series 5, vol. 195, 7 May 1926, col. 611.
26. NAS, Walter Elliot Papers, Acc.6721, box 13, *Scotsman*, 6 March 1926.
27. NAS, HH/1/891. Report of proceedings of annual general meeting of the Convention of Royal Burghs, April 6 1926.
28. Hansard, Commons, Series 5, vol. 14, 2 March 1910, col. 847.
29. Ibid., vol. 26, 1 June 1911, col. 1249.
30. Ibid., vol. 17, 17 June 1910, cols. 1581, 1557.
31. *Whitaker's Almanack*, 1890 and 1914.
32. Hansard, Series 4, vol. 32, 28 March, 1895, cols. 354–5.
33. John Sandars Papers, fols. 121–4, letter from A.G. Murray to Balfour, 5 October 1903.
34. Craik Papers, MS.7175, f. 45, letter from A. G. Murray to Balfour, October 5 1903.

35. NAS, HH/1/887. Convention of Royal Burghs, Status of the Office of Secretary for Scotland. Report of deputation to the Prime Minister on 23 February 1925.
36. Hansard, Commons, Series 5, vol. 119, 5 August 1919, cols. 304–5, 312–13.
37. Report from the Select Committee on Ministers' Remuneration, House of Commons, 170, 1929–30, VI, 287.
38. Gilmour Papers, GD 383/67/13, Robert Bruce to Gilmour, 22 March 1936.
39. H.J. Hanham, 'The development of the Scottish Office', in J.N. Wolfe (ed.), *Government and Nationalism in Scotland*.
40. CAB 37/73, no. 166, 19 December 1904.
41. Hansard, Series 5, vol. 62, 15 May 1914, col. 1473.
42. Ibid., Series 4, vol. 191, 25 June 1908, col. 119.
43. Ibid., vol. 109, 19 June 1902, col. 1151.
44. Robert Munro, *Looking Back: Fugitive Writings and Sayings*, p. 282.
45. John Percival Day, *Public Administration in the Highlands and Islands of Scotland*, pp. 36–7.
46. Lady Pentland, *The Rt. Hon. John Sinclair, Lord Pentland GCSI: A Memoir*, p. 94.
47. McKinnon Wood Papers, letter from John W. Gulland MP to Wood, 22 May 1915.
48. C.T. Carr, *Delegated Legislation*, p. 6.
49. Sir Cecil T. Carr, *Concerning English Administrative Law*, p. 25.
50. Report of the Committee on Ministers' Powers, April 1932, Cmd.4060.
51. NAS, HH/45/38. Letter to departments from J.H.E. Woods, secretary to the Committee on Ministers' Powers, 16 November 1929.
52. Ibid., William K. Dickson to the Committee on Ministers' Powers, 30 November 1929.
53. Sir Cecil T. Carr, *Concerning English Administrative Law*, p. 26.
54. Hansard, Commons, Series 5, vol. 350, 19 July 1939, col. 395.
55. NAS, Walter Elliot Papers, Acc.6721, box 12, *Times*, 7 April 1925.
56. Sir Alexander McEwen, *Towards Freedom*, p. 125.
57. Hansard, Commons, Series 5, 28 February 1928, col. 279.
58. H.J. Paton, *The Claim of Scotland*, p. 79.
59. Report of the Committee on Scottish Administration October 1937, Cmd.5563, p. 19, para. 37.
60. NAS, Elliot Papers, Acc.6721, box 14, *Edinburgh Evening News* 27 August, 1927; *Glasgow Herald* 5 October, 1927, *Morning Post*, 6 October 1927.
61. Ibid., box 17, *Glasgow Herald*, 2 May 1928.
62. David Marquand, *Ramsay MacDonald*, p. 493.
63. Report of the Committee on Scottish Administration October 1937, cmd.5563, p. 52, para. 107.
64. NAS, HH/1/820. Additional Parliamentary Under Secretary of State for Scotland, initialled for 7/12/38 and 9/12/38.
65. Ibid.
66. John Sandars Papers, fols. 72–80, letter from Linlithgow, 13 March 1905.
67. Iain MacLean, *The Labour Movement in Clydeside Politics, 1914–22*, p. 323.
68. McKinnon Wood Papers. *Alliance News* April 1927, article by Charles Roberts.
69. Christopher Harvie, *No Gods and Precious Few Heroes*, p. 28.

70. Papers of Ronald Munro Ferguson, Vt. Novar. Letter to Prime Minister from Novar, 12 November 1924.
71. Sir John Gilmour Papers, GD 383/70/18x. Article in press by P. J. Dollan, 'Miner Who Refused Peerage', 4 March 1938.
72. Dunfermline Public Library, William Adamson Papers, *The Dunfermline Press*, 29 February 1936.
73. John Sandars Papers, MS Eng. Hist. c.733, fols. 50–1, 55–8. 12 November 1900, Balfour of Burleigh to AJB; 13 November 1900, AJB to B of B; 14 November 1900, B of B to AJB.
74. Lady Francis Balfour, *A Memoir of Alexander Hugh Bruce, Lord Balfour of Burleigh KT, 6th Baron*, p. 74.
75. John Sandars Papers, fols. 63–4, 1 June, 1901.
76. Papers of Ronald Munro Ferguson, Vt. Novar. Baldwin to Novar, 9 November, 1924.
77. Ibid.
78. Ibid., Novar to Baldwin, 12 November 1924.
79. Keith Middlemas and John Barnes, *Baldwin: A Biography*, pp. 145–7.
80. Ibid., pp. 224–8.
81. Gilmour papers, GD 383/43/35. Letter from J.J. to Gilmour, 29 September 1932.
82. E.M.M. Taylor, *The Politics of Walter Elliot, 1929–36*, quoted Chamberlain Papers 18/1/501, Chamberlain to Ida, 23 September 1925.
83. Sir Colin Coote, *A Companion of Honour – The Story of Walter Elliot*, p. 85.
84. John Malcolm McEwen, Unionist and Conservative MPs, 1914–39, p. 173.
85. Gilmour Papers, GD 383/17/18. Letter to A. Bartlett Glen from Gilmour, 21 October 1922.
86. Keith Middlemas and John Barnes, *Baldwin: A Biography*, p. 279.
87. Gilmour Papers, GD 383/20/5. Letter to Gilmour from Blair, 7/11/24.
88. Ibid., GD 383/43/76. Letter from Fergusson to Gilmour, 30 September 1932.
89. Interview with Sir William Murrie, January 1983.
90. Gilmour Papers, GD 383/65/14–16. Letter from Maxwell to Gilmour, 17 November 1935.
91. Herbert Sidebotham, *Political Profiles From British Life*, p. 241.
92. Elliot Papers, Acc.6721, *The Weekly Dispatch*, 9 June 1928 names Elliot as a possible Speaker to succeed J.H. Whitely. *Sunday Times* 12 May 1929 predicted that Elliot would go farthest of the young MPs of that Parliament despite being at the 'Relatively Obscure' Scottish Office. *Daily Express*, 6 December 1929 carried an article by Iain C. Lees, 'A Cabinet to Govern Scotland', in which it was stated that Elliot would make a 'Good Prime Minister for Scotland's First Parliament'.
93. E.M.M. Taylor, *The Politics of Walter Elliot, 1929–36*, pp. 191–2.
94. George Pottinger, *The Secretaries of State for Scotland*, p. 52.

10 Conclusion

1. James Mitchell, *Conservatives and the Union*, Edinburgh, Edinburgh University Press, 1990; James Mitchell and Lynn Bennie, 'Thatcherism, and the Scottish Question', in *British Elections and Parties Yearbook*, 1995,

London, Frank Cass, pp. 90–104 and *'Politics in a Cold Climate'*, S. Kendrick and D. MC Crone, 'Politics in a Cold Climate: The Conservative Decline in Scotland', *Political Studies*, vol. 37, 1989, pp. 589–603.

2 B. Guy Peters, , *Institutional Theory in Political Science* London, Pinter, 1999, p. 63.

3. Theda Skocpol, *Protecting Soldiers and Mothers: The Political Origins of Social Policy in the United States,* Cambridge, Cambridge University Press,1992; D.S King, *Actively Seeking Work: The Politics of Unemployment and Welfare Policy in the United States* Chicago, University of Chicago Press,1995; S. Krasner, 'Approaches to the State: Alternative Conceptions and Historical Dynamics', *Comparative Politics*, vol. 16, 1984, pp. 223–46.

4. Krasner, *op. cit.* Much of the debate on institutional development has borrowed from economics. The notion of 'increasing returns' is useful, that once set on a path a policy or institution will find it increasingly attractive to stick with this rather than change direction radically. Additionally, timing and the sequence of events are important (see Paul Pierson, 'Path Returns, Path Dependence, and the Study of Politics', *American Political Science Review*, vol. 94, no. 2, 2000 though see S.J. Liebowitz and S.E. Margolis, *Winners, Losers and Microsoft,* revised edition, Oakland, California, Independent Institute 2001 especially pp. 19–44 for an alternative view of path dependency). Pierson draws on Levi in making a distinction between broader and narrower conceptions of path dependence: the former refer to the relevance of preceding stages in a temporal sequence, in other words quite simply that what went before will influence what happens later; the latter conception means that when a 'country or region has started down a track, the costs of reversal are very high'. (Margaret Levi, 'A Model, a Method, and a Map: Rational Choice n Historical Analysis', in M.I. Lichbach and A.S. Zuckerman (eds), *Comparative Politics: Rationality, Culture and Structure*, Cambridge, Cambridge University Press) It is this narrower conception that is most useful both generally in the study of politics but also specifically in the study of Scottish central administration.

5. Margaret Levi, 'A Model, a Method, and a Map: Rational Choice n Historical Analysis', in M.I. Lichbach and A.S. Zuckerman (eds.), *Comparative Politics: Rationality, Culture and Structure* Cambridge, Cambridge University Press, p. 28.

6. B. Guy Peters, *Institutional Theory in Political Science,* London, Pinter, 1999, p. 76.

7. S. Rokkan and D. Urwin 'Introduction: centres and peripheries in western Europe' in S. Rokkan and D. Urwin (eds) *The Politics of Territorial Identity: Studies in European Regionalism,* London: Sage, 1982, p. 11.

8. See especially Pierson, *op. cit.*

9. Peter Hall, *The Power of Economic Ideas*, Princeton, N.J., Princeton University Press, 1989; 'The Movement from Keynesianism to Monetarism: Institutional Analysis and British Economic Policy in the 1970s' in S. Steinmo, K. Thelen, and F. Longstreth (eds), *Structuring Politics: Historical Institutionalism in Comparative Politics* Cambridge, Cambridge University Press, 1992; B. Guy Peters, *op. cit.,* p. 164.

10. Paul Pierson, 'Path Returns, Path Dependence, and the Study of Politics', *American Political Science Review*, vol. 94, no. 2, 2000, p. 253. However, see S.J. Liebowitz and S.E. Margolis, *Winners, Losers and Microsoft*, Revised edition, Oakland, California, 2001, see pp. 19–44 for the demolition of what the authors call 'The Fable of the Keys'.

11. Ibid.

12. Lindsay Paterson, *The Autonomy of Modern Scotland* Edinburgh, Edinburgh University Press, p. 116.

13. Most notably Jeffrey Pressman and Aaron Wildavsky, *Implementation*, Implementation, 3rd edition, University of California Press, Berkeley, 1984 and M. Lipsky, 'Street Level Bureaucracy and the Analysis of Urban Reform' *Urban Affairs Quarterly*, vol. 6, 1971, pp. 391–409 and *Street Level Bureaucracy*, Russell Sage, New York, 1980.

14. NAS, ED 7/5/22, Lloyd George. Transcript of proceedings of meeting between Lloyd George and deputation from Scottish MPs, 18 June 1912.

15. John Macintosh, review of 'The Scottish Political System', in *Political Quarterly*, vol. 44, 1973, p. 369.

16. Ibid.

17. Sir Andrew Grierson, 'Scottish Self Government', *Public Administration*, vol. 11, 1933, pp. 172–90.

18. Laura Cram, *Policy-Making in the European Union*, London, Routledge, 1997, p. 5 refers to what had been deemed the EU's 'cheap talk' in its development of social policy ambitions which in time proved very real and in that sense expensive.

19. Those who criticised James Kellas's notion of a Scottish political system including those who were strong advocates of a Scottish Parliament. See Neil MacCormick's review of the first edition of the book in *Scottish International*, vol. 6., 1973.

20. One of the earliest and most succinct formulations of this was James Porteous, *Unionist Policy for Scotland: A Criticism*, Edinburgh, Scottish Convention. A more recent example was Lyndsay Paterson, *The Autonomy of Scotland*, Edinburgh, Edinburgh University Press, 1994.

21. Charles Loch Mowat, *Britain Between The Wars*, p. 142.

22. Salisbury to Richmond, 7 August, 1885. Quoted in 'The Creation of the Scottish Office' *Juridical Review*, 1965, p. 229.

23. NAS, SOE 1/61. Memo. prepared for Col. Colville's use for an address to the St Columba's Church Literary Society on 10 November 1936.

24. Michael Fry, *Patronage and Principle* Aberdeen, Aberdeen University Press, pp. 255–6. In an earlier book, *Conservatives and the Union* Edinburgh, Edinburgh University Press, pp. 126–28 I quoted this passage but commented on it more critically than I would now.

Bibliography and Sources

I was fortunate in being able to interview Sir William Murrie, who had been a junior Scottish Office official in the inter-war period, in January 1983. The main primary source were public records held in the National Archives of Scotland in Edinburgh and the Public Records office in Kew, London. Over 100 files were consulted and just under 100 are referred to in footnotes throughout the book. Official reports and debates in Hansard and in the contemporary press have been used extensively. In addition, various private papers were consulted and are listed below. For the most part I relied on primary materials. Many secondary sources were consulted though most have not been referenced as primary sources have been preferred.

Private papers

William Adamson Papers, Dunfermline Public Library.
Asquith Papers, Bodleian Library, Oxford, MS Asquith.
Sir Henry Craik Papers, National Library of Scotland, MS 7174.
Educational Institute of Scotland Papers, Register House, Scottish Records Office, Edinburgh, GD 342.
Walter Elliot Papers, National Library of Scotland, Acc.6721.
Sir John Gilmour Papers, Register House, Scottish Records Office, GD 383/17.
Tom Johnston Papers, National Library of Scotland, Acc.5862.
Viscount Novar (Ronald Munro-Ferguson), National Library of Scotland.
Prime Ministerial Letters to the Queen, Bodleian Library, Oxford, CAB 41.
John Satterfield Sandars Papers, Bodleian Library, Oxford, MS Eng. Hist. C.713–77.
Scots Secretariat Files, National Library of Scotland, Acc.3721.
Scottish Landholders Federation Files, West Register House, Edinburgh, GD 325.
Thurso (Sir Archibald Sinclair) Papers, Churchill College Archive Centre, Cambridge, Thrs I.
Thomas McKinnon Wood Papers, Bodleian Library, Oxford.

Newspapers and periodicals

Aberdeen Free Press.
Alliance News.
British Medical Journal.
Civil Service Opinion.
Daily Express.
Dunfermline Press.
Edinburgh Evening News.
Educational News.
Glasgow Herald.

Graham's Handbook 1911 edition.
Morning Post.
North British Agriculturalist.
Roxburgh's The Law of Education in Scotland.
Scotsman.
Scottish Educational Journal.
Shanghai Times.
Sunday Times.
Times.
Times of India.
Weekly Dispatch.
Whitaker's Almanack, 1890.
Whitaker's Almanack, 1914.

Official publications and reports

Camperdown, Report of Inquiry into Civil Departments in Scotland, Parliamentary Papers, 1870, vol. 18.
Civil Service Commissioners, 47th report, 1903, Cd.1695.
Civil Service Commissioners, 51st report, 1907, Cd.3602.
Civil Service Commissioners, 54th report, 1910, Cd.5277.
Civil Service Commissioners, 56th report, 1912, Cd.6332.
Correspondence between Chancellor of the Exchequer and the Secretary for Scotland in regard to the Allocation of the Grant in aid of Local Taxation for the year, 1888–89. Parliamentary Paper, June 1888, C.5418.
Highlands and Islands Medical Service Committee. Report to the Lords Commissioners of His Majesty's Treasury, December 1912, Cd.6559.
MacDonnell Commission, 1913, Cd.6740.
Report from the Select Committee on Education, Science, and Art (Administration) July 1884, C.312.
Report from the Select Committee on Ministers' Remuneration, House of Commons, 170, 1929–30, VI, 287.
Report from the Select Committee on the Remuneration of Ministers, House of Commons, 15 December, 1920, Cd.241.
Report of Committee on Scottish Administration (Gilmour), October 1937, Cmd.5563.
Report of Deputation to Prime Minister on 23 February, 1924. Published by the Convention of Royal Burghs, March 1925.
Report of Her Majesty's Commissioners for Inquiry into the Housing of the Working Classes (Scotland), 1885, C.4409.
Report of the Commissioners appointed by the Lord Commissioners of Her Majesty's Treasury to inquire into certain Civil Departments in Scotland, March 1870.
Report of the Committee on Ministers' Powers, April 1932, Cmd.4060.
Report of the Committee on Scottish Administration (Gilmour) October 1937, Cmd.5563.
Report of the Committee on Scottish Health Services (Cathcart) Report, 1936, Cmd.5204.

Report of the Machinery of Government Committee, 1918, Cd.9320.

Report of the Royal Commission on the Housing of the Industrial Population of Scotland, 1917, Cd.8731.

Report of the Scottish Departmental Committee on the North Sea Fishing Industry, Report 1, 8 January, 1914, Cd.7221.

Report on Local Taxation in Scotland C.7575, 1895.

Report on Revenue and Expenditure (England, Scotland and Ireland), Return, 1 July 1914, Cd.387.

Royal Commission on Local Taxation, Final Report on Local Taxation (Scotland), 1902, Cd.1067.

Royal Commission on Mines, second reading, 1909, Cd.4820.

Royal Commission on Poor Laws and Relief of Distress (Scotland), 1909.

Royal Commission on the Civil Service (MacDonnell) Report, 1914, Cd.7338.

Royal Commission on the Poor Laws and Relief of Distress, Report on Scotland, 1909, Cd.4922.

Second Report of the Argyll Commission inquiring into the schools of Scotland, Elementary Schools C.3845, 1867.

White Paper on Revenue and Expenditure (Scotland's Relations), December 1932.

Books and articles

Addison, Christopher, *Four and a Half Years,* vol. 2, London, Hutchison & Co, 1934.

Allen, C.H., 'The Study of Scottish Politics: A Bibliographical Sermon', *Scottish Government Yearbook, 1980*, Edinburgh, Paul Harris, pp. 11–41.

Atkinson, Mabel, *Local Government in Scotland*, Edinburgh, Blackwood & Sons, 1904.

Bagehot, Walter, *The English Constitution*, London, Fontana, 1981 [1867].

Balfour, Lady Frances, *A Memoir of Alexander Hugh Bruce, Lord Balfour of Burleigh KT, 6th Baron*, London, Hodder & Stoughton, 1924.

Bone, T.R., *School Inspection in Scotland, 1840–1966*, London, University of London Press, 1968.

Boyle, Lawrence, *Equalisation and the Future of Local Government Finance*, Edinburgh, Oliver & Boyd, 1966.

Brand, Jack, *The National Movement in Scotland*, London, Routledge and Kegan Paul, 1978.

Bridges, Sir Edward, *Treasury Control*, London, Athlone Press, 1950.

Brown, John, 'Scottish and English Land Legislation, 1905–11', *Scottish Historical Review,* vol. 47, pp. 72–85.

Bunbury, Sir Henry (ed.), *Lloyd George's Ambulance Wagon: Being The Memoirs Of William J. Braithwaite, 1911–1912*, London, Methuen, 1957.

Carr, C.T., *Delegated Legislation*, Cambridge, Cambridge University Press, 1921.

Carr, Sir Cecil T., *Concerning English Administrative Law*, London, Oxford University Press, 1941.

Chamberlain, Sir Austen, *Politics From Inside – An Epistolary Chronicle 1906–1914*, London, Cassell, 1936.

Checkland, Sydney and Olive Checkland, *Industry and Ethos*, London, Edward Arnold, 1984.

Christie, Robert, *Injustice to Scotland Exposed, in a Letter to the Scottish Representatives in Parliament*, Edinburgh, Thomas Constable & Co., 1853.

Cockburn, Lord Henry, 'The Powers and Duties of the Lord Advocate of Scotland', *Edinburgh Review*, vol. 39, 1824. [unattributed at the time].

Connor, Walker, 'The Politics of Ethnonationalism', *Journal of International Affairs*, vol. 27, 1973, pp. 1–21.

Coote, Sir Colin, *A Companion of Honour – The Story of Walter Elliot*, London, Collins, 1965.

Coupland, Sir Reginald, *Welsh and Scottish Nationalism*, London, Collins, 1954.

Craik, Henry, *The State and its relation to Education*, London, Macmillan, 1884.

Craik, Henry, 'A Minister for Education', *Fortnightly Review*, vol. 37, April 1885, pp. 476–90.

Crowley, D.W., 'The Crofters Party, 1885–1892', *Scottish Historical Review*, vol. 35, 1956, pp. 110–26.

Davie, George Elder, *The Democratic Intellect*, Edinburgh, Edinburgh University Press, 1982.

Day, John Percival, *Public Administration in the Highlands and Islands of Scotland*, London, University of London Press, 1918.

Donaldson, James, 'The Scottish Education Department', *Scottish Review*, vol. 21, 1893, pp. 183–207.

Donaldson, Sir Henry, 'Address on the Scotch Education Department to the Education section of the British Association' at Dundee, printed in booklet form, *St Andrews Citizen*, 14 September 1912.

Douglas, Charles M. and Henry Jones, *Scottish Education Reform*, Glasgow, James MacLehose & Sons, 1903.

Egremont, Max, *Balfour: A Life of Arthur James Balfour*, London, Collins, 1980.

Ferguson, William, *Scotland: 1689 to the Present*, Edinburgh, Mercat Press, 1987.

Findlay, Ian Russell, *Sir John Struthers KCB – Secretary of the Scotch/Scottish Education Department (1904–1922) – a study of his influence upon Scottish educational development*, unpublished Dundee University Ph.D, 1979.

Finlay, Richard, *Independent and Free*, Edinburgh, John Donald, 1994.

Fraser, W.I.R., *An Outline of Constitutional Law*, London, Hodge, 1938.

Gibb, Andrew Dewar, *Scotland in Eclipse*, London, Humphrey Toumlin, 1930.

Gibson, E.L., *A Study of the Council for Wales and Monmouthshire, 1948–1966*, unpublished University College of Wales Aberystwyth LLB, 1968.

Gibson, John, *The Crown and the Thistle*, Edinburgh, HMSO, 1985.

Gilbert, Martin, *Winston S. Churchill*, Companion Part I, vol. 5, London, Heinemann, 1979.

Gowan, Ivor, *Government in Wales*, Aberystwyth, University College of Wales Aberystwyth, 1965.

Grierson, Sir Andrew, 'Scottish Self Government', *Public Administration*, vol. 11, 1933, pp. 172–90.

Grierson, Sir Andrew, 'One Hundred Years of Scottish Local Government', *Public Administration*, vol. 13, 1935, pp. 230–41.

Haldane, R.B., 'Preface' in Charles M. Douglas and Henry Jones (eds), *Scottish Education Reform*, Glasgow, James MacLehose & Sons, 1903.

Hall, Peter, *The Power of Economic Ideas*, Princeton, N.J., Princeton University Press, 1989.

Hall, Peter, 'The Movement from Keynesianism to Monetarism: Institutional Analysis and British Economic Policy in the 1970s' in S. Steinmo, K. Thelen, and F. Longstreth (eds), *Structuring Politics: Historical Institutionalism in Comparative Politics*, Cambridge, Cambridge University Press, 1992.

Hanham, H.J., 'The Creation of the Scottish Office, 1881–87', *Juridical Review*, 1965, pp. 205–44.

Hanham, H.J., *Scottish Nationalism*, London, Faber, 1969.

Hanham, H.J., 'The development of the Scottish Office', in J.N. Wolfe (ed.), *Government and Nationalism in Scotland*, Edinburgh, Edinburgh University Press, 1969, pp. 51–70.

Harvie, Christopher, *No Gods and Precious Few Heroes*, London, Edward Arnold, 1981.

Heald, David, *Territorial Equity and Public Finances: Concepts and Confusion*, Glasgow, Strathclyde University Studies in Public Policy no. 75, 1980.

Heald, David, *Public Expenditure*, Oxford, Martin Robertson, 1983.

Heasman, D.J., 'The Ministerial Hierarchy' Parliamentary Affairs, vol. 15, 1961–62, pp. 307–30.

Hunter, James, *The Making of the Crofting Community*, Edinburgh, John Donald, 1976.

James, Robert Rhodes, *Rosebery: A Biography of Archibald Philip, Fifth Earl of Rosebery*, London, Weidenfeld & Nicolson, 1963.

Journal of Jurisprudence, vol. 1, 1857.

Journal of Jurisprudence, vol. 31, September 1887.

Keating, Michael and Arthur Midwinter, *The Government of Scotland*, Edinburgh, Mainstream, 1983.

Keir, David, *The House of Collins*, London, Collins, 1952.

Kellas, James, *The Scottish Political System*, 3rd edition, Cambridge, Cambridge University Press, 1984.

King, D.S., *Actively Seeking Work: The Politics of Unemployment and Welfare Policy in the United States*, Chicago, University of Chicago Press, 1995.

King, Preston, *Federalism and Federation*, London, Croom Helm, 1982.

Krasner, S., 'Approaches to the State: Alternative Conceptions and Historical Dynamics', *Comparative Politics*, vol. 16, 1984, pp. 223–46.

Laura Cram, *Policy-Making in the European Union*, London, Routledge, 1997.

Lees, Iain C., 'A Cabinet to Govern Scotland' *Daily Express*, 6 December 1929.

Levi, Margaret, 'A Model, a Method, and a Map: Rational Choice n Historical Analysis', in M.I. Lichbach and A.S. Zuckerman (eds), *Comparative Politics: Rationality, Culture and Structure*, Cambridge, Cambridge University Press, 1997.

Levitt, Ian, *Welfare and Scottish Poor Law, 1890–1914*, unpublished Edinburgh University Ph.D, 1983.

Lipsky, Michael, *Street Level Bureaucracy*, New york, Russell Sage foundation, 1980.

Liebowitz, S.J. and S.E. Margolis, *Winners, Losers and Microsoft*, Revised edition, Oakland, California, 2001.

MacCormick, Neil, 'The Scottish Political System', review in *Scottish International*, vol. 6, 1973.

MacDonald, Mary and Adam Redpath, 'The Scottish Office, 1954–79', *Scottish Government Yearbook, 1980.*

MacGillivray, Duncan, 'Fifty Years of Scottish Education: Retrospect and Outlook', in John Clarke (ed.) *Problems of National Education*, London, Macmillan & Co. 1919.

Mackintosh, John, *The Devolution of Power*, London, Chatto & Windus, 1968.

MacLean, Iain, *The Labour Movement in Clydeside Politics, 1914–22*, unpublished D.Phil, Oxford, 1972.

Marquand, David, *Ramsay MacDonald*, London, Jonathan Cape, 1977.

McEwen, John Malcolm, *Unionist and Conservative MPs, 1914–39*, unpublished London University Ph.D, 1959.

McEwen, Sir Alexander, *Towards Freedom*, London, William Hodge & Co. Ltd., 1938.

Middlemas, Keith and John Barnes, *Baldwin: a biography*, London, Weidenfeld & Nicolson, 1969.

Midwinter, Arthur, Michael Keating, James Mitchell, *Politics and Public Policy on Scotland*, Basingstoke, Macmillan, 1991.

Milne, Sir David, *The Scottish Office*, London, Allen and Unwin, 1957.

Mitchell, James, *Conservatives and the Union*, Edinburgh, Edinburgh University Press, 1990.

Mitchell, James, *Strategies for Self-Government*, Edinburgh, Polygon, 1996.

Molyneaux, James, 'Speech to Unionist Party conference', Copy obtained from author, 19 November, 1983.

Morgan, Alexander, *The Rise and Progress of Scottish Education*, London, Oliver & Boyd, 1927.

Morgan, Alexander, *Makers of Scottish Education*, London, Longmans, Green, 1929.

Morgan, K.O., *A Study of the attitudes and Policies of the British Political Parties Towards Welsh Affairs, Disestablishment of the Church, Education and Governmental Devolution in the Period 1870–1920*, unpublished Oxford University D.Phil., 1957.

Mowat, Charles Loch, *Britain Between The Wars*, London, Methuen & Co, 1955.

Munro, A. Campbell, 'Public Health Administration in England and Scotland: Points of Contrast and Contact', *Public Health Administration*, vol. 11, October 1898, pp. 5–24.

Munro, Robert, *Looking Back: Fugitive Writings and Sayings*, London, Thomas Nelson, 1930.

Murray, S.M., *A Short Manual of the Education (Scotland) Act, 1908*, Edinburgh, Blackie & Son, 1909.

O'Halpin, E., *Sir Warren Fisher: Head of the Civil Service, 1919–1939*, unpublished Cambridge University Ph.D., 1982.

Omond, George W.T., *The Lord Advocates of Scotland*, vol. II, Edinburgh, Hamilton, 1883.

Parris, Henry, *Constitutional Bureaucracy*, London, George Allen & Unwin, 1969.

Paterson, Lindsay, *The Autonomy of Modern Scotland*, Edinburgh, Edinburgh University Press.

Paton, H.J., *The Claim of Scotland*, London, George Allen & Unwin, 1968.

Peters, B. Guy, *Institutional Theory in Political Science*, London, Pinter, 1999.

Pierson, Paul, 'Path Returns, Path Dependence, and the Study of Politics', *American Political Science Review*, vol. 94, no. 2, 2000, pp. 251–67.

Pottinger, George, *The Secretaries of State for Scotland, 1926–76*, Edinburgh, Scottish Academic Press, 1979.

Pressman, Jeffrey and Aaron Wildavsky, *Implementation*, Implementation, 3rd edition, Berkeley, University of California Press, 1984.

Pryde, George S., *Central and Local Government in Scotland since 1707*, London, Historical Association, 1960.

Rait, Sir Robert and George S. Pryde, *Scotland*, 2nd edition, London, Ernest Benn, 1954.

Randall, P.J., *The Development of Administrative Devolution in Wales from the Establishment of the Welsh Department of Education in 1907 to the Creation of the post of Secretary of State for Wales in October 1964*, unpublished University of Wales M.Sc., 1969.

Randall, P.J., 'Wales in the Structure of Central Government', *Public Administration*, Autumn 1972, vol. 50, pp. 353–72.

Reid, Sir Thomas Wemyss, *Memoirs and Correspondence of Lyon Playfair*, London, Cassell & Co, 1899.

Rokkan, S. and D. Urwin 'Introduction: centres and peripheries in Western Europe' in S. Rokkan and D. Urwin (eds), *The Politics of Territorial Identity: Studies in European Regionalism*, London, Sage, 1982.

Rose, Richard, *Understanding the United Kingdom*, London, Longman, 1982.

Scotland, James, *A History of Scottish Education*, vols 1 and 2, London, University of London, 1969.

Scott, A. MacCallum, 'The Government of Scotland' in the *Scots Magazine*, October 1925, pp. 11–18.

Selby-Bigge, Sir Lewis, *The Board of Education*, London, G.P Putnam's & Sons, 1927.

Sidebotham, Herbert, *Political Profiles From British Life*, London, Houghton Mifflin, 1921.

Skocpol, Theda, *Protecting Soldiers and Mothers: The Political Origins of Social Policy in the United States*, Cambridge, Cambridge University Press, 1992.

Smellie, K.B., *A History of Local Government*, London, Unwin university Books, 1968.

Smith, B.C., *Field Administration: An act of decentralisation*, London, Routledge & K.Paul, 1967.

Smith, B.C., *Decentralisation*, London, George Allen and Unwin, 1985.

Smith, Rev. John, *Broken Links in Scottish Education*, London, James Nisbet & Co, 1913.

Smith, Sheriff W.C., 'Imperial Grants as Adjustments of Taxation' *Proceedings of the Philosophical Society of Glasgow*, vol. 30, 1898–99, Glasgow, John Smith and Son, 1899.

Smith, William C., *The Secretary for Scotland*, Edinburgh, Blackwood & Sons, 1885.

Spinner, Thomas J., *George Joachim Goschen: The Tranformation of a Victorian Liberal*, London, Cambridge University Press, 1973.

Stevenson, Andrew L., *The Development of Physical Education in the State Schools of Scotland, 1900–1960*, unpublished Aberdeen University M.Litt., 1978.

Stewart, J. Henderson, 'A Plan for "Cinderella Scotland" ', *The People's Journal*, 24 December, 1938.

Taylor, E.M.M., The Politics of Walter Elliot, 1929–36, unpublished Edinburgh University Ph.D, 1980.

Thomas, Ian, *The Creation of the Welsh Office: Conflicting Purposes in Institutional Change*, Glasgow, Strathclyde University Studies in Public Policy, 1981.

Turner, Arthur, *Scottish Home Rule*, Oxford, Basil Blackwell, 1952.

Walker, J.H., *The Ad Hoc Administration of Education in Scotland, 1872–1929*, unpublished Glasgow University Ph.D., 1970.

Watkins, Sir Percy, *A Welshman Remembers*, Cardiff, William Lewis, 1944.

Whyte, W.E., *The Case for the Reform of Local Government in Scotland*, address delivered at Glasgow University, 11 February 1926.

Willson, F.M.G., 'Ministries and Boards: Some Aspects of Administrative Development Since 1832' *Public Administration*, vol. 33, 1955, pp. 43–58.

Winnifrith, Sir John, *The Ministry of Agriculture, Fisheries and Food*, London, Allen & Unwin, 1962.

Zebel, Sydney H., *Balfour: A Political Biography*, London, Cambridge University Press, 1973.

Index

Aberdeen Press and Journal   70
Acland, Arthur   57
Adamson, Willie   89, 106, 123, 184, 186, 199, 200
Addison, Christopher   87, 91
Administrative devolution   129, 210, 211, 212, 213, 214
Advisory Council (education)   58–64, 73
Aglen, John   x, 133
Agriculture   6, 7, 74–81, 101, 140, 141
Alness, Lord see Robert Munro
Animal diseases   75, 78, 79, 91
Anstruther, Sir Robert   21
Argyll, Duke of   15
Asquith, H.H.   46, 47, 48, 78, 98, 182, 183, 188, 193
Atholl, Duchess of   195
Atkinson, Mabel   13

Bagehot, Walter   6, 51
Baldwin, Stanley   150, 170, 186, 190, 199, 201
Balfour of Burleigh, Lord   28, 32, 40, 57, 58, 60, 61, 64, 158, 159, 164, 184, 192, 199, 200, 201
Balfour, A.J.   9, 28, 34, 35, 36, 74, 75, 182, 183, 184, 190, 198, 200, 201
Ballantyne, W.M.   144
Bank of England   151
Barnett formula   211
Barr, Rev. James   185, 196
Battle of the Braes, Skye (1882)   34
Baxter, William   20, 21, 22
Bellairs, Commander   187
Blair, P.J.   116, 176, 203
Board of Agriculture   74, 75, 76, 78, 79, 80, 81, 87, 88, 90, 102, 104, 112, 114, 125, 127
Board of Education (England and Wales)   61, 95, 163, 168, 171, 177, 186

Board of Education (Scotland)   14, 15, 16, 40, 59, 65
Board of Supervision   12, 13, 22, 115, 151
Boards (in Edinburgh)   3, 8, 12–14, 20, 21, 22, 23, 40, 46, 71, 92, 94, 85, 96, 98, 99, 103, 109, 110, 139
Bonar law, Andrew   183, 199, 201, 203
Bone, T.R.   60
Boys, William   105, 107
Brand, Jack   2, 216
Bright, John   45
British Medical Journal   102
Brown, James   111
Bruce, Robert   190
Buchan, John   132
Bunbury, Sir Henry   86

cabinet   24, 25, 26, 30, 34, 35, 36, 37, 38, 41, 44, 47, 61, 82, 88, 98, 182, 183, 188, 197, 199, 200, 201, 206, 214
Caldwell, James   38, 41, 70, 157
Cameron, Dr Charles   40
Campbell, Sir George   43, 44
Campbell-Bannerman, H.   45, 46, 78
Camperdown Commission on Civil Service Departments in Scotland (1870)   13, 21, 22, 23, 24
Camperdown, Lord   21, 28
Carr, C.T.   193, 194
Chamberlain, Austen   65, 74
Chamberlain, Neville   202, 203, 205
Chancellor of the Exchequer   31, 41, 82, 120, 121, 150, 159, 162, 168, 178, 189, 196, 197, 201, 206
Chief Secretary for Ireland   21, 22, 35, 46, 96, 189
Church of Scotland   3, 12, 50, 209
Churchill, Winston   47, 196
Civil Service Commissioners   94
Civil Service Confederation   111
Clark, Dr Gavin   158

Clerke, Sir William   21
Clyde, James   54
Collins, Sir Godfrey   9, 123, 131, 132, 133, 140, 145, 180, 184, 186, 197, 203, 204, 205, 214
Colville, John   184, 200, 205, 214
Committee of the Privy Council for Scottish Education   5, 14, 16, 17, 28, 32, 41, 50–55, 57, 61, 101, 141, 145
Committee on Scottish Health Service (Cathcart)   140, 142
confederal state   3
Congested Districts Board   80, 81
Connor, Walker   73, 217
Conservatives/Conservative Party   4, 8, 26, 28, 43, 45, 71, 74, 75, 78, 102, 110, 111, 189, 203, 204, 205
Convention of Royal Burghs   19, 25, 27, 45, 110, 186, 187, 190
Cooper, Charles   25
Cooper, Lord   120, 137
Coote, Colin   203
Coupland, Sir Reginald   19, 219
Court of session   20, 53, 54, 190
Cowan, W.H.   70
Craik, Sir Henry   14, 55, 56, 57, 58, 59, 60, 63, 64, 66, 70, 150, 155, 158, 159, 162, 173, 174, 190
Craufurd, Edward H.J.   21
Crofters   34, 74, 76, 83
Crofters Commission   75, 76, 80, 81
Cross, Sir Richard   25, 34

Dalhousie, Earl of   182, 184, 198
Dalziel School Board vs. SED   52, 53, 60
Dalziel, Sir Henry   47, 70
Davie, George Elder   50
Day, John Percival   ix, 192, 193
Department of Agriculture (Scotland)   137, 140, 179, 202
Department of Health (Scotland)   131, 141, 146, 179, 202
Deputy Clerk Register   102, 108, 109, 112
Devonshire, Duke of   57
Dewar, Sir John   81, 82
Dicey, A.V.   194

Dodds, Sir James   80, 94, 95, 96, 97, 98
Donaldson, James   58, 59, 61, 62
Douglas, W.S.   142
Dover House   61, 67, 70, 71, 92, 93, 94, 108, 114, 116, 123, 124, 127, 130, 131, 135, 138, 139, 200, 205
Duke, R.N.   132, 133, 137, 142
Dunlop, Jim   80

Edinburgh Review   18
Education   6, 7, 24, 30, 31, 32, 33, 50–73, 101
Education (Scotland) Act, 1872   15, 16, 51, 53
Education (Scotland) Act, 1918   52, 60, 61, 64, 70, 78, 83, 90, 158, 163, 166, 167, 169–173, 175, 191
Educational Institute of Scotland   32, 58, 62, 63, 64, 68, 176
Elliot, Walter   9, 88, 101, 119, 120, 121, 134, 142, 145, 147, 184, 187, 188, 196, 197, 200, 203, 204, 205
Emigration   79, 120
Erskine, John   133
Eton   198

Faculty of Advocates   108
federal/federalism/federation   3, 10, 211
Fergusson, Sir James   20
Finance   8
Financial Secretary to the Treasury   82, 156, 157, 170, 182, 196
Findlay, Ian Russell   59, 66
Fisher, Sir Warren   53, 144, 145, 150
Fisheries   101, 140, 141
Fishery Board   14, 40, 46, 67, 106, 107, 110, 112, 113, 116, 125, 135, 140, 144
Fleming, David   203
Fleming, Lord   133
Fraser, W.I.R.   113
Fry, Michael   215

Geddes reports/cuts   102, 175, 176, 187
General Board of Control (Lunacy)   14, 22, 82, 90, 116, 125, 135, 139, 140, 141

Gibb, Andrew Dewar   118
Gibson, John   ix
Gilmour Committee   x, 17, 71,
    117–148, 195, 196, 197, 203
Gilmour, Sir John   105, 106, 109, 110,
    111, 112, 114, 124, 133, 142, 184,
    187, 190, 202, 203, 204, 205, 214
Gladstone, W.E.   17, 21, 25, 26, 28,
    31, 32, 43, 44, 92
Glasgow Herald   59, 144, 147,
    169, 190
Goschen formula   9, 149–181, 202,
    208, 211
Gray, Professor Alexander   133,
    134, 142
Greig, Robert   103
Grierson, ir Andrew   ix, 217
Gulland, John   192, 193

Haldane, R.B.   61, 62, 64, 86, 87,
    92, 109
Hamilton Committee   142–145, 147
Hamilton of Dalzell, Lord   78
Hamilton, Sir Horace   117, 142, 143
Hamilton, Sir Robert   133
Hanbury, R.W.   156
Hanham, H.J.   12, 29, 191
Harrow (school)   198
Harvie, Christopher   199
Hawkins, R.T.   171, 176, 177
Health   6, 7
Hewart, Lord   194
Highland Land League   34
Highlands and islands   6, 7, 74, 81–83
Highlands and Islands (Medical
    Service) Board   82, 83
Highlands and Islands Medical
    Fund   82
Highton, John   134, 136
historic institutionalism   207, 208, 209
Hogge, James   48, 63, 186, 190
Home Office/Secretary   14, 17, 19,
    20, 21, 22, 23, 25, 26, 29, 33, 34,
    35, 36, 37, 38, 41, 42
home rule   25, 43, 44, 47, 49, 70, 80,
    98–100, 109, 110, 114, 115, 118,
    121, 134, 144, 147, 176, 187, 195,
    204, 213
Hope of Granton, Charles   18
Hope, Harry   70, 88, 186

Hope, Major John   174
Horne, Sir Robert   178
Housing   84, 85, 123
Hozier, J.H.C.   157
Hunter, William   45, 153

Inspectorate (schools)   65, 66, 72
Insurance Commission   82, 83, 85,
    86, 90
Ireland/Irish Question   25, 47, 49,
    109, 110, 121

James, Robert Rhodes   25
Jeffery, John   ix, 86, 134, 135, 136,
    138, 139, 140, 202
Johnston, Tom   9, 113, 133, 135, 142,
    196, 197
Journal of Jurisprudence   19

Keeper of the Registers and Records of
    Scotland   109, 112
Keith, Henry   168, 169, 176, 177,
    187, 188
Kellas, James   x, 1, 5, 212
Kerr, Dr John   63
Keynes, John Maynard   150
Kidd, James   203
King, D.S.   207
King, Preston   2, 216
Kirkwood, Davie   119, 180
Krasner, S.   207

Labour Party   47, 69, 70, 93, 99, 100,
    102, 109, 110, 111, 115, 116, 133,
    142, 203
Laird, Patrick   ix, 95, 116, 124, 127,
    128, 129, 130, 131, 134, 137, 138,
    142, 147, 212
Lamb, Sir John   89, 90, 123, 133, 137
land reform   75, 76
Laurie, Professor S.S.   58, 59, 62
law and order   34, 35, 72, 74
Leishman, James   62
Levi, Margaret   208
Levitt, Ian   ix, 12, 13, 85
Liberals/Liberal Party   26, 28, 39, 43,
    44, 47, 48, 70, 72, 76, 88, 99, 100,
    109, 110, 133, 169, 186, 189, 191,
    193, 203
Linlithgow, Marquess of   41, 184, 198

Lloyd George, David 76, 168, 194, 199, 203
local government 7, 101, 116, 139
Local Government Board (England and Wales) 13, 33, 39, 85, 189
Local Government Board (Scotland) 24, 26, 28, 46, 67, 71, 82, 84, 85, 87, 89, 90, 97, 115
Local Taxation Accounts 151–154, 155, 160–161, 162, 171, 174
Lord Advocate 14, 15, 17, 18, 19, 20, 22, 23, 24, 34, 35, 36, 39, 48, 53, 54, 79, 89, 102, 109, 139, 145, 189, 203
Lord Chancellor 82, 102, 109, 194
Lothian, Marquess of 26, 27, 37, 38, 39, 40, 153, 182, 184
Lunacy Board *see* General Board of Control
lunacy, 14, 22, 82, 90, 101, 106, 140, 192

MacCrae, Sir George 87, 97
MacDonald, George 66, 70, 137, 171, 176, 177
MacDonald, J.H. 34, 36
MacDonald, Ramsay 145, 190, 196, 202
MacDonnell, Lord 80, 87, 96
Macdougall, Sir J. 102
Mackinder, Halford 88
Mackintosh, John 2, 212
MacLean, Neil 178, 180
MacLeod of MacLeod, Reginald 186
MacMillan, Hugh 109
MacPherson, Ewan 103, 104, 105
MacPherson, James 191
Marriot, Sir John 187
Maxwell, Sir John Stirling 204, 205
May Committee 175
May, Sir Erskine 43
McKechnie, Sir William 131, 137
McKinnon Wood, Thomas 54, 55, 70, 81, 82, 103, 168, 174, 182, 183, 184, 185, 193, 199
McLaren, Duncan 21, 22
McLean, Iain 185, 199
McNicoll, N.F. 144
Menzies, Sir Walter 168, 169
Milne, Sir David ix, 131, 202

Ministry of Transport 74
Molyneaux, James 1, 216
Moncrieff, James 20, 23
Montrose, Duke of 147, 204
Morgan, Alexander 58, 153
Morning Post 182
Morton, A.C. 54, 65, 188
Mowat, C.L. 213
Muir Mackenzie, Lord 101, 102
Muirhead, Roland 80
Munro, Robert (Lord Alness) 87, 88, 89, 90, 133, 170, 183, 184, 185, 192, 198, 199
Munro-Ferguson, Ronald (Viscount Novar) 41, 48, 65, 70, 71, 99, 100, 101, 112, 124, 168, 184, 199, 201, 203
Murray, Andrew Graham 65, 109, 184, 189, 190, 198
Murrie, Sir William x, 114, 134, 204

National Association for the Vindication of Scottish Rights 19, 20, 149
National Farmers Union (Scotland) 104
National insurance 7
National Party of Scotland 118, 204
nationalism 2, 4, 20, 21, 47, 48, 73, 99, 110, 118, 129, 207
Northcote, Sir Stafford 17
Northcote-Trevelyan 7, 23, 92, 96
Northern Ireland Office 1
Novar, Viscount See Munro Ferguson

Office of Works 69
Ogilvie, Grant 55, 56
Omond, George 24, 219

Parliament/Parliamentarians (Westminster) 8
Parliamentary sovereignty 212
Parliamentary Under Secretary (of State for Scotland 88, 89, 100–102, 105, 196–197
Paterson, Lindsay 212
path dependency 207, 208, 209, 211
patronage 8, 22, 23, 80, 87, 92, 93, 94, 96, 97, 98, 107, 112, 210
Pearson, Sir Charles 157

Peck, J.W.   134, 142, 143
Pentland, Lord *see* John Sinclair
Permanent Under Secretary   104, 117, 135–138, 141, 143, 147
Pirie, Duncan   46, 47, 63, 67, 68, 69, 70, 98
Playfair, Sir Lyon   31, 40
Pottinger, George   177, 202, 206
pressure groups   4, 5
Prime Minister   17, 27, 28, 35, 44, 48, 101, 182, 183, 186, 187, 189, 190, 191, 195, 197, 199, 200, 201, 204, 205, 206
Prison Commissioner for Scotland   14, 107, 114, 126
Prisons   101, 107
Pryde, George S.   12
Public opinion   4

Rae, Sir James   133, 144
Register House   102, 107–109, 110, 112, 125
Registrar General for Scotland   108, 141
Reorganisation of Offices (Scotland) Act, 1928   93, 95, 111–114, 116, 117, 122
Reorganisation of Offices (Scotland) Act, 1939   113, 117, 129, 147, 148, 200, 202
Richmond and Gordon, Duke of   1, 16, 28, 33, 182, 184, 188, 191
Ritchie, Charles   159
Rokkan, Stein   x, 3, 9, 211
Rose, P.J.G.   95, 142
Rose, Sir Arthur   137, 205
Rosebery, Lord   23, 25, 26, 28, 32, 33, 44
Ross, Willie   9
Royal Commission on Education in Scotland, 1867   15, 16
Royal Commission on Housing, 1917   83, 84, 85
Royal Commission on Poor Laws and Relief of Distress (Scotland), 1909   81, 85
Royal Commission on Scottish Affairs (Balfour), 1954   7, 74, 79

Royal Commission on the Civil Service (MacDonnell) 1914   72, 73, 80, 87, 90, 92–98, 101, 102, 103, 106, 113, 116
Runciman, Walter   166

Salisbury, Lord   4, 28, 34, 39, 40, 42, 43, 45, 150, 183, 198, 208, 214
Samuel, A.M.   196
Sandon, Viscount   16
Science and Art Department (SED)   55–58
Scotch/Scottish Education Department (SED)   14, 15, 16, 31, 32, 52, 53, 54, 55, 56, 57, 58, 59, 60, 62, 63, 64, 65, 66, 67, 68, 69, 70, 71, 72, 73, 82, 90, 100, 126, 128, 129, 131, 132, 135, 136, 150, 154, 155, 156, 157, 158, 162, 163, 164, 166, 167, 168, 169, 170, 172, 175, 176, 177, 195, 198, 199
Scots Secretariat   187
Scotsman   25, 62, 66, 144, 145, 169, 176
Scottish Board of Health   82, 83–90, 100, 102, 103, 104, 105, 106, 110, 112, 113
Scottish Educational Journal   177
Scottish Grand Committee   42, 43–45, 47, 49, 118, 119, 121, 142, 147
Scottish Home Department   127, 140, 141, 144, 146
Scottish Home Rule Association   11, 111
Scottish Land Court   80, 126
Scottish Local Government Board   46
Scottish Miners Federation   84
Scottish Parliament   6
Scottish political system   212, 213
Scottish Secretary created   11, 13
Scottish view/dimension   6, 7, 8, 49, 68, 74, 93, 129, 209, 210, 212
Secretaries of State Act, 1926   187, 196
Secretaryship of State, raising status of   183–191
SED and 'bureaucratic despotism'   58–64
SED and transfer to Edinburgh   64–72
Selby-Bigge, Sir Lewis   163, 218

Shaw, Lord 53
Simon, John 120
Sinclair, John (Lord Pentland) 41, 46, 47, 69, 76, 78, 79, 84, 85, 106, 184, 191, 193, 198, 199
Sinclair, Sir Archibald 115, 133, 138, 177, 184, 202
Skelton, Noel 115, 129
Skelton, Sir John 85, 151
Skocpol, Theda 207
Small Landholders legislation 67, 76, 78, 79, 191
Smellie, K.B. 153
Smith, B.C. 216
Smith, Sheriff W.C. 154
Smith, William ix, 13, 23, 24, 26
Solicitor General 109, 133, 189, 203
St. Andrews House 30, 71, 118, 145, 200
Steel, G.A. 133
Stewart, F.O. 130, 131
Stewart, J. Henderson 119, 147, 195
Stewart, James 105
Struthers, Sir John 53, 57, 58, 59, 60, 62, 63, 64, 65, 66, 68, 69, 70, 72, 73, 166, 168, 169, 170, 176
Sutherland, Angus 76, 106

Tait, Thomas 145
Tennant, H. 184, 185
Thomson, F.C. 114, 176
Thorburn, W. 157
Times 26, 27, 182, 196, 205
Treasury 8, 37, 53, 66, 68, 80, 81, 82, 86, 88, 90, 103, 111, 121, 130, 133, 143, 144, 145, 146, 150, 151, 154, 155, 156, 157, 158, 162, 163, 164, 167, 168, 169, 170, 171, 172, 173, 174, 175, 177, 178, 180, 182, 186, 196, 212
Treaty of Union, 1707 11, 207
Trevelyan, Sir George 44, 45, 56, 72, 184
Turner, Arthur 118

union state 3, 8, 9, 10, 12, 208, 209, 210, 211
Unionists/Unionist Party 70, 99, 100, 110, 114, 116, 133, 147, 176, 193, 203
unitary state 2, 3, 208, 211, 212
Ure, Alexander 53, 79
Urwin, Derek x, 3, 9, 211, 217

Wales 7, 216
Wall Street Crash 175
Watson, Cathcart 78
Watson, William 203, 218
Watt, Henry 99
Webb, Sidney 115
Wedderburn, Sir David 24
Weir, James 189, 192
Welsh Office 1
Wemyss, Earl of 27, 39
Wheatley, John 199
Whitehall view/dimension 6, 7, 8, 49, 72, 92, 100, 109, 111, 113, 115, 129, 209, 210, 212
Whyte, W.E. 122
Willson, F.M.G. 23
Wilson, D.M. 166, 167

Young, George 15, 16, 23
Younger, George (late C20th) 215
Younger, Sir George 47, 70, 99, 100